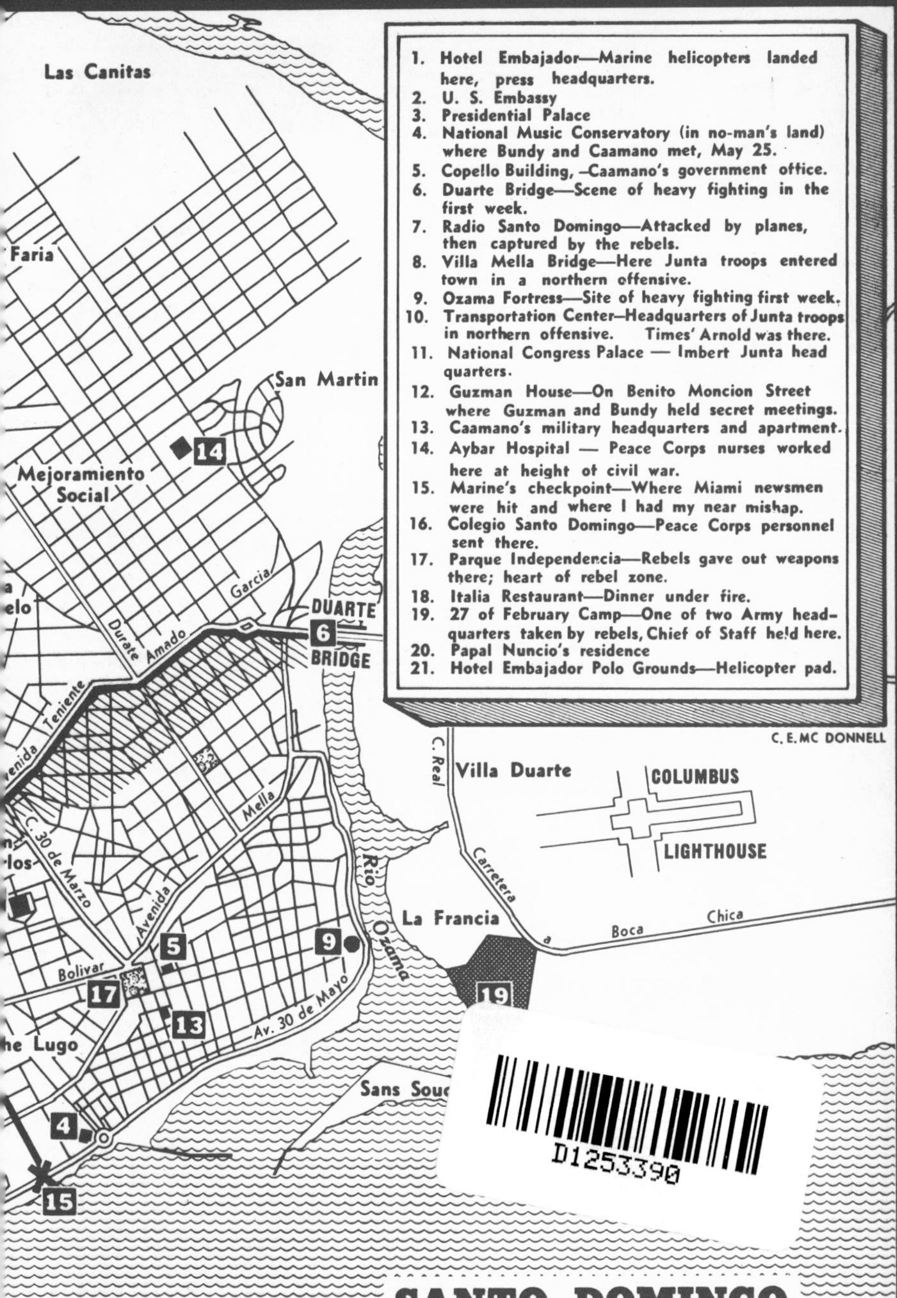

1. Hotel Embajador—Marine helicopters landed here, press headquarters.
2. U. S. Embassy
3. Presidential Palace
4. National Music Conservatory (in no-man's land) where Bundy and Caamano met, May 25.
5. Copello Building, –Caamano's government office.
6. Duarte Bridge—Scene of heavy fighting in the first week.
7. Radio Santo Domingo—Attacked by planes, then captured by the rebels.
8. Villa Mella Bridge—Here Junta troops entered town in a northern offensive.
9. Ozama Fortress—Site of heavy fighting first week.
10. Transportation Center–Headquarters of Junta troops in northern offensive. Times' Arnold was there.
11. National Congress Palace — Imbert Junta head quarters.
12. Guzman House—On Benito Moncion Street where Guzman and Bundy held secret meetings.
13. Caamano's military headquarters and apartment.
14. Aybar Hospital — Peace Corps nurses worked here at height of civil war.
15. Marine's checkpoint—Where Miami newsmen were hit and where I had my near mishap.
16. Colegio Santo Domingo—Peace Corps personnel sent there.
17. Parque Independencia—Rebels gave out weapons there; heart of rebel zone.
18. Italia Restaurant—Dinner under fire.
19. 27 of February Camp—One of two Army head-quarters taken by rebels, Chief of Staff held here.
20. Papal Nuncio's residence
21. Hotel Embajador Polo Grounds—Helicopter pad.
Las Canitas
Faria
San Martin
Mejoramiento Social
Garcia
Durate
Amado
Teniente
DUARTE BRIDGE
C. Real
Villa Duarte
COLUMBUS
LIGHTHOUSE
Mella
C. 30 de Marzo
Avenida
Rio
Ozama
La Francia
Carretera
a
Boca
Chica
Bolivar
Av. 30 de Mayo
Sans Souc
C. E. MC DONNELL
SANTO DOMINGO
Sea

DOMINICAN DIARY

BOOKS BY TAD SZULC

TWILIGHT OF THE TYRANTS
THE CUBAN INVASION (WITH KARL E. MEYER)
THE WINDS OF REVOLUTION
LATIN AMERICA
DOMINICAN DIARY

DOMINICAN DIARY

BY TAD SZULC

DELACORTE PRESS
NEW YORK

LIBRARY OF CONGRESS CATALOG CARD NUMBER: 65–26188
PRINTED IN THE UNITED STATES OF AMERICA
FIRST PRINTING
BOOK DESIGN BY BARBARA LUTTRINGHAUS

JACKET PHOTO CREDITS: FRONT--UPI: BACK—MAGNUM-RAPOPORT

to the Peace Corps volunteers
in Santo Domingo

INTRODUCTION

At 7:10 P.M., Eastern Standard Time, the radio set in the wheelhouse of the U.S.S. Wood County, an LST attached to the Caribbean Amphibious Task Force, crackled ominously, then a voice coming from afar in the tropical night said: "Close the coast. Prepare to land."

It was Wednesday, April 28, 1965, and the command, transmitted to all ships of the Navy's Task Force 44.9, was a Presidential flash ordering United States Marines to go ashore in the Dominican Republic. The order, issued by President Johnson in Washington, was the beginning of the first United States military intervention in the Dominican Republic since 1916.

The initial landing by 405 Marines to cover the evacuation of American citizens from Santo Domingo, where a bloody civil war had been raging for days, was to be followed by a major military build-up that ultimately brought the United States forces in the Dominican Republic to a peak strength of nearly 22,000 men.

President Johnson's decision to intervene—and subsequently to escalate the mission of the American troops—will presumably go down as one of his most controversial actions. Among the still unanswered questions is whether the intervention saved the Dominican Republic from Communism or whether in the long run it helped Communism.

The President's decision was preceded and followed by political and diplomatic confusion as the Administration seemed to favor one side and then another, saying one thing and doing another, in its desperate attempts to settle the Dominican crisis.

A long time may elapse before the final consequences of the President's decision to intervene and his Administration's subsequent policies can be judged in terms of the future of the Dominican Republic and of United States relations with Latin America.

Meanwhile the landing of American troops was the central event in the struggle that swept the Dominican Republic's ancient capital of Santo Domingo in the spring of 1965.

As a correspondent for The New York Times I stood on the flying bridge of the Wood County when the Presidential order was flashed to the fleet. The next morning I landed in Santo Domingo behind the first contingent of Marines. For the next four weeks I covered the Dominican civil war and witnessed an extraordinary spectacle of heroism and dedication, brutality and death, political blunders and intrigues played out by a fantastic cast of characters.

It was a story that few of the newsmen who were in Santo Domingo in those days are likely to face again—or to forget.

PRINCIPAL DRAMATIS PERSONAE

In the Order of Their Appearance

Donald Reid Cabral .... Dominican provisional president, overthrown on April 25, 1965.

Brigadier General Marco Rivera Cuesta .... Army Chief of Staff, taken hostage by rebels.

W. Tapley Bennett, Jr. ...... United States Ambassador to the Dominican Republic, a man surprised by the events.

Brigadier General Antonio Imbert Barreras .... Killer of Dictator Trujillo, who went dove-hunting the day before the revolution and later became the chief of the Junta.

Jack Hood Vaughn .... Assistant Secretary of State for Inter-American Affairs, who was also surprised by Dominican developments.

William B. Connett, Jr. .... Counsellor of the U.S. Embassy, who for three days held the key role of Chargé d'Affaires in Santo Domingo.

José Rafael Molina Ureña .... For two days provisional president in the rebel regime.

Juan Bosch .... Former Dominican President, ousted in 1963, and the inspirational leader of the 1965 revolt, who returned to Santo Domingo in September, 1965.

Brigadier General Elias Wessin y Wessin .... Troop commander at San Isidro base, who overthrew Dr. Bosch in 1963 and sought to destroy the rebels in 1965; a recalcitrant protégé of U.S.

Carmen Bosch .... Wife of Juan Bosch and an influential adviser.

Lieutenant Colonel Miguel Angel Hernando Ramirez	Military leader of the pro-Bosch revolt, but not for long.
Lieutenant Colonel Francisco Caamaño Deñó	He became the leader.
Silvestre Antonio Guzmán	Former Minister of Agriculture, who was insulted at U.S. Embassy, but later almost became the U.S.–backed president.
Thomas C. Mann	Under Secretary of State for Economic Affairs, who disliked Dr. Bosch and played a key role in conduct of U.S. policy during the crisis.
Monsignor Emanuele Clarizio	Papal Nuncio in Santo Domingo, a brave man and tireless mediator.
Malcolm McLean	Energetic U.S. press attaché in Santo Domingo.
Rafael Herrera	Editor of *Listin Diario*.
Lieutenant Colonel Manuel Ramon Montes Arache	Commander of Dominican Navy's frogmen, a key rebel commander.
Commodore Francisco J. Rivera Caminero	Dominican Navy commander, later a key figure in Imbert Junta.
Brigadier General Jesus de los Santos Cespedes	Junta Air Force commander.
Major General Robert York	Commander of U.S. 82nd Airborne Division.
Benjamin J. Ruyle	Chief of Political Section at U.S. Embassy, a well-informed official.
Hector Aristy	The rebels' "Minister of the Presidency," an influential and very intriguing figure.
André Rivière	French veteran from Indochina and soldier of fortune; a top rebel commander, killed in action.
Colonel Pedro Bartolomé Benoit	President of the San Isidro Junta; he asked for U.S. intervention.
Vice Admiral William F. Raborn, Jr.	C.I.A. Director, sworn in the day of the intervention.
George W. Ball	Under Secretary of State.

McGeorge Bundy .... Special Assistant to the President for National Security Affairs, a key negotiator in Santo Domingo.

Robert S. McNamara .... Secretary of Defense.

Bill Moyers .... Special Assistant to the President.

Raul Leoni .... President of Venezuela, and a critic of the intervention.

Benno Varon .... Israeli Ambassador to the Dominican Republic, a highly informed diplomat.

L. Robert Satin .... Peace Corps Director in the Dominican Republic; a man who got around.

Fidelio Despradel Roque ...... A leader of the 14th of June Movement; regarded by U.S. as an influential pro-Communist among the rebels.

Ellsworth Bunker .... U.S. Ambassador to the O.A.S. Council; later a negotiator in Santo Domingo.

Phil Tucker .... A lieutenant in U.S. Marines, a cool troop commander.

John Bartlow Martin .... Former U.S. Ambassador to the Dominican Republic; LBJ's special envoy during the revolt.

José A. Mora .... Secretary-General of O.A.S., a stubborn peacemaker.

Ricardo M. Colombo .... Argentine Ambassador to O.A.S., chairman of first O.A.S. committee.

U Thant .... U.N. Secretary-General.

Jaime Benítez .... Chancellor of University of Puerto Rico, and a participant in the Dominican talks.

Jottin Curi .... "Foreign Minister" of the rebel regime.

Abe Fortas .... Washington attorney and the secret "middleman" in negotiations; later Supreme Court Justice.

Brigadier General Jacinto Martinez Araña .... Tough Junta commander who directed the northern attack.

Anthony M. Solomon .... Assistant Secretary of State for Economic Affairs, and in charge of Dominican economy.

Lieutenant General Bruce Palmer .... U.S. military commander in the Dominican Republic.

Major General Indar Jit Rikhye .... U.N. Military observer.

Cyrus R. Vance .... Deputy Secretary of Defense.

Lieutenant Colonel Rafael Fernandez Dominguez .. A rebel leader, killed in firefight.

José Antonio Mayobre .... A Venezuelan diplomat, the U.N.'s eyes and ears in Santo Domingo.

General Hugo Panasco Alvim .. Brazilian commander in chief of the Inter-American Peace Force.

. . . AND . . .

Boy and girl Peace Corps Volunteers, U.S. Marines and paratroopers, diplomats and embassy secretaries, American and foreign news correspondents, CIA and FBI agents, rebels and Junta soldiers, American carpetbaggers, Hotel Embajador waiters, middlemen, taxi drivers, spear-bearers-at-large . . . and the citizens of Santo Domingo. . . .

THE FIRST WEEK

Saturday, April 24th.

Rebellion broke out in Santo Domingo on the morning of Saturday, April 24. I was at home in Washington working on a book, a common spare-time occupation of Washington correspondents. Oddly enough, I was writing about the first U.S. military intervention in Santo Domingo in 1916. When my telephone rang I was busy describing Major General Smedley Butler, now an obscure historical figure, who led the American occupation forces in those days.

The telephone call was from New York. Trouble had broken out in Santo Domingo and The Times wanted me to get down there to cover whatever was developing.

A check by phone with the Dominican desk officer at the State Department confirmed that something indeed was happening in Santo Domingo. The first reports from the United States Embassy there, which largely matched the news transmitted by the wire services, said a group of civilian and military rebels had apparently captured the principal radio station in the Dominican capital as well as two army headquarters buildings.

The information was that the rebels had demanded the return to power of former President Juan Bosch, who had been overthrown by a military coup d'état on Sept. 25, 1963. But according to both the embassy and the wire services, the situation was still unclear in the afternoon hours of Saturday.

The information then being cabled to the State Department from our embassy in Santo Domingo is important in evaluating subsequent United States attitudes. In fact, as it developed later, the reporting from the embassy to the State Department—and to the White House—became a key factor in creating a state of mind among Administration officials that led before too long to a series of decisions culminating in the massive military intervention by U.S. forces in the Dominican Republic.

What had actually happened in Santo Domingo, according to the first reports, was that a small commercial radio station there had broadcast late in the morning a bulletin announcing a revolution and the downfall of the Government of President Donald

Reid Cabral. Although it was a Saturday and most of the residents of Santo Domingo were at home, large crowds quickly poured into the downtown streets to celebrate the ouster of the civilian but military-backed regime that had been in power since the overthrow of the constitutional Bosch Government 19 months earlier.

Reid Cabral had not been a hated figure like Generalissimo Rafael Leonidas Trujillo Molina, the late dictator. But a deep sense of malaise had been developing for a long time among Dominicans. At least some of them seemed to want a return to the democratic rule that had come to the Dominican Republic for the first time in 38 years with the election of Dr. Juan Bosch in December, 1962. In addition, Dominicans had become restless under the financial austerity program imposed by Reid Cabral at the prodding of the United States and the International Monetary Fund. Among the measures that had annoyed Dominicans were restrictions on imports and a head tax on travel abroad. But there were other grievances, too.

Ever since Trujillo had been assassinated on May 30, 1961, Dominicans had been promised democracy and a better life, more job opportunities, more food, more schools—in a word a better future. But as time went on, from Government to Government through the seven changes of regime that occurred between Trujillo's assassination and the downfall of President Bosch, very little had been accomplished to make the Dominican Republic, a potentially wealthy country, the "showcase of democracy" it was supposed to become with the end of tyranny. It was not really anybody's fault: the nation had been shattered by the brutal Trujillo dictatorship and could not achieve stability. Reid Cabral probably meant well but the forces loose in Dominican society worked against him—as they had worked against Dr. Bosch.

Most of the military officers were holdovers from Trujillo's forces. Some of the older generals and colonels resented Reid Cabral because he had ended certain of their special privileges and had apparently attempted to curtail the traditional corruption among the Dominican armed services. Some of the younger officers, although they had helped or tacitly accepted the overthrow of President Bosch, were now having second thoughts about the political fate of their country and had engaged in conspiracies to bring back the deposed President.

And finally there was the irritation of a nine-month drought. For weeks there had been virtually no water supply in Santo Domingo, a city of nearly 400,000 people, and this helped fray tempers and put the population on edge. In the opinion of many Dominicans, the drought provided additional fuel for the fury with which the revolution was to erupt.

So when that first bulletin was heard in Santo Domingo over the small commercial radio station—a bulletin announcing something that had not yet actually happened, the overthrow of the Reid Cabral Government—people responded with joy. Afterward a housewife told me that her own reaction had been that "the captains have kicked out the colonels." To others the seeming success of the revolution meant new hope for the future. The Dominicans, for so long betrayed and humiliated by fate, are, if nothing else, a people who thrive on hope.

At this point, however, the revolt in reality was far from successful. It was not until a few hours later that a group of civilian and military rebels succeeded in capturing Radio Santo Domingo, which is the Government's radio and television broadcasting center and is not to be confused with the little commercial station that had prematurely reported the Reid Cabral regime's downfall. From Radio Santo Domingo the insurgents announced that a rebel movement to bring Dr. Bosch back to power had been initiated.

Simultaneously it became known that military rebels had seized two military barracks, the 16th of August Camp and the 27th of February Camp. One of the camps—their names, incidentally, commemorate patriotic dates—is across the Ozama River from Santo Domingo and the other is about 20 miles away. By midafternoon, therefore, it had become clear that some sort of important movement was under way. In downtown Santo Domingo the cheering crowds, some people among them setting off firecrackers, clashed with the Government's police. A policeman was killed and an 18-year-old boy, apparently a bystander, also died.

In Washington another check with the State Department's Dominican desk disclosed that the military rebels had taken as a hostage the army chief of staff, Brigadier General Marco Rivera Cuesta, and his deputy, Colonel Maximiliano Americo Ruiz Batista.

However, the State Department official, quoting reports from our embassy in Santo Domingo, told me that even so the rebellion did not seem to amount to much. He reported that loyal forces had recaptured Radio Santo Domingo, imprisoning eight of the rebels, and that President Reid Cabral had issued an ultimatum to the military insurgents holding the two army camps to surrender by 5 o'clock in the afternoon or face an attack by loyalist troops.

That the U.S. Embassy in Santo Domingo so obviously underestimated the potential of the revolution is a vital point in examining future events. First the embassy was caught unawares by the revolution and then it proceeded to minimize its importance until, suddenly, matters got out of hand.

The first intriguing question is why the embassy was taken by surprise. With an active political staff and a contingent of Central Intelligence Agency operatives, the embassy, it might be assumed, would have been aware that a conspiracy was in the works. In addition, the United States had in Santo Domingo regular military attachés and 13 Army, Air Force and Navy officers attached to the Military Assistance Advisory Group, whose job it was to work with the Dominican armed forces and keep in touch with their leaders. That a conspiracy of some type was in progress had not been much of a secret for weeks in Santo Domingo, a city renowned even by Latin American standards for the high quality of its grapevine and the inability of its inhabitants, whether plotters or friends of plotters, to keep anything confidential. This was a heritage of the 30 years of the Trujillo regime, when the grapevine was the only means of remaining reasonably well informed.

At least a week earlier a newspaper man who represents The New York Times on a part-time basis in Santo Domingo had advised us that trouble might be brewing in the Dominican Republic. El Caribe, the leading Santo Domingo newspaper, had published several page one stories in April about reports of military conspiracies and unexplained troop movements in the vicinity of the Presidential Palace. And finally President Reid Cabral himself had learned enough about the likelihood of trouble to have moved on Thursday, April 22, to dismiss from active duty seven air force officers apparently involved in the plotting.

It was the removal of these officers that precipitated the Saturday revolution. The plot to restore Dr. Bosch to power had been set in motion as far back as September, 1964, and the target date was to have been June 1, 1965. The plotters' primary intention was to prevent the elections scheduled for September, 1965, which Reid Cabral was suspected of planning to rig to insure his own victory. But the President's apparent discovery of the conspiracy panicked the rebels and caused them to act at once—if they were to act at all.

All of this, however, seemed unknown to our embassy—and thereby hangs the tale of the first major U.S. blunder in the situation.

The embassy was denuded of its top personnel. Ambassador W. Tapley Bennett Jr. had left Santo Domingo for the United States on Friday, the day before the revolution began, for consultations in Washington and to visit his family. Mr. Bennett explained to me later that he had flown to the United States because he knew trouble was approaching and thought this would be his last opportunity to discuss calmly the various contingency plans with the Administration. But the fact remains that when the revolt broke out on Saturday Mr. Bennett was visiting his mother in Georgia and only the next day was able to fly to Washington to begin consultations on a crisis that had already exploded.

Before his departure for the U.S. Mr. Bennett actually did mention in his regular weekly report—the embassy's "weeker" that went by air pouch to Washington on Thursday—that there were again rumors that some generals might try to overthrow Reid Cabral during the weekend. But the Ambassador did not seem to take these predictions seriously, remarking that they were the usual Santo Domingo rumors.

The military men attached to the United States establishment in Santo Domingo were just as remiss in their surveillance as the Ambassador. Eleven of the 13 members of the Military Assistance Advisory Group had gone to Panama for a routine conference. On Friday, the day before the revolt's outbreak, the embassy's naval attaché went dove hunting in the Cibao Valley with Brigadier General Antonio Imbert Barreras, a man who was shortly to become the chief American instrument in the ensuing chaos.

William C. Ide, director of the United States Economic Mission to the Dominican Republic, was in Washington attending a conference. And in Washington the office of the Assistant Secretary of State for Inter-American Affairs, Jack Hood Vaughn, was empty. Mr. Vaughn, as unaware of the Dominican situation as his subordinates in Washington and in Santo Domingo, had gone to the Mexican resort of Cuernavaca to attend a meeting of Western Hemisphere intellectuals.

The embassy was in the hands of Chargé d'Affaires William B. Connett Jr., a Foreign Service officer who had been in Santo Domingo for only five and a half months. Mr. Connett suddenly found himself in the commanding position of reporting on the crisis and recommending action until Ambassador Bennett finally succeeded in returning to his post three and a half days later.

It was Mr. Connett, then, who advised the State Department that the revolt seemed to have fizzled out. Although the rebels had ignored the ultimatum to surrender by 5 P.M., President Reid Cabral made a radio speech from the Presidential Palace at 10 P.M. announcing in effect that the situation was under control and that the revolutionaries at the two army headquarters now had until 6 o'clock the next morning to surrender.

This information, too, was dutifully passed on to the State Department by Mr. Connett. The department's officials in turn assured inquiring newsmen in Washington that the situation hardly seemed to merit a reporter's interrupting a weekend for an emergency trip to the Dominican Republic.

In Santo Domingo, however, matters were taking a different turn. In the early evening, even before President Reid Cabral made his reassuring broadcast, civilian and military groups had begun organizing for the next phase of their rebellion. Students and other civilians had started a telephone campaign, calling up friends and acquaintances and urging them to go back into the streets to demand the ouster of the Reid Cabral Government. About midnight someone got into a firehouse in Santo Domingo and sounded a siren, adding to the tension and confusion.

In the two military camps held by the rebels the insurgent officers were assuring callers that their revolt was only beginning and that they were not intimidated by the Reid Cabral ultimatum. They continued to hold General Rivera Cuesta, the army chief of staff, as a hostage. One of the rebels explained that the troops had risen under the command of younger officers when the general had attempted earlier in the day to arrest four officers whom he suspected of being part of the conspiracy.

This was the end of the first day of the Dominican crisis, the start of the insane violence to come. To the United States Government it was still a routine and low-priority situation.

Sunday, April 25th.

After 17 years of marriage I am beginning to believe in feminine intuition. Despite the reassuring reports from the State Department Saturday night, my wife told me that she had that "funny feeling" that something serious was afoot in the Dominican Republic. Much as she hated to see me go off on another assignment, she added, she thought I had better get ready for it. I followed her advice, made airline reservations from Washington to San Juan, Puerto Rico, obtained some cash—not an easy undertaking on a Saturday night—and went to sleep. Sunday morning, as I drove to the airport to leave for San Juan, a radio news bulletin told me that the Reid Cabral Government had fallen in Santo Domingo. There were no details but it was now obvious that a major story was developing. I felt I had done well in heeding my wife's intuition and taking off in the general direction of the Dominican Republic.

On my arrival in San Juan four hours later I discovered that all commercial flights to Santo Domingo had been interrupted. I had originally hoped to catch the first flight from Puerto Rico to the Dominican Republic, which shares the neighboring island of Hispaniola with Haiti, but the agent at the counter of Pan American World Airways informed me that the Government forces had closed the Dominican Republic's Punta Caucedo International Airport to airline traffic. Caribair, a small airline flying between San Juan and Santo Domingo, had the same information. And the counter of the Compania Dominicana de Aviación was deserted. A penciled sign said in Spanish: "All flights to Santo Domingo are canceled until new orders." The Dominican Republic was thus isolated from the outside world and I was stuck in San Juan, only one hour's flying time away from my story but unable to reach it. I made a perfunctory check with the Air Taxi service at the San Juan airport in the faint hope of being able to hire a light plane for the trip to Santo Domingo, but the girl at the counter shook her head. No, she said, because of insurance risks they would not venture to fly into a closed airport. This was the beginning of days of intense frustration for me and the other newsmen who followed me to San Juan.

I moved into a hotel and checked on the latest information from Santo Domingo. It appeared that during the night military commanders from both sides—the rebels and the loyalists—had decided that the time had come for the ouster of President Reid Cabral. Consequently the loyalist forces had refused to obey Reid Cabral's order to attack the two rebel-held army camps. A decision seems to have been reached that a military junta would be established immediately and new elections scheduled within three or six months.

On the strength of this decision, which appeared to have been taken unanimously by all the military leaders, Reid Cabral agreed to resign about 10 o'clock Sunday morning. The military told him that he and his closest collaborator, Ramón Cáceres, and their wives should remain at the Presidential Palace for their own safety.

But then, suddenly, the whole situation changed again. The young military commanders who had set off the revolt the day before took control of the Presidential Palace and announced that, instead of a military junta, they were now pressing for the restoration of constitutional government and specifically for the return to the presidency of Juan Bosch, who was living in exile in San Juan. The young commanders had no confidence that a junta containing former Trujillo generals would really bring democracy back to the Dominican Republic.

Pending Dr. Bosch's return, the rebels installed before noon Sunday José Rafael Molina Ureña to serve as Provisional President.

Mr. Molina Ureña had been President of the Chamber of Deputies during the Bosch regime and under the provisions of Article 131 of the 1963 Constitution he was next in line for the presidency of the country in the absence of the President and the Vice President of the Dominican Republic and the President of the Senate.

This swift move by the young officers led to an instant split within the military establishment—as the loyalist commanders reacted with fury against what they considered a betrayal. This, then, was the real beginning of the civil war in the Dominican Republic.

Unable to fly to Santo Domingo, I began at once looking for Dr. Bosch in San Juan. I had known him before his election to the presidency in 1962 and I had seen him several times during his term in office—before the military ousted him in September, 1963.

Juan Bosch is one of the most interesting, intriguing and disconcerting men I have ever met in my 10 years as a newspaper correspondent in Latin America. There is a sense of dignity and history about him—and also a sense of tragedy and defeat. I could never escape the impression during his presidency that he did not really believe he was the ruler of a nation and always expected to fall from power at any moment. I am not even sure that the complicated human being that is Juan Bosch did not subconsciously desire to see himself thrown tragically out of office.

The important thing to remember about Juan Bosch, I think, is that he is a writer and a good one. But, perhaps like all good writers, Juan Bosch tends—or overtends—to identify himself with his characters and the tragedies his tales invariably spin.

In his very fine biography of King David, unfortunately not available thus far in English, Bosch draws a tragic portrait of David that with slight adaptations of personality could be a portrait of himself. One day in May, 1963, during his first major crisis as President in connection with a Dominican-Haitian dispute, Bosch sat on the terrace of his home in Santo Domingo reading to me a few pages from the King David book. He read intently and it seemed as if he were reading his own autobiography.

Bosch has also written a history of the 30 years of the Trujillo tyranny. He wrote it in exile shortly before Trujillo was assassinated in 1961. The main point he makes is that the Dominican Republic is a nation that has been cursed by fate since 1492, when Columbus set foot on its soil. Bosch recounts the beginnings of his island home, speaks of Columbus's abandonment of his first site, goes on to discuss the slavery that was imposed upon the aboriginal Indians of Hispaniola by the Spanish conquerors and tells the tragic story of how the Dominican Republic had to turn back to Spain for help against the Haitians who had invaded it from the west. It was the only instance of a former Spanish colony in Latin America requesting the ex-colonizer to return and resume its occupation. And then, of course, there was the terrible hurricane of 1930 and finally the Trujillo era.

Somewhere in this book Juan Bosch remarks that the Dominican Republic is a nation born in tragedy from a poisoned womb. And in his excellent collection of short stories about Dominican life he highlights the tragic and helpless lives of the peasants in the sugar-cane fields.

Juan Bosch, then, has been the narrator of Dominican tragedy. In the end he himself became associated with one of the greatest tragedies to befall his country in this century.

In his mid-50's, Juan Bosch is a rather impressive figure. Not really tall, he creates the illusion of height through erect bearing. His white hair and his blue eyes, which look piercingly at one, enhance his air of statesmanship.

Outwardly he is self-possessed, self-controlled, seemingly nerveless. In conversation he is extraordinarily self-assured, as if never doubting of the wisdom of his moves. But probably there are—there must be—deep inner conflicts within this restless man.

Having lived 24 years in exile during the Trujillo dictatorship, he came back to the Dominican Republic late in 1961 to offer himself as a candidate for the presidency. In his years abroad he had lived in Puerto Rico, in Cuba, in Venezuela and in Costa Rica, mainly writing and becoming a self-taught political scientist. He had even lectured in political science at an institute for labor leaders and politicians in San José, Costa Rica.

Running for the presidency in 1962, Juan Bosch won presumably because he impressed the Dominican people with his appearance, with his gifts of oratory and possibly above all with his championing of social reform. That social reform was needed in the Dominican Republic after the three decades of Trujillo rule was obvious to anyone. Most of the good sugar and cattle land had belonged to the Trujillo family. Most industries had directly or indirectly been in the hands of the dictator, his relatives or henchmen. The country had been a personal fief of the Trujillos and at the tyrant's downfall it was clearly necessary to give the Dominican Republic back to its people.

To the United States under the Kennedy Administration the Dominican Republic, liberated—not without American help—from the Trujillos, appeared to offer a wonderful opportunity to construct a "showcase of democracy" in the Caribbean as a contrast to neighboring Communist Cuba. Alliance for Progress programs were enthusiastically applied to the Dominican Republic even before Dr. Bosch's election and more so after he became President.

To nobody's great surprise Bosch won with 62 per cent of the votes. He carried Santo Domingo by an overwhelming margin and did well in the agricultural areas of the central valley where he was born in 1909. The election was a great national event: the people were voting freely for the first time in 38 years and they were proud of it. Dr. Bosch came to Washington to meet President Kennedy and to set in motion cooperation with the United States.

Lyndon B. Johnson, then Vice President of the United States, and Hubert H. Humphrey, then majority whip in the Senate, came to Dr. Bosch's inauguration on Feb. 27, 1963. There are photographs showing Mr. Johnson warmly embracing Dr. Bosch after his swearing-in ceremony. The United States Government was generous with praise and expressions of hope for the success of the Dominican Republic's first democratic regime in nearly 40 years.

After his election President Bosch remarked dryly: "I was not elected because I have blue eyes but because I am a social reformer."

Yet Bosch's social and other reforming was not quite a success—if one can make such a definitive judgment when a man has had but seven months in office. Bosch began on a small scale to redistribute some of the land that had once belonged to the

Trujillos and was now held by the Dominican state. This did not involve taking over land from private owners—as often has to be the case elsewhere in Latin America—but it was a complicated labor of resettlement and teaching farmers how to work the land they now possessed.

Juan Bosch, unfortunately, was not a practical man or a good administrator. He surrounded himself with a Cabinet that by no stretch of the imagination could be described as first rate. He allowed personal friends with strange (to say the least) business contacts to be in the Cabinet or in his immediate entourage. He signed contracts for foreign loans with private groups under conditions that international financial institutions described as bizarre, not to say catastrophic. In other fields his Congress passed a new Constitution that angered segments of the clergy and some of the more rightist elements because it established the institution of divorce. The new Constitution also forbade the banishment of Dominicans from their own country, no matter what the grounds.

President Bosch's relations with the powerful military establishment that had survived Generalissimo Trujillo's assassination were not felicitous either. He sent the army at one point to the Haitian border in what appeared to be a plan to invade Haiti and topple its dictator, François Duvalier. The military did not take very kindly to this idea. Some Dominicans suspected that the Haitian crisis was a diversion to turn attention away from domestic problems.

Then, inevitably, Bosch came under attack on the grounds that he was harboring or protecting Communists. Although no proof was ever offered by anyone that Dr. Bosch actually favored Communists or had brought any of them into his Government on any level, the opposition press, radio and television, the military hierarchy and the leaders of rightist groups began a powerful and well-financed campaign to make it appear that Dr. Bosch was at best a dupe of the Communists. He was blamed for not exiling Communists or suspected Communists and for allowing other Communists to re-enter the Dominican Republic. But it was forgotten that Bosch—as a democratic social reformer—was also the target of furious attacks from Fidel Castro's Cuba.

The argument of this independent-minded President was that a democratic society had to take a risk with its enemies and try to defeat them politically—through improving democratic institutions and living standards—instead of applying police methods that in a country as sensitive as the Dominican Republic could easily become reminiscent of the Trujillo rule. In any event, as Bosch pointed out, the rightist Council of State Government that had preceded his own regime was quite generous in letting Communists organize and freely enter the country.

In September, 1963, the lines were drawn. The military elements at the air force base at San Isidro, across the Ozama River from the capital, had made up their minds that Bosch had to go. The chief spokesman for this group was Colonel Elias Wessin y Wessin, who commanded the powerful units of the Armed Forces Training Center. He had the support of the aviation personnel stationed at San Isidro and of the air arm's infantry and armored forces. Under Trujillo's rule the dictator's son Ramfis had been allowed to build a private and separate army around the air force and now this élite group loomed as the most powerful single armed element in the Dominican Republic—and it was poised to destroy Bosch.

When the showdown came Bosch tried to dismiss Colonel Wessin y Wessin. Instead the colonel led the revolt that ousted the President—and again Bosch left for exile. The Kennedy Administration reacted with predictable anger, severing diplomatic relations and cutting off all aid to the Dominican Republic. To John F. Kennedy the coup represented a betrayal of the democratic principles of the Alliance for Progress.

But pressures on the Administration mounted to resume relations with the junta that had replaced the democratic Bosch regime. Even before President Kennedy's assassination the United States had considered restoring diplomatic ties to help the junta in its fight against a small band of pro-Castro guerrillas. These guerrillas, members of the 14th of June Movement, went into the hills after Dr. Bosch's overthrow. They did so even though the 14th of June Movement had boycotted the 1962 elections and later had sharply criticized Dr. Bosch in a parroting of the official Havana line. But the junta's reports of the guerrillas' strength were deliberately exaggerated to impress the U.S.

One of President Johnson's first actions in the field of Latin American affairs was to resume diplomatic relations with the Dominican Republic. Mr. Johnson explained to a delegation of Congressional leaders that this was necessary in view of the danger posed by the "Castro guerrillas." A few weeks later Dominican troops liquidated the guerrillas, killing even those who had surrendered. Among the dead was the head of the 14th of June Movement, Manuel Tavares Justo. So brutal was the slaying of the captured guerrillas that the junta's President, Emilio de los Santos, an elderly and highly respected gentleman, resigned in protest.

Now on this sunny April Sunday of 1965, exactly 19 months after he had been thrown out of office, Juan Bosch was getting ready for a triumphant return to the presidency of the Dominican Republic. I found him in his modest second-floor apartment on Sixth Street in the Rio Piedras section of San Juan, not far from the University of Puerto Rico, where he worked as a writer-in-residence.

The apartment was full of Dr. Bosch's friends and followers, members of his Dominican Revolutionary Party. It was a joyful bedlam, with the friends embracing the former President and congratulating him on what seemed to be his victory. His wife, Carmen, and his niece and former secretary, Milagro Ortiz, were busy packing the family's belongings. Open suitcases with clothing in them were laid out on the floor.

The atmosphere was electric. There was a feeling of anticipation, a sense of urgency, a readiness to return to the homeland.

Bosch expected to be able to return to the Dominican Republic the next day, perhaps even this same night. He was awaiting a military aircraft from the Dominican Republic to carry him back. It was believed it would arrive momentarily.

Mrs. Bosch turned to her husband, pointed to me with a smile and said: "Here is another passenger to go on our plane."

Bosch was the only outwardly calm person in all the joyful confusion. We got away from the crowd and sat in one of the bedrooms, talking of the past and discussing the new situation.

Bosch seemed fully in command of the revolution. He had spoken by phone with Acting President Molina Ureña in Santo Domingo and told of having instructed Molina Ureña to appoint as

Secretary of Defense Colonel Miguel Ángel Hernando Ramirez, whom he described as one of the top leaders of the uprising that had begun in Juan Bosch's name. Bosch spoke of Colonel Hernando Ramirez and the other young officers as idealistic military men who had been forced to accept his overthrow in 1963 but who had never really come to terms with that collapse of democracy in Santo Domingo.

Other names, too, began to emerge from the conversation. There was Colonel Francisco Caamaño Deñó, another young officer among those instrumental in engineering the uprising. A telephone call from Santo Domingo, one of many being received by Bosch, told of Colonel Caamaño's announcing the rebel victory early Sunday and saying that "the former President will be brought back to power in the shortest possible time."

Although Dr. Bosch was nominally the head of the revolution that had been set in motion to bring him back to power, it appeared that he did not actually know when it was to start. On Saturday, when the revolt began, Bosch and his immediate family had been spending a quiet weekend at the resort of Luquillo. Only when word of the uprising was received from Santo Domingo did Dr. Bosch drive back to San Juan to assume his role of commander of the rebellion by remote control.

Now he sat in a rocking chair in the bedroom, chain-smoking and saying that the revolution had been "inevitable" since early 1964. By then, he declared, it had become clear that the Dominican economy was being ruined and corruption and inefficiency were spreading under the Government of Donald Reid Cabral.

"The rebellion," he said, "was fundamentally a movement of the people" and "an episode in the struggle of the Dominican people to rid themselves of an oligarchical minority."

But in Santo Domingo, despite the enthusiastic telephone reports to San Juan, things were not completely in hand. In midafternoon aircraft under the control of Wessin y Wessin, by now a brigadier general, strafed and hurled rockets at the Presidential Palace, where Mr. Molina Ureña and his command had established themselves. Other planes from the San Isidro Air Force Base raided one of the rebel army barracks on the outskirts of the capital.

At first the news of the air attacks did not seem to disturb the Bosch family. Mrs. Bosch remarked: "It is all for the best. Let them learn that democracy has its price in blood."

And, indeed, in the ancient Dominican capital blood was flowing freely. Rebel army units and civilian bands were firing across the city at the positions of the Wessin forces. Planes streaked overhead, machine gunning the streets and dropping bombs on the rebels and the civilian population. Casualties were mounting and hospitals were filling up with the wounded.

Possibly as a reaction against the air raids and in anticipation of attacks by Wessin's tanks and infantry, the rebel military command issued orders Sunday afternoon to begin arming pro-rebel civilians. At first weapons ranging from pistols and rifles to submachine guns and .50-caliber machine guns were issued only to veterans of the armed forces and each recipient had to sign a receipt. By late Sunday night, however, arms depositories in the city were thrown open to anyone who wanted to grab a weapon. It has been estimated, but can never be proved, that as many as 20,000 weapons were given out to civilians. Filling stations in Santo Domingo began giving away gasoline free for the manufacture of Molotov cocktails. The rebel city was arming itself against the assault by the Wessin forces.

It is a matter of argument whether the order to arm the civilians was given by the rebel military commanders on their own initiative or whether they were influenced by Communists and pro-Communists. The military leaders have insisted throughout that the order to arm the civilian population came from them. Some United States sources insist this could only have been the idea of the Communists, seeking to capitalize on the pro-Bosch revolt. Actually, in downtown Santo Domingo signs were painted in black and red on walls saying "Weapons for the People." The signature was P. S. P.—the initials in Spanish of the Communist-led Socialist Popular Party. Captured vehicles and tanks had the word "pueblo"—the people—painted on them. To some American observers this indicated that Communists were in command—or at least wielding strong influence over the rebellion—but this is at best arguable. The term "the people," after all, is not, or should not be, Communist property.

Nonetheless the fact remains that by Sunday night thousands of people were armed in Santo Domingo—not only men but also women and teen-agers. Even boys of 12 and 13 were carrying rifles they could hardly handle. More weapons were made available and two truckloads of arms from the army barracks on Santo Domingo's outskirts were brought to the Parque Independencia, one of the city's main squares. There people were simply told to help themselves to weapons.

Meanwhile the events of the last 24 hours seemed to have convinced the United States Embassy in Santo Domingo of two things. One was that a return of Dr. Bosch would mean "Communism in the Dominican Republic in six months." The second was that U.S. forces would have to be used in support of General Wessin's troops if the pro-Bosch rebellion was to be defeated.

These two basic judgments, which the embassy arrived at even before the rebellion could be identified politically in any way, went far to shape subsequent United States attitudes and policies. It was Ambassador Bennett who had long felt that the Bosch influence would be pernicious for the Dominican Republic, and in his absence his staff members apparently shared this view. During the 13½ months he had spent in Santo Domingo, Ambassador Bennett had largely confined himself to contacts with the Reid Cabral Government, business and land-owning groups supporting it and some of the military officers loyal to it. He had had little, if any, contact with the opposition—whether democratic groups like Bosch's Dominican Revolutionary Party and the Christian Democrats or the extreme left-wingers. Thus, in a sense, the situation in terms of Juan Bosch had been prejudged at the embassy even before the rebellion erupted.

This bias—or judgment—was reflected immediately in the telegrams to the State Department from Chargé d'Affaires Bill Connett. After having first been surprised by the revolt and then having minimized it, Mr. Connett by late Sunday was beginning to hint in his messages that the pro-Bosch uprising was a Communist danger. He reported "armed leftists on street corners" without explaining, however, how he knew they were necessarily "leftists." Thus the seed of the idea of a major intervention—one not limited just to saving or protecting American lives—came into being at the embassy little more than 24 hours after the rebellion had erupted.

Having had practically no contacts with the opposition during the preceding year, embassy personnel had virtually no links to the rebel leadership. Some of the lower-ranking embassy officials sought to telephone acquaintances in the Dominican Revolutionary Party and other moderate groups. But it was impossible or deemed undesirable to try to establish contact or rapport with the rebels now entrenched at the Presidential Palace, only a few blocks from the building housing the embassy.

It appears that most of the information being received by Mr. Connett—information that served as a basis for his reports to Washington—came via telephone from friends and acquaintances (often persons identified with the deposed Government), from rebel broadcasts and from paid informants of the Central Intelligence Agency. The C.I.A.'s station chief in Santo Domingo, Edwin N. Terrell, and his four permanent associates had their offices in a back room in the embassy. It was to their cubicles, beginning late Saturday and continuing throughout Sunday, that the C.I.A.'s paid informers and other individuals streamed. Among them were leftist members of the Dock Workers Union and the Transportation Workers Union as well as characters who defied all description.

As an example of the embassy's hostile attitude toward the rebellion virtually as soon as it began, there is this account of an interview held at the embassy Sunday afternoon. The account is by Enriquillo del Rosario, formerly Dr. Bosch's Ambassador to the United States.

Mr. del Rosario told me that at 5:45 P.M. he went to the embassy with three ranking officials of the Dominican Revolutionary Party to seek American good offices to halt the Wessin air attacks. His companions were Silvestre Antonio Guzmán, a wealthy Cibao Valley planter who had been Dr. Bosch's Minister of Agriculture and who was to figure prominently in subsequent negotiations with the United States; Máximo Lovatón Pitaluga, chairman of the Santo Domingo chapter of the party, and Antonio Martinez, the party's secretary general.

They were received by the embassy's second secretary, Arthur E. Breisky, who, according to Mr. del Rosario, called the rebels "irresponsible" and charged that they were part of a "Communist movement."

Mr. Lovatón reportedly replied that "you know perfectly well that there is no Communism in this movement" because it is "principally a military movement."

To this Mr. Breisky was said to have retorted that "now you ask for U.S. help after having sent your people into the streets." Then, Mr. del Rosario said, the U.S. diplomat added: "If I had the power of Wessin, I would use it."

In San Juan that same afternoon Dr. Bosch complained to me that althought the revolt was now more than 24 hours old, he had not been contacted by any U.S. Government official. He said he had hoped to work again with the U.S. but now was wondering if the U.S. wanted to work with him.

Meanwhile, in Washington, officials who had at first been ready to accept the information that Reid Cabral had "weathered the storm" were now receptive to the suggestions from the Santo Domingo embassy that Bosch's return would mean extremism or Communism "in six months" and must be prevented at all costs. According to persons in Washington familiar with the hectic hours of late Sunday afternoon, it was then that the initial discussions about a United States military intervention in Santo Domingo began to be held.

A telegram from the State Department to the embassy late Sunday said: "We are very concerned with your reports of pro-Communist and anti-United States statements. Please keep us informed."

In the absence of the Assistant Secretary of State for Inter-American Affairs, Jack Hood Vaughn, it was the Under Secretary of State for Economic Affairs, Thomas C. Mann, who moved into the State Department's seventh-floor operations center to coordinate the United States' response to the crisis. Mr. Mann, who had served as Assistant Secretary for Inter-American Affairs until recently, had a Washington reputation as a "hardliner," a man not necessarily disturbed by the existence of military governments in Latin America and an inexorable foe of Communism. Some of Mr. Mann's associates have said that his main standard in defining Latin Americans was to ask, "Is he a Communist or isn't he?"

In any event, if Chargé d'Affaires Connett's first judgment that the pro-Bosch revolt posed a Communist threat was not immediately accepted in Washington, it certainly received serious consideration. The Johnson Administration felt that the United States could not afford "another Cuba" in the Caribbean and contingency planning to avert such a possibility was at once set in motion. Thus Sunday evening in Washington the stage was set for future events, while in Santo Domingo heavy fighting continued far into the night.

Monday, April 26th.

Monday, the third day of the revolution, was a day of confusion in Santo Domingo, San Juan and Washington.

In the Dominican capital General Wessin y Wessin was pressing his advantage against the rebels in the air and in ground attacks on their positions. Beginning at 6:30 A.M. Wessin's aircraft from the San Isidro base bombed and strafed Santo Domingo in successive passes. A twin-engined Canberra bomber loosed rockets at the National Palace. Other planes strafed Radio Santo Domingo's transmitter facilities and went after the two military barracks in rebel hands. Then General Wessin concentrated the full power of his air attack on the vicinity of the bridge connecting Santo Domingo with the suburb of Duarte and the outlying areas toward the San Isidro base.

Working in pairs, P-51 fighters zoomed low over the city on strafing runs. Bullets rained along the streets of downtown Santo Domingo, where rebels and civilians joined in firing at the attacking planes and running for cover.

Then the rebel command thought up tactics to counteract the air attacks. First someone suggested that the population bring into the streets any mirrors they could find and place them facing upward to reflect the rays of the sun into the eyes of the pilots of the diving P-51's. This was intended to blind them. Next, rebel soldiers and civilians begun rounding up families of the San Isidro pilots, using them virtually as hostages. They took them before the television cameras of Radio Santo Domingo and made them appeal to their fathers, husbands or brothers to desist from the bombing and strafing. According to certain unverified reports, some of the relatives were also taken to the Duarte bridge to further discourage the pilots from attacking the area.

Finally Santo Domingo's Archbishop Octavio Beras and the diplomatic corps jointly appealed to General Wessin to halt the air attacks in view of the heavy casualties. Whether in response to this appeal or not, the air attacks stopped about 12:30 P.M.

But heavy fighting went on in the eastern part of Santo Domingo. The rebels were well entrenched in the section known as Ciudad Nueva, which lies along the eastern end of the seaside boulevard and curves around at the point where the Ozama River flows into the Caribbean. Further north the rebels controlled the narrow streets and old houses along the river all the way to the Duarte bridge and, beyond the bridge, the section of new housing projects. The only important enclave held by the loyalists in that part of the city was the historic Ozama Fortress bordering the river about half a mile south of the Duarte bridge. Hundreds of riot-control policemen loyal to the deposed Government—they were known as the Cascos Blancos, meaning white helmets—were defending the fortress against rebel attacks. The fortress was one of the major depositories of weapons in Santo Domingo.

The loyalist forces also held the National Police Palace, which is a block from the Presidential Palace in the residential area of the city and just a few blocks from the United States Embassy. Otherwise the rebels had the run of the capital. But in a real sense it could not be said that they controlled the city. Although Mr. Molina Ureña was nominally the Acting President, operating from the Presidential Palace, there was no established authority in Santo Domingo. It was a city in revolution—a city in civil war—and authority was in the hands of each army patrol or group of armed civilians who roamed the streets on foot or in commandeered jeeps, cars or "publicos," which are the Santo Domingo buses. Toward the end of the day the patrols became joint units composed of army personnel and armed civilians. They manned improvised checkpoints here and there, stopping cars and occasionally arresting people.

Thus far there was no clear ideological content or form in this revolution. The only slogans heard in the streets or over the rebel-controlled radio and television were exhortations for the "Constitution" and for "Bosch." But officials at the United States Embassy, watching rebel TV, began developing the uneasy feeling that the tone of the broadcasts was becoming disconcertingly reminiscent of the early days in Havana after Castro's assumption of power.

The broadcasters were giving the addresses of officials of the deposed Government and of "counterrevolutionaries," implying in effect that rebels ought to go and get them—or do something unpleasant with them. Over rebel television, which for some reason sounded more radical than the rebels' radio broadcasts, young army officers were denouncing their superiors, mainly the old colonels and generals associated first with the Trujillo regime and now with the forces at San Isidro.

It was this TV activity that presumably led the embassy to become even more convinced that the revolution might be Castroite or Communist in character or inspiration, even though there was no visible Communist-type leadership in the movement up to that point. In the circumstances the embassy threw its entire support to the forces of General Wessin regardless of the fact that the Wessin forces clearly represented a highly unpopular element in the eyes of a great many Dominicans.

It appeared to be one of those unfortunate—and seemingly inevitable—situations in which the United States, once bitten by Communism in Cuba, was allowing itself to be impelled in the direction of unpopular military groups rather than run the risk that democratic forces might not defeat the Communists in a revolutionary situation. To be sure, there can be no quarrel with this concern over Communism in light of the widespread subversive activities undertaken by Castro all over Latin America in recent years. But the point made early in the Santo Domingo crisis by some Americans and many Dominicans was that the United States tended prematurely to put all its eggs in one basket—in this case, General Wessin's basket—before the situation could be clarified and better strategic planning to face the Communist problem could be undertaken.

In fact, the embassy was so concerned that there might be interference with what it hoped would be a Wessin victory that

Ambassador Bennett, while still in Washington, reportedly recommended against providing U.S. military transportation back to Santo Domingo for the Papal Nuncio, Msgr. Emanuele Clarizio. The Nuncio, who had been visiting Rome earlier in April, was caught in San Juan by the revolution and, because the International Airport was closed, asked U.S. authorities for a military lift to the Dominican Republic as soon as possible. But Mr. Bennett seemed to fear that the Nuncio, who had a reputation as a liberal, might in some manner favor the rebels because of his earlier friendship with Dr. Bosch. He suggested that Msgr. Clarizio await the resumption of commercial transportation, but in the end he was overruled and the Nuncio later played an important role in seeking to end the civil war.

The case can be made here that while it may be easy to control Communism, or an apparent threat of Communism, through initial forceful measures, these may lead to the aggravation of the long-run Communist problem. It is the story of the U.S. propensity for closing off all options and alternatives to non-Communists caught up in revolutionary events.

In any event, the United States Embassy was squarely on the side of General Wessin. Its military attachés were at San Isidro with the Wessin command, relaying to the embassy battle reports and requests for assistance. Among the requests emanating from General Wessin's headquarters was one for communications equipment, particularly for walkie-talkies so that the action of the loyalists' tanks against the rebels could be better coordinated.

It is not clear whether the embassy recommended actual help to the Wessin forces as early as Monday. But a long telegram from Chargé d'Affaires Bill Connett that afternoon told the State Department that while direct United States intervention in the Dominican civil war might be inadvisable because of Dr. Bosch's popularity, the pro-Bosch movement had to be stopped by other means—or there would be "extremism in six months" in the Dominican Republic. The telegram implied in effect that at least logistical support should be given the Wessin forces. All the while the Johnson Administration was speaking of United States neutrality in the conflict.

In war-torn Santo Domingo the battle for control of the Duarte bridge raged all afternoon and early into the evening as tank-supported Wessin forces sought to thrust across the bridge and break into the city. But the rebel army forces and their civilian allies, armed with weapons of every description and the gasoline bombs known as Molotov cocktails, fought hard and the tanks did not make much headway, though several times Wessin armor crossed the bridge.

In San Juan, meanwhile, utter frustration gripped the newspaper correspondents gathered there. Unable to fly to the Dominican Republic on regular airlines, most of us spent much of our time trying desperately to charter light planes. A few newsmen succeeded in obtaining aircraft that took them to within a few miles of the International Airport in Santo Domingo, but they were chased away by radio warnings from the control tower that they might be fired upon if they attempted to land. A television camera crew flew to Port-au-Prince, Haiti, in the hope of being able to enter the Dominican Republic from there. But that too failed as the Dominican border was closed and it also proved impossible to fly from the Haitian capital to Santo Domingo. The more inventive among us tried to charter fast boats to sail from the western tip of Puerto Rico to the Dominican Republic. But it was a long and risky crossing of the turbulent waters of the Mona Passage and none of the owners or captains of the fishing or pleasure craft available in the Mayagüez area were willing to ferry desperate correspondents. I reserved berths aboard a merchant vessel that was to sail from San Juan for Santo Domingo the next day, but in the end this was another project that had to be abandoned.

Unable thus far to cover the story directly, we tried to do it by telephone from San Juan to Santo Domingo, an effort that was reasonably rewarding.

I established my headquarters at the offices of The San Juan Star, an English-language daily newspaper, where I was given the use of a desk, a typewriter and a telephone. There I went on for two more days covering the Dominican civil war by phone. I worked alongside Louis Uchitelle, the young and enterprising San Juan bureau chief of The Associated Press, and we succeeded in talking to Santo Domingo 10 or more times a day. The telephone exchange there was in rebel hands and it was not too difficult getting press priority calls through.

Among our good sources of news in Santo Domingo was the embassy's information officer, Malcolm McLean, whom I had known for many years, first in São Paulo, Brazil, and then in the Dominican capital. McLean, who knew many people in Santo Domingo, managed to keep fairly well abreast of events and his journalistic background enabled him to provide us with quick, sharp and succinct information. Another good source was Rafael Herrera, editor of Listin Diario, a newspaper which had opposed the Reid Cabral Government even though it belonged in part to one of the deposed President's closest business associates. Still another source was the city editor of El Caribe, the other morning newspaper in Santo Domingo. Finally there was Jeanette Diedrich, the wife of our stringer in Santo Domingo. Her husband was with us in San Juan but Jeanette, a bright Haitian girl who had learned journalism by watching Bernie Diedrich operate, was able to give us several daily reports on the situation in the residential part of Santo Domingo. She also monitored rebel and loyalist radio broadcasts and passed on to us the gist of what was being said. There were other friends and acquaintances we telephoned and, with everything put together, we had at the end of each day a fairly accurate picture of what was going on in the embattled Dominican capital.

A certain inventiveness was required to keep this operation going as more and more newsmen tried to telephone Santo Domingo, overtaxing the limited phone circuits. Lou Uchitelle and I devised the system of asking each person to whom we spoke in Santo Domingo to get his telephone operator back after we had completed our conversation and ask the operator to ring the next number we wanted in Santo Domingo. In this manner we succeeded in talking to as many as 10 persons during a single telephone call to Santo Domingo. All this cost money, but on such occasions newspapers and press services can be generous and I do not believe our auditors in New York batted an eye when confronted with bills for phone calls between San Juan and Santo Domingo, including one bill for $1,100.

All this, of course, had a touch of complete unreality about it.

Whenever we were sitting in The San Juan Star office, talking on the telephone to Santo Domingo and then writing our stories to be phoned on to New York, we could almost feel the battle going on across the water. It was, in fact, not uncommon during some of the telephone calls to hear gunfire and bomb explosions in the background. But as soon as we left the newspaper office our sense of near-participation in the Dominican civil war immediately vanished. San Juan, as usual, was full of tourists and busy with its own bustling life. At night, when some of us would make our way to a restaurant or a bar for a late meal or a drink between filing stories, we would run into gay vacationers from the mainland, dancing, drinking and singing—completely oblivious of the tragedy that had brought us, the newsmen, to San Juan.

One night at a hotel bar a girl from Pittsburgh said to me, "And what brings you to San Juan?" I replied, "Why, the Santo Domingo war," thinking she would know all about it. But she had not seen a newspaper since she left her secretarial job back in Pennsylvania and she could not have cared less. Here again was that sense of unreality about everything we were doing in San Juan.

In the small apartment on Sixth Street in Rio Piedras where Juan Bosch lived, the plans for an immediate return to Santo Domingo had been shelved. The packed suitcases were no longer in evidence. Bosch was now awaiting the outcome of the battle being waged in his name. Carmen, his wife, told me at one point: "You cannot risk so lightly the life of the constitutional President."

When the whole story of the Dominican civil war is written, the question whether Juan Bosch should have risked an immediate trip to his homeland will remain a point of great controversy. There are many people who feel that if Bosch had taken the risk and gone to Santo Domingo the first day or even the second day, much of the fighting might have been averted. If nothing else, he might have filled the tremendous political void that existed at the outset of the rebellion. Since the Wessin forces controlled both the International Airport in Santo Domingo and the San Isidro Air Force Base, Bosch obviously could not have flown directly from San Juan. But suggestions had been made to him that he go by private plane to some other point in the Dominican Republic and then be taken into the capital. However, his judgment was to refuse to do so and he remained in San Juan, always in touch with his rebellion by telephone but tragically far removed from it.

In Washington concern over the situation in Santo Domingo mounted from hour to hour. President Johnson was reading personally all the reports from the embassy, the C.I.A. and other sources. He was becoming increasingly worried about the safety of the Americans living in Santo Domingo, and by late Monday plans were under consideration not only for an evacuation of Americans and a Marine landing to protect their departure but also for a large military intervention. The President was to say at his news conference in Washington on June 17th that the decision to land Marines to help in the evacuation had been considered from Saturday, the first day of the rebellion.

From all that is known now about the planning in Washington Sunday and Monday, it is clear that the Administration was thinking simultaneously in terms of an evacuation and of a political-type military intervention. The first, obviously, would be designed to protect American lives. The second was being thought of in terms of preventing what it was already feared might be a "new Cuba." The embassy's reporting and the nervousness in the State Department were having their effect.

The six-ship Caribbean Amphibious Task Force led by the U.S.S. Boxer, a helicopter carrier, had moved to the vicinity of Santo Domingo Saturday night. The 1,500 Marines aboard the ships, which also carried tanks, armored vehicles and artillery, were in readiness. Such readiness was routine. The Caribbean Task Force and its Marines had been alerted each time a dangerous political situation developed in the Caribbean, be it in the Dominican Republic, Haiti or elsewhere, to say nothing of Cuba.

But this time, as it quickly became clear, the Marines were facing a situation that would send them into action. The Department of Defense and the Joint Chiefs of Staff began alerting units in the United States for what might come. A Marine brigade at Camp Lejeune and the 82nd Airborne Division at Fort Bragg, both in North Carolina, were given preliminary word Sunday or Monday to stand by for action.

On Monday, as I returned to my hotel room from The San Juan Star about 11 o'clock at night, I decided to make a few final checks by telephone with Santo Domingo before advising New York that the story was complete for the day. First I talked to my friend Rafael Herrera at Listin Diario, which he still kept trying to publish every day despite gunfire all around his printing plant. Rafael described for me the heavy fighting late in the day at the Duarte bridge during which a few of the Wessin tanks actually succeeded in entering the city but were stopped at the barricades erected by the rebels at the Santo Domingo approaches to the bridge.

Rafael then went on to tell me about the continuing arming of civilians and about the 15,000 Molotov cocktails that he estimated were now in the hands of the city's population. He said that the armed civilians were an extremely disturbing element and that the situation could get even more out of hand than it was now.

Then I called Malcolm McLean at our embassy. Like all the other embassy staff members, McLean was spending most of the night in his office and, as before, he was extremely well informed. He had been driving around Santo Domingo earlier in the evening and he told me that he had been stopped several times by patrols of armed civilians. After he showed his diplomatic credentials he was allowed to continue on his way. But Malcolm and the others at the embassy felt the situation in the Dominican capital was becoming increasingly dangerous.

It was at this point that he told me, rather casually, that the decision had been made to begin evacuating Americans from Santo Domingo the next morning. He said the embassy had recommended a "voluntary" evacuation because of a feeling that no one could any longer guarantee the safety of Americans in the capital.

He told me the plans were for the U.S.S. Raleigh, one of the ships of the Caribbean Amphibious Task Force, a vessel with a helicopter landing platform, to stand close off Santo Domingo and for helicopters to fly to the Hotel Embajador in the western residential section of the city to fetch the evacuees. He said American residents were being informed by telephone and other means to begin gathering at the hotel at 6 o'clock in the morning to be processed for evacuation. Malcolm also said that both the

Wessin command at San Isidro and the rebel commanders at the Presidential Palace had offered assurances that there would be no interference with the planned evacuation.

This was a major new development in the Dominican crisis, involving the United States directly for the first time. It had not yet been announced from Washington and I grabbed the telephone to call in a new lead for the late editions of The New York Times. The story in the next morning's paper began:

> *SAN JUAN*, P. R., Tuesday, April 27—The United States Navy will begin later today to evacuate American citizens who want to leave the Dominican Republic in view of the mounting threat of a breakdown in public order.
>
> A spokesman at the United States Embassy in Santo Domingo said in a telephone conversation that about 500 of the 2,500 United States citizens in the country were expected to leave.

Tuesday, April 27th.

Tuesday was to be another crucial day in the quickening Dominican crisis—with the United States involvement growing every hour.

It was crucial in Santo Domingo, where the civil war was reaching furious proportions; in Washington, where United States planners were moving closer and closer to a major intervention; in Fort Bragg, North Carolina, where the 82nd Airborne Division was placed on full alert; and in San Juan, where Juan Bosch was fighting for his political life—and for the life of his revolution.

In the Dominican capital fighting resumed in full force early in the morning. General Wessin's aircraft returned to their attacks on the Duarte bridge and his tanks and infantry continued the effort to break into the rebel-held city. Lou Uchitelle and I went back to the telephones and the accounts from Santo Domingo again described fierce but disorganized fighting. Before noon, as I was talking to Rafael Herrera, the editor of Listin Diario, he suddenly exclaimed "Hold on, something is happening" and ran away from his phone. Over the open line I could hear the sound of explosions. Then Rafael returned and said: "I just came back from the roof. It looks as if the navy has turned against the rebels and it is bombarding the city."

Rafael checked the situation a few more times, made some telephone calls of his own and came back with the report that ships of the tiny Dominican Navy had sailed from the harbor and, standing less than two miles off shore, had lobbed three shells into Santo Domingo in the general direction of the Presidential Palace, where Acting President Molina Ureña was holding out.

This apparent defection of the navy's few frigates and destroyers to General Wessin's side turned out to be a crucial element in subsequent events. Until Tuesday morning it had been assumed that the navy was with the rebels. In fact, the navy's élite corps of frogmen had become the chief commando group in the rebel forces and later the personal guard of the rebel leadership. The commander of the highly trained frogmen, Lieutenant Colonel Manuel Ramón Montes Arache, was one of the principal leaders of the pro-Bosch rebellion.

However, Commodore Francisco J. Rivera Caminero, the new commanding officer of the navy, had decided to throw his forces on the side of General Wessin. Messages between the embassy in Santo Domingo and the State Department in Washington Sunday and Monday had disclosed growing concern over the navy's role and one of the principal functions of the embassy's naval attachés had become to persuade Commodore Rivera Caminero to cast his lot with the loyalist troops or at least remain neutral. To judge from the lobbing of shells into the Presidential Palace area Tuesday morning, the attachés' efforts had proved successful.

The air force, under Brigadier General Jesus de los Santos Cespedes, had been solidly with the loyalists from the beginning.

Meanwhile the evacuation of Americans from Santo Domingo had begun even as Wessin's aircraft were bombing the Duarte bridge area in the eastern part of the city and the navy was firing at the midtown section. At about 6 o'clock in the morning hundreds of American residents—as well as many dependents of our embassy and military personnel—started gathering at the Hotel Embajador. The seven-story modernistic white hotel is in the westernmost residential section of Santo Domingo, miles from where the fighting was going on. It overlooks the Caribbean and is less than a mile from the shore.

Embassy officials and American volunteers set up desks in the cavernous lobby of the hotel to check the documents of the evacuees and to process them for the trip out of the Dominican Republic. At Haina, a sugar port six or seven miles west of the hotel, two ships of the Caribbean Task Force had moored earlier in the day to take the evacuees aboard. The vessels were the Wood County, an LST (Landing Ship Tank), and the Ruchamkin, a high speed assault transport known as an APD.

Four Marine helicopters flew from the U.S.S. Boxer to the polo grounds adjoining the Hotel Embajador to help in the evacuation. The helicopters brought ashore unarmed Marine communication teams whose personnel proceeded to set up radio communications at the United States Embassy, about two miles from the hotel, and at the San Isidro Air Force Base, General Wessin's headquarters. These radio facilities proved to be of great assistance in the forthcoming phase of the Dominican crisis.

About 10 o'clock in the morning, as the processing for the evacuation was moving apace, a band of rebels, some in army uniforms and some in civilian clothes, suddenly invaded the hotel grounds and then burst into the lobby. They said they were looking for "counterrevolutionaries" and particularly for Rafael Bonilla Aybar, a television commentator and newspaper publisher who had been one of the foremost influences behind the movement that overthrew Dr. Bosch in 1963. The rebels apparently had heard that Bonilla was among the persons who were to be evacuated by the United States and they had come to get him.

In the confusion that developed the rebels fired at several windows and balconies of the upper stories of the hotel. The fire was returned from one of the balconies. Inside the lobby the rebels fired several submachine-gun bursts into the ceiling and, for some unclear reason, forced the American civilians to line up against the walls. Nobody was hurt and the rebels presently departed. However, the embassy's reports on this incident must have been greatly exaggerated because President Johnson later spoke of armed rebels running up and down the hotel's corridors firing into rooms and closets. Actually, nothing of the sort had occurred, but this overwrought reporting by the embassy evidently helped increase the President's concern and pushed the United States closer to the ultimate decision to intervene militarily in the Dominican Republic.

After the rebels left the hotel the bulk of the evacuees were taken in a convoy to Haina under the guard of loyalist policemen. They traveled in trucks, buses and embassy vehicles. Some others were transported by helicopter. By 3:15 P.M. the operation was completed and 1,172 Americans were evacuated. The Wood County and the Ruchamkin left for San Juan, Puerto Rico.

Seven Marine helicopters were left overnight at the polo grounds by the Hotel Embajador in case any further emergency evacuations were necessary. Although it was not announced at the time, a detachment of armed Marines remained with the helicopters.

Back in the United States the military machine had been getting into high gear for a major operation. In a move that apparently coincided with the decision in Washington Monday night to set the evacuation from Santo Domingo in motion, the 82nd Airborne Division at Fort Bragg was placed on high alert. According to a chronological account of events later made available to newsmen in Santo Domingo by the Joint Information Bureau of the U.S. Armed Forces, Maj. Gen. Robert York, commanding general of the Airborne Division, briefed his subordinates at 4 A.M. Tuesday—hours before the evacuation began—to prepare for a "parachute assault" on the Dominican Republic.

The mission, as described by General York, would be to secure the San Isidro Air Force Base, then take the highway leading from the base to the Ozama River and establish positions on the Duarte bridge leading into Santo Domingo. Since no Americans resided on the eastern bank of the Ozama River and the evacuation was being processed at the westernmost end of the capital, it appeared that this contingency plan was no longer designed to protect the American residents but rather to support the Wessin forces in their effort either to break into Santo Domingo or to prevent the rebels from spilling out over the bridge into Wessin-held territory.

Meanwhile Ambassador Bennett returned to his post in Santo Domingo. He flew in on an Air Force jet from Washington to the Punta Caucedo International Airport, held by the Wessin forces, and from there was lifted by helicopter to the garden of the United States Embassy. At noon he bounced up the steps of the embassy just as Wessin aircraft were making another strafing run over the city. Looking up at the sky, the Ambassador shouted that someone should get those planes out of there because the air attacks were causing too many casualties.

One of the Ambassador's first acts after he got behind his desk was to send a telegram to Washington recommending that walkie-talkies and other communications equipment be flown in for the Wessin forces. He indicated that the availability of such equipment could spell the difference between victory or defeat for Wessin.

But in the course of the afternoon the rebels' situation deteriorated.

Supported by his P-51 fighter planes, General Wessin was again attacking the Duarte bridge position in force. In mid-afternoon the fighting reached the most serious proportions since the beginning of the civil war. Wessin tanks reached the middle of the bridge and were firing almost point blank at the resisting rebels. Among the latter was Colonel Francisco Caamaño Deñó, one of the top military leaders of the revolt and the man who the day before had announced the rebels' victory. He was fighting on the bridge with his friend Hector Aristy, a young politician and playboy who a few days later was to have a key role in the development of the rebellion. A rebel marine, standing next to Colonel Caamaño, had his leg shot off by the enemy.

About the same time the rebels heard that an army regiment from San Cristobal, a city and army base about 15 miles west of Santo Domingo, had driven into the western section of the capital, setting up camp at the old International Fair Grounds just below the Hotel Embajador. This force was commanded by Brigadier General Salvador Augusto Montás Guerrero, one of the former Trujillo generals. Montás Guerrero, who had been watching the development of the civil war from San Cristobal for three days, had apparently made up his mind to side with the Wessin command and so brought his troops into Santo Domingo. Although this force did not immediately go into action, it nonetheless represented a flanking movement from the west against the rebels.

Working frantically through our telephones from The San Juan

Star, Lou Uchitelle and I were told about the arrival of the San Cristobal regiment by our priceless reporter on the scene, Rafael Herrera, who suggested that this new event might well tip the scales against the rebel movement.

And, in fact, this is what apparently had begun to happen. Shortly after 4 P.M. a group of eight or nine rebel military leaders suddenly arrived at the United States Embassy and asked to see Ambassador Bennett. The group was led by Colonel Miguel Ángel Hernando Ramirez, who on Sunday had been named Defense Minister of the Provisional Government and who was regarded as the top military chief of the rebellion. Colonel Caamaño, however, was not in the group, presumably because he was fighting on the Durate bridge. After checking their weapons at the door at the Ambassador's request, the rebel officers entered Mr. Bennett's private office and proceeded to tell him that they believed "there had been enough bloodshed" and a solution should be found for the civil war.

According to Mr. Bennett's subsequent account, they asked him to mediate in negotiations with General Wessin. The Ambassador said he had no authority to negotiate or mediate, but since he was in touch with the Wessin headquarters he could pass on to the San Isidro commander whatever proposals for a truce the rebels might have. Then, still according to Mr. Bennett's account, the rebel officers said it would also be necessary to persuade Acting President Molina Ureña that the time had come to recognize defeat and seek terms. They asked if the embassy could be of assistance in conveying this view of the rebel military commanders to the Acting President. The Ambassador agreed and assigned Benjamin J. Ruyle, chief of the embassy's political section and one of the best-informed and best-connected officials in the embassy, to undertake this mission.

The Presidential Palace is only a few blocks from the embassy and Mr. Ruyle drove there in a few minutes under intermittent firing. He found the sprawling yellow palace that had once housed the dictator Trujillo apparently unoccupied. There were no rebel troops in sight and as he entered the building Mr. Ruyle noted the shattered windows and the rubble in the garden, on the staircases and in the corridors—mute testimony to the air raids of past days.

Though the palace appeared empty, Mr. Ruyle finally found Acting President Molina Ureña in a room off the main corridor in the right wing of the building. Mr. Molina Ureña was sitting dejectedly in an armchair surrounded by a group of rebel leaders. There were military men and civilians among them and Mr. Ruyle's impression was that they were an exhausted bunch. They were unshaven, their eyes were bloodshot and their attire consisted of bits of uniforms combined with other clothing.

Mr. Ruyle conveyed the message from the rebel officers who had spoken to Mr. Bennett. At first Mr. Molina Ureña refused to accept defeat. But, according to the embassy's account of this incident, the other men in the room finally persuaded the Acting President to face reality. Mr. Ruyle went back to the embassy.

Shortly afterward, about 5 P.M., Acting President Molina Ureña and 17 or 18 rebel military commanders arrived at the embassy to see Ambassador Bennett. This time Colonel Caamaño came along. Again the officers left their weapons at the door with the small Marine contingent that is permanently attached to the embassy and went into the Ambassador's private office.

The discussion there was at best chaotic. Some people sat on the green leather couch and the upholstered chairs. Others paced up and down the spacious room. Mr. Molina Ureña sat on a corner of the sofa talking to the Ambassador. Again the rebels told Mr. Bennett that there had already been too much bloodshed and that an end had to be found for the four-day-old revolution. Again the Ambassador was asked to mediate between the rebels and the Wessin forces and again he told the rebel delegation that he had no authority to do so.

From here on the accounts of what happened next vary considerably. Colonel Caamaño's own version is that Mr. Bennett told the group that "this is not the time to negotiate, this is the time to surrender." According to the colonel, the Ambassador also told the rebels that they had brought all this upon themselves and had no choice now but to surrender to the Wessin command without any conditions. This, Colonel Caamaño was to say later, was an insult to the military honor of the rebel officers.

Mr. Bennett, however, denies Colonel Caamaño's version. He says that he did not demand a surrender and did not insult—and certainly had no intention of insulting—the rebels. Mr. Bennett says he simply told the rebels that since he had contact with General Wessin's command he would be glad to assist in the settlement of the civil war by communicating with the San Isidro base and then letting the rebels and the loyalists negotiate themselves. But Colonel Caamaño's memory of this discussion is one of the American Ambassador arrogantly telling the rebels to surrender. This impression played an important role in defining the future relationship of the rebel command toward Mr. Bennett personally. The Ambassador recalls that at the end of the interview, as the rebel leaders were leaving the room, Colonel Caamaño, whom the envoy did not remember ever having met before, stopped at the door and said to him: "Let me tell you, we shall go on fighting no matter what happens."

Curiously, however, no mention of Colonel Caamaño or his parting remark appears in the long dispatch to the State Department in which Ambassador Bennett narrated the afternoon's events at his office. In fact, Colonel Caamaño had not yet been mentioned at all in embassy telegrams.

As the meeting with the United States Ambassador broke up, Mr. Molina Ureña shook hands with Mr. Bennett, left the building and got into a car that was to take him to the Colombian Embassy, where he requested and received political asylum. Some of the rebel military commanders tarried around the American Embassy, apparently hoping they could remain there in asylum. However, embassy officials pointed out to them that the United States, not being a party to inter-American conventions on political asylum, did not grant refuge to Latin Americans engaged in political strife. One by one, reluctantly, the officers left and vanished in the falling dusk. For all practical purposes, the rebellion seemed to have collapsed.

I received a fairly detailed account of these happenings by telephone from a good news source in Santo Domingo about 8 P.M. This is just about the deadline time for the first edition of The New York Times. I called The Times shortly before 9 P.M., as soon as I could arrange my notes, and told the assistant foreign editor on duty what had happened at the embassy and of the impression that the revolt had collapsed, suggesting that I write a new lead on the story for the next edition. But the editor shot back at me: "How quickly can you start dictating?"

"Right away," I said.

"Okay," he said. "We'll put you on to a rewrite man and if you can dictate a few paragraphs we'll replate the first edition with the collapse of the revolution."

Breathlessly I dictated the story paragraph by paragraph. Each paragraph was torn out of the rewrite man's typewriter and rushed to the foreign copy desk and then to the composing room. In its first edition The Times was exclusive with the apparent collapse of the revolution and the dramatic role the United States Embassy had played in it.

Lou Uchitelle also had this story and in a short time it was spread throughout the world over the wires of The Associated Press. Within minutes Juan Bosch was apprised of it. He had gone to a local television station to appear on a program discussing the future of the Dominican Republic in light of what was still being regarded as a probable victory for the rebels. The A.P. bulletin on what had just happened in Santo Domingo was handed to Dr. Bosch as he entered the TV station. He turned pale, told the station officials he was canceling his appearance and left for his home in Rio Piedras. But from his car he told a local reporter that "the people in Santo Domingo will go on fighting anyway." I doubt that anyone took this prediction seriously at that moment.

In Washington, as my colleague John W. Finney wrote in The Times, "Administration officials were expressing relief over the apparent collapse of the insurrection led by young army officers supporting the return of former President Bosch." The Administration apparently felt it would be academic at this stage to maintain the fiction of neutrality.

Wednesday, April 28th.

To everybody's complete surprise, the rebels went on fighting despite their apparent collapse the night before. While Colonel Hernando Ramirez and some of the other rebel officers were going into asylum at foreign embassies, Colonel Caamaño had assumed command of the movement—apparently in the absence of anyone else—and had moved downtown to reorganize the rebel forces. Thus he suddenly became the standard-bearer of the revolution and, to his own surprise, its top leader.

There was firing all Tuesday night in the old part of Santo Domingo, but it was generally assumed that these were small clashes involving die-hard rebel groups or the "*Tigres*," bands of armed hoodlums. Yet by Wednesday morning it had become obvious that the rebels had not only reorganized themselves during the night but had also gained new spirit and a new determination to win.

How this was accomplished remains one of the unsolved mysteries of the revolution. Colonel Caamaño and Hector Aristy are reluctant to discuss what happened during the night hours after the discussions at the U.S. Embassy. Aristy, who began to emerge as the principal civilian spokesman of the rebel movement, told me later that he had refused to go with Colonel Caamaño to the second Tuesday conference at the embassy. He and Caamaño had been fighting on the Duarte bridge Tuesday afternoon, but when the colonel rejoined his colleagues in the rebel leadership for the negotiations at the embassy Aristy went back downtown. This is when the first steps toward the regrouping of the rebels may have been taken.

It is the opinion of many Americans, as well as of foreign diplomats and observers, that it was at this time that the Communist and Castro-type groups may have played their most important role in the Dominican rebellion by assisting Caamaño to regroup his forces.

There is no actual proof of this, but those who believe it claim that the Communists were probably the only ones with sufficient organization to provide the leadership necessary for the regrouping of the rebels.

Information sent to Washington by the embassy spoke of "leftists" or Communists in the rebel command or manning rebel checkpoints. But neither the embassy nor the C.I.A. was able at that point to name any of those "leftists" or Communists.

It is known, of course, that activists from the Popular Socialist Party, the official Communist Party in the Dominican Republic, from the Dominican Popular Movement, a pro-Peking splinter Communist group, and from the 14th of June Movement, the pro-Castro organization, had infiltrated the rebel movement from the beginning. But as a foreign diplomat was to remark later, "While obviously all the Communists were rebels, it does not necessarily follow that all the rebels were Communists."

So while the possibility obviously cannot be excluded that the Communists and their associates indeed played a crucial role in regrouping the rebels, the fact remains that the rebels had a number of their own highly competent military leaders who were in a position to act in reorganizing the collapsing movement.

There was, in the first place, Colonel Caamaño himself, an officer trained by the Marines in the United States. There was Colonel Montes Arache, the commander of the frogmen, and there was his closest associate, André Rivière, a French veteran from Indochina, a colorful soldier of fortune and one of the most interesting figures in the rebel movement.

Be it as it may, by Wednesday morning the rebels were fighting again—and suddenly with considerable success. They turned the downtown business district of Santo Domingo and the maze of narrow streets in the old part of the capital—which, curiously, is known as Ciudad Nueva, the New City—into their main stronghold. As part of a defense plan credited to André Rivière, many a house in the downtown area had become a tiny fortress. Machine guns were installed on roofs and rebel units with rifles, submachine guns and pistols manned street corners and patrolled the downtown thoroughfares. Except for the Ozama Fortress near the Duarte bridge downtown and for the Presidential Palace and the National Police Palace toward the western residential districts, where the San Cristobal regiment had moved during the night, the whole of Santo Domingo was under rebel control. The rebels held all the utilities and facilities in the city, such as the power plant, the telephone exchange, the banks and just about everything else, though except for the telephones most did not function. And the reorganized rebels were again pressing their attacks against the Ozama Fortress, that great depository of weapons.

There was firing everywhere and nobody seemed safe. As a foreign ambassador recounted later, machine-gun bullets were raining into his garden all morning from all directions. His 5-year-old son, watching the bullets from behind a wall inside the building, innocently asked whether he could go out and play with "these things."

His mother cried, "Good heavens, no!"

But the child insisted, "But, Mommy, even if I promise not to touch them?"

From the polo grounds at the Hotel Embajador American helicopters were flying a shuttle service to the U.S.S. Boxer, ferrying out additional evacuees, who were filling the hotel.

Downtown armed civilian groups were attacking police stations. At the corner of Espaillat Street and George Washington Boulevard, which skirts the seacoast, eight dead policemen lay on the sidewalk by the police station for seven hours before someone picked them up. Then two of Wessin's Vampire jets swooped low over the city, bombing the rebel zone.

Now firmly in control of the situation in their part of the city, the rebels were organizing district commands. Contrary to reports from the embassy to Washington, however, these were not Communist-type political action committees but rather military defense commands.

Barricades were rising across the streets and avenues leading to the rebel strongholds. The rebels now had at least 12 tanks, captured both from the Wessin aviation forces and from loyalist army units. The word "PUEBLO" was painted on the sides of the tanks.

In the story I had written Tuesday night describing what had then appeared to be the collapse of the rebel movement, I forecast that the loyalists would now establish a military junta so there would be at least a semblance of government in the country. The prediction was right but I had erred in saying that General Wessin himself would be the top man in the junta. Since General Wessin was anathema not only to the rebels but also to a great many other Dominicans, and as his name seemed the symbol of a returning dictatorship, the United States Embassy, which rather visibly sponsored the creation of the junta, prevailed in having a group established in which the controversial general did not personally appear.

Instead a virtually unknown air force officer, Colonel Pedro Bartolomé Benoit, was picked as president of the junta. Colonel Enrique Apolinario Casado Saladin represented the army on the junta. Captain Olgo Manuel Santana Carrasco represented the navy.

This junta, of course, was a government on paper only. It functioned at the San Isidro Air Force Base but it had no control over the Dominican capital and presumably over the rest of the country, where military commands and the people at large seemed to be awaiting the outcome of the struggle in Santo Domingo before choosing sides. Dominicans, conditioned to caution by the three decades of Trujillo's dictatorship, often tend to be fence-sitters.

However, for the United States and its embassy in Santo Domingo, the junta had the advantage of being a body with which Washington could deal in some manner.

Administration officials discussed the possibility of formally recognizing the San Isidro junta but this still seemed politically risky. Nevertheless, the U.S. proceeded to act as if the Benoit group was indeed a real government.

And the junta wasted no time in fulfilling its assigned role in the Dominican drama. First it confirmed the establishment of martial law over the capital—though it was not in a position to enforce it—and then it began broadcasting orders and threats to the rebels to surrender or be destroyed. However, the junta was in no position to destroy the rebels, who were on the offensive.

Privately the junta was desperately pressing the embassy for communications equipment and other assistance. Ambassador Bennett, aware that the embassy's protégés were suddenly losing, cabled the State Department at 1:48 P.M. that Wessin's communications problem was "critical." He told Washington that "these people are facing leftist forces" and asked rhetorically "what would be the effect on the morale of the air force and the others" if the U.S. denied the requested help.

Shortly afterward Mr. Bennett sent another urgent message making it abundantly clear that not only did he regard the pro-Bosch revolt as a Communist movement but that he now envisioned an outright U.S. military intervention. This, it must be remembered, was at a time when the Administration in Washington was talking publicly about nothing more serious than protecting the American citizens in Santo Domingo. Ambassador Bennett cabled the State Department:

"I regret that we may have to impose a military solution to a political problem. . . . While leftist propaganda will fuzz this up as a fight between the military and the people, the issue is really between those who want a Castro-type solution and those who oppose it.

"I don't want to overdramatize, but if we deny the communications equipment, and if the opposition to the leftists lose heart, we may be asking in the near future for a landing of Marines to protect U.S. interests and for other purposes. What does Washington prefer?"

As the messages flew furiously between the embassy and Washington, the State Department cabled a reply to Mr. Bennett, telling him the Administration was reluctant to intervene to "safeguard law and order" unless "the outcome is in doubt." It noted that the embassy had reported earlier that the Wessin forces were winning but it said: "We're taking steps to have the walkie-talkies ready when needed."

The Administration was still reluctant to espouse the Ambassador's viewpoint entirely. But now events were moving rapidly.

Colonel Benoit sent a radio message to Ambassador Bennett—the Marines who had landed the day before with communications equipment had set up a radio link between San Isidro and the embassy—informing him that the junta was in no position to guarantee the safety of Americans or other foreigners in Santo Domingo. Therefore, Colonel Benoit's message said, the junta was requesting a United States intervention.

This request, if nothing else, provided the legal justification for a United States landing if Washington chose to play it that way. It was somewhat reminiscent of the 1958 situation in Lebanon, where United States Marines landed at the request of President Camille Chamoun to help him restore order.

About the time Ambassador Bennett received the junta's radio request for a U.S. intervention, Marine Corps pathfinders from the Boxer were landing at the port of Haina so the Marines could measure the beach for amphibious landings. This, incidentally, was even before the junta's intervention request was formalized and before President Johnson took the official decision to have the Marines go ashore at all.

The Marines brought along medical supplies, particularly pain killers and anesthetics, for hospitals in Santo Domingo, which by then were completely out of them. The Boxer emptied its medical stores to provide emergency assistance to the overcrowded hospitals. The supplies were handed by the Marines at the Haina beach to Peace Corps representatives, who arranged for their delivery to the Dominican Red Cross and the hospitals downtown.

In mid-afternoon a formal note from Colonel Benoit was delivered to Mr. Bennett at the embassy.

"We ask you for a temporary intervention and for assistance in restoring order," the note said.

Now the stage was fully set for the next move by the United States. Ambassador Bennett telephoned the White House and told President Johnson that the situation was getting completely out of hand, that the junta was requesting a temporary intervention and that he, personally, favored a landing by the Marines.

There was intermittent sniper fire, apparently by irregulars or plain hoodlums, around the embassy when Mr. Bennett spoke to the President. Somehow the idea was conveyed to the President that the embassy was at that moment under direct and heavy machine-gun fire. As Mr. Johnson later related the episode, Mr. Bennett and his secretary were under their desks as the Ambassador spoke to the White House.

But embassy officials said later that at no time had the embassy building been fired upon by machine guns. For that matter, despite many subsequent sniper firings, there were never any bullet marks on the embassy's walls. However, the image of the situation at the embassy and around it at that time presumably crystallized in the President's mind the decision to land troops. It was seemingly another case of the President's being fed exaggerated and inaccurate information which he accepted in good faith.

Ambassador Bennett confirmed his request for intervention with a telegram to the State Department shortly before 6 P.M. At the White House the President acted at once.

Shortly before receiving Ambassador Bennett's telephone call the President had met with the new director of the C.I.A., Vice Admiral William F. Raborn Jr., retired, who had been sworn into his job at 12:30 P.M. that same day. The admiral told the President the C.I.A. had identified three known Communists in the rebel leadership but he provided no names. There is a firm belief in some official quarters in Washington that President Johnson had made up his mind to order the landing when he received the admiral's report on the Communists. Always mindful of President Kennedy's experience with Cuba—particularly in the Bay of Pigs episode in 1961—Mr. Johnson was obviously unwilling to take any chances with a possible new Communist movement or take-over in the Caribbean.

When Ambassador Bennett's telegram arrived the President was in his office with Admiral Raborn, Secretary of State Dean Rusk, Under Secretary of State George W. Ball, McGeorge Bundy, Special Presidential Assistant for National Security Affairs, Secretary of Defense Robert S. McNamara and Special Assistant Bill Moyers.

Interestingly Vice President Hubert H. Humphrey was not invited to attend that meeting or, for that matter, any of the top-level decision-making White House conferences on the Dominican crisis. In fact he had not participated in any of the crucial policy decisions since some time before Feb. 6, when air strikes were ordered against North Vietnam. Only in the seventh week of the Dominican crisis, in June, was Mr. Humphrey invited back to the "inner sanctum" White House meetings. Likewise Senator J. W. Fulbright, chairman of the Foreign Relations Committee, was not consulted on the decision to land troops in Santo Domingo and was apprised of it only after it had been ordered.

Following his conversation with Ambassador Bennett and the arrival of the Ambassador's telegram, the President turned to Mr. McNamara. He instructed him to order the Chairman of the Joint Chiefs of Staff, General Earle G. Wheeler, to pass on the word to his commanders to proceed with the plans for a landing. Secretary McNamara replied that General Wheeler had already ordered his commanders to stand by for a landing and that the Presidential order could be carried out at once. After all, the Marines had already measured the Haina beach for amphibious landings and Marine helicopter crews were already familiar with the polo grounds at the Hotel Embajador.

While this part of the Dominican drama was being played out in Washington, the correspondents in San Juan were finally given hope of reaching the scene of the civil war after days of frustrating coverage from Puerto Rico. Shortly before noon Commander Russell Bufkins, the Public Information Officer of the Tenth Naval District in San Juan—known as the Caribbean Sea Frontier—advised us that we could be taken at our own risk to the fleet off the Dominican coast aboard one of the Task Force ships bringing evacuees in from Santo Domingo. He said that chances were good that we could be transferred the next morning to the Boxer and then shuttled by helicopter to the Hotel Embajador if this did not interfere with military operations and if Ambassador Bennett had no objections to our presence ashore.

Whether to accept the Bufkins offer became a major problem for most of us. He had told us that we would probably get to Santo Domingo the next morning but, of course, he could not guarantee this. Therefore we ran the risk of being stuck, perhaps for days, aboard the ship that was to take us to the fleet or aboard the Boxer. That might isolate us completely while other newsmen in the meantime might find some way to fly into Santo Domingo and beat us to the story. If we stayed in San Juan in the hope that one of the Santo Domingo airports would open quickly, we might get to the Dominican Republic ahead of the group to be transported by the Navy.

It was one of those agonizing situations in which a newsman must rely entirely on instinct, becoming a winner if he makes the right decision, often purely on guesswork, and a loser if he doesn't. News that Jules Dubois of The Chicago Tribune, a personal friend of General Wessin, had succeeded in landing during the morning at San Isidro aboard a chartered plane with the permission of the junta added to the urgency of our dilemma. Since none of the other correspondents then in San Juan were personal friends of the loyalist general, the chances of other authorized charter flights appeared dim. I consulted with The New York Times and after the decision was tossed back to me as being the man on the spot I made up my mind to risk the Navy expedition. Before driving to San Juan's Army Embarkation Port, from where we were to leave, I dictated a quick story that covered the day's events in Santo Domingo up to that moment, including the resumption of fighting by the reorganized rebel forces and the creation of the San Isidro junta.

The vessel that was to take us to the fleet—and on to the Dominican Republic—was the Wood County, a relatively new LST (Landing Ship Tank). With a full load displacement of 7,800 tons, she was the largest ship of her kind ever built. Despite her awkward bulk she could make 17 knots and we were told we would reach the Boxer within 14 hours.

We boarded the Wood County about 6 P.M., just as President Johnson in Washington was making his decision to order the Marine landing. But when the LST sailed from the San Juan harbor we found ourselves isolated from our story.

There were 22 of us, 20 Americans and 2 Britons. The latter were Robin Stafford of The London Daily Express and his photographer, Harry Benson. Twelve of us were reporters or radio and television correspondents, the others were photographers and network cameramen.

Darkness was falling over the Caribbean and we were one hour out of San Juan when the Presidential flash ordering the landing reached us. I was standing with two other reporters on the flying bridge of the Wood County when we suddenly heard the radio set in the wheelhouse broadcasting the message: "Close the coast. Prepare to land."

We had been talking for days about the possibility of a United States landing or intervention in some form in the Dominican Republic. But to hear the actual order to land was suddenly to be faced with the reality of a possible war. It was 7:10 P.M. and the die was cast.

I turned to the ship's Executive Officer on the flying bridge and asked rather stupidly: "Is this really serious?"

"You're damned right," he said.

I asked him whether he had ever before heard such a Presidential flash. He said he had once, during the Cuban missiles crisis in

1962, when the Navy was ordered to stand by for a landing, although one never actually took place.

We had no way of knowing, of course, whether the Dominican landing had been announced in Washington. This was close to the deadline time for the first edition of The Times and I wondered whether there was any way of transmitting the news of the intervention to New York. But our skipper, Lieutenant Commander James R. Allingham, told us pleasantly but firmly that he could not authorize us to use the LST's communications facilities for filing stories. I think that never before in my newspaper career had I felt so frustrated by isolation. I remembered one of my first lessons in journalism—it's absolutely worthless to have the greatest story in the world if you cannot transmit it to your newspaper.

Dinner in the enlisted men's mess was a melancholy affair for us as we wondered if we would be able to communicate with our papers and wire services in the foreseeable future. A great story was breaking barely 100 miles away and all we could do was eat Navy chow in an LST in the Caribbean. But the Marines and the sailors around us did not seem to take the situation nearly as seriously as we did. To them it seemed like just another of those interminable routine landing exercises and they ate heartily, joking and talking about everything under the sun except the Dominican operation.

After dinner Commander Allingham turned the ship's office over to us as a place to work. It was air conditioned, which was a blessing in the overheated LST plying the tropical sea.

Later we went on deck with our transistor radios to try to find out what was happening in Santo Domingo and Washington. Now the ship was completely darkened, cruising under wartime conditions with running lights turned off. It was a beautiful, clear night and we could see the lights of the Puerto Rican coast receding in the distance. Then we tuned in the Voice of America from Washington and discovered that the world had learned about the Dominican landing without any help from us. President Johnson had gone on radio and television to announce his decision and we heard him on our radios aboard the Wood County.

These were the President's words:

I've just concluded a meeting with the leaders of the Congress. I reported to them on the serious situation in the Dominican Republic. I reported the decisions that this Government considers necessary in this situation in order to protect American lives.

The members of the leadership expressed their support of these decisions.

The United States Government has been informed by the military authorities in the Dominican Republic that American lives are in danger. These authorities are no longer able to guarantee their safety and they reported that the assistance of military personnel is now needed for that purpose.

I've ordered the Secretary of Defense to put the necessary American troops ashore in order to give protection to hundreds of Americans who are still in the Dominican Republic and to escort them safely back to this country.

This same assistance will be available to the nationals of other countries, some of whom have already asked for our help.

Pursuant to my instructions, 400 Marines have already landed. General Wheeler, the Chairman of the Joint Chiefs of Staff, has just reported to me that there have been no incidents.

We have appealed repeatedly in recent days for a cease-fire between contending forces in the Dominican Republic in the interest of all Dominicans and foreigners alike.

I repeat this urgent appeal again tonight.

The Council of the O.A.S. has been advised of the situation by the Dominican Ambassador and the Council will be kept fully informed.

Mr. Johnson's decision to land the Marines was taken by him personally and a small group of close advisers. The Congressional leaders of both parties were called to the White House to be apprised of a decision already taken. In telling them what he had decided, the President repeated the account of how Ambassador Bennett and the embassy had been under machine-gun fire, how Americans were being attacked and how the lives of United States citizens in Santo Domingo were in danger.

According to persons at the Congressional leaders' meeting, President Johnson spoke at length about Ambassador Bennett and his high qualities as a diplomat. He said, as he did in his nationwide radio and television speech, that the landing was solely for the protection of American and foreign lives. He also passed on to the Congressional leaders the information given him earlier by Admiral Raborn that at least three Communists had been identified by the C.I.A. in the rebel command. The Republican Minority Leader, Senator Everett McKinley Dirksen of Illinois, reported this later to newsmen in Washington. As it turned out, however, this annoyed the President because the Administration was not yet ready to "surface" the so-called Communist angle in the rebellion. Although State Department briefing officers, presumably acting on the basis of early reports from Chargé d'Affaires Bill Connett and then Ambassador Bennett, had been hinting for the last few days that there was Communist infiltration—if not domination—in the rebels' "constitutionalist" movement, the Administration was not quite prepared officially to make the Communist charge.

This report by Senator Dirksen was the beginning of a long chain of confusion and contradiction surrounding the Administration's position in the Dominican crisis. There was another inconsistency that bothered some of us aboard the Wood County listening to the Voice of America's account of the events in Washington. This was the fact, mentioned by the President, that it was the Dominican Ambassador to the Organization of American States who had advised the O.A.S. Council of the over-all situation, including the U.S. decision to land. Since there had been no established government in the Dominican Republic since the overthrow of the Reid Cabral regime and since nobody had extended diplomatic recognition to the San Isidro junta, it appeared odd to us that the Dominican Ambassador, José Antonio Bonilla Atiles, could be in the position of informing the O.A.S. Council of the happenings in Santo Domingo and United States counter-measures.

In fact, it was at that urgently convened meeting of the O.A.S. Council this Wednesday night that the other Latin American Governments had been informed of the United States intervention. President Johnson and Administration spokesmen insisted subsequently that there had been no time to advise the O.A.S. of the planned landing. This omission was to become one of the principal problems the United States had to face in its relations with Latin America.

At stake was the whole principle of nonintervention on a unilateral basis by one American nation in the affairs of another. This principle was at the very heart of the inter-American system and the O.A.S. Charter. Venezuela's President Raul Leoni—a friend of the United States and an advocate the year before of strong O.A.S. action against Cuba for her intervention in Latin American affairs—was to write in the July, 1965, issue of Foreign Affairs: "Such actions as the one in the Dominican Republic tend to revive the era of unilateral intervention, which one supposed had been left far behind by the evolution of international life."

"They place in serious jeopardy the principles and essential norms that constitute the legal basis of the O.A.S.," President Leoni continued. "Venezuela, I repeat, will not countenance unilateral intervention. We favor multilateral or collective action when necessary to guarantee or reestablish the democratic basis of member states, or to oppose subversive activities from abroad that threaten the security and independence of an American state. Such was the case when the Soviet Union established missiles on Cuban territory, clearly threatening the peace and security of the hemisphere. And today we adhere to the same attitude regarding the situation in the Dominican Republic."

While a case can certainly be brought against the Johnson Administration for failing, or omitting, to inform the Latin American governments in advance of the plan to land in the Dominican Republic, I think it is fair to say that the overwhelming majority of newsmen covering the Dominican strife at that time felt that, diplomatic niceties notwithstanding, the President had no choice but to order the landing.

As we knew from our telephone contacts in the Dominican Republic and were to see ourselves the next day, there had been a complete breakdown of order in Santo Domingo. My own feeling is that no President of the United States could have done less than to send in a limited number of troops to protect the American citizens in the war-torn city. The question whether this should have been followed by a larger intervention for political purposes, no matter how disguised, was one we were to face later.

While we listened to the Voice of America, Marine helicopters had been ferrying 405 Marines from the U.S.S. Boxer to the polo grounds by the Hotel Embajador. Simultaneously ships of the Navy's Caribbean Amphibious Task Force moved to shore near Haina in preparation for landing tanks, armored personnel carriers, artillery and the other heavy equipment of the Marines.

When the initial Marine force arrived at the Hotel Embajador in helicopters, a platoon was immediately dispatched to help guard the United States Embassy. Since military vehicles had not yet been landed, the platoon was driven from the hotel in pickup trucks and sedans belonging to the embassy and the U.S. Agency for International Development mission.

No sooner had the Marine platoon arrived at the embassy and established a perimeter around its compound than snipers began firing at them. Close to 8 P.M. the unidentified snipers, shooting at the embassy gardens from roofs, including that of the Maternity Hospital across the street, put the area under virtual siege. The snipers were more intent on hitting the Marines than the embassy building, but one bullet went through the shutters protecting the windows of the room occupied by C.I.A. operatives assigned to the embassy. Nobody was hurt, however.

Under fire within minutes of their arrival, the Marines shot back, killing seven snipers. One of these was shot out of a tree by a Marine who accompanied the platoon commander, Lieutenant Phil Tucker, on one of his rounds of the embassy compound. The dead snipers could not be identified because their companions dragged away their bodies under cover of darkness.

There was intermittent fire around the embassy all night and the Marine platoon had to establish close cooperation with a detachment of Dominican policemen stationed in the area. The embassy had to provide interpreters so that the Marines and the Dominican policemen could understand each other in such matters as passwords that would allow either to move in the darkness. That night the password was "Seventeen" and the response was "Ten."

Even as the first Marines were landing in Santo Domingo to protect American citizens, Ambassador Bennett was sending new telegrams to Washington urging, in effect, even stronger action.

One of his late-afternoon telegrams had reported that banks in the rebel section downtown were being looted. As it turned out, no such looting took place, although some crudely counterfeit $10 bills appeared in the city later in the week.

At 7:30 P.M. Mr. Bennett sent a telegram marked for Under Secretary of State Mann, who turned out to be his principal ally in the ensuing political battle over the Santo Domingo crisis.

The message said that "United States lives are in danger" and passed on the following oral message from the junta president, Colonel Benoit: "The situation is deteriorating rapidly. Request urgent reply my official request for assistance."

Mr. Bennett added that he was sending the embassy's air attaché by helicopter, presumably to San Isidro, to get a full statement of Colonel Benoit's needs. He remarked that doubtlessly the attaché would be able to get to the junta's headquarters.

Half an hour later, at 8 P.M., Ambassador Bennett sent another telegram to Washington. He reported a "breakdown" of the junta forces, adding that they were "incapable of resisting."

He then made what turned out to be perhaps the most crucial single recommendation emanating from the embassy in the whole crisis:

"I recommend that serious thought be given to armed intervention to restore order beyond a mere protection of lives. If the present loyalist efforts fail, the power will go to groups whose aims are identical with those of the Communist Party. We might have to intervene to prevent another Cuba."

On the Wood County Commander Allingham addressed his crew and the 170 Marines aboard, telling them of the mission that might lie ahead of them. A Marine officer spoke on the ship's public address system, warning the Marines of snipers and of "those crazy Dominicans."

Below deck noncoms were breaking out ammunition boxes and passing bullets out to the Marines. The latter, who had been aboard ship for six weeks on their routine Caribbean patrol, were now cleaning their guns and other equipment in anticipation of the action they would face tomorrow.

After midnight the newsmen left the deck one by one and straggled down below to their bunks. We still did not know whether Ambassador Bennett would authorize our landing in Santo Domingo the next day and we felt uncertain about our immediate future as we went to sleep.

Thursday, April 29th.

We were awakened at 6 A.M. by a Marine private who shook each of us by the shoulder and handed us a mimeographed shipboard bulletin containing the latest news of the Santo Domingo crisis.

In the enlisted men's mess the conversation at breakfast was about the U.S. intervention, its pros and cons and its possible consequences.

We were, of course, unaware of the recommendations for a large-scale political intervention that were streaming from our embassy in Santo Domingo to Washington or of the Administration's reactions. As far as our little contingent aboard the Wood County was concerned, the Marine battalion that had gone ashore the night before had been dispatched solely to protect the lives of American citizens in the Dominican capital, as the President had said.

Inevitably a few of the American reporters got into good-natured but lively arguments with our British colleagues about the wisdom of the Marine landing. Robin Stafford and Harry Benson, the two London Daily Express men, were critical of the landing. We defended it and, with the slightest touch of perversity, reminded them of the British action in Suez almost nine years earlier.

"Well, now you know how it feels," Robin said.

Topside it was the beginning of another beautiful and sizzling day over the Caribbean. Preparations were being made for a landing or whatever else might come. Helmeted sailors were checking the two 3-inch guns on the Wood County's bow. The Marines, also helmeted, had their full battle gear, including weapons. Some were standing by to prepare heavy equipment for a landing, including the fuel trucks fastened to the forward deck and the Beachmaster amphibious vehicles.

Shortly after 8 A.M. we came into sight of the Boxer. Faintly discernible beyond her was the Dominican coast. U.S. destroyers and assault transports were plying the waters back and forth.

One of the newsmen standing on the flying bridge thought of turning on his transistor radio. To our utter amazement we found ourselves listening to official communications in open language concerning the activities in Santo Domingo. Then another reporter discovered that we could hear the ship's radio from another point on the flying bridge and thus monitor the fleet conversations. What we heard was most revealing as to the part the United States was already playing in the Dominican civil war. In fact, this was our first direct exposure to what was really happening.

After a while, from what was being said, we were able to identify the origin of the different shortwave broadcasts. Shade Tree One turned out to be the U.S. Embassy in Santo Domingo. Shade Tree Two was San Isidro, where a United States armed forces radio dispatcher had obviously been assigned. And Shurade —a radio corruption of the word Charade—was the U.S.S. Boxer.

A message from ashore, either from the embassy or from San Isidro, told the fleet: "The port is supposed to be secure but you may want to keep cannon cocked."

About 8:30 A.M. the embassy passed on to the fleet this information: "I have the message that the suppression attack is being initiated at 0845 local. . . . This is definitive from Shade Tree One—This is Shade Tree One."

The "suppression attack," obviously, was a reference to another assault on the rebels being planned by the Wessin forces.

Then the embassy, the American dispatcher at San Isidro and the Boxer became engaged in lengthy exchanges about the needs of the junta and what was being done about this by United States authorities.

Most of the discussion concerned the radio equipment about which Ambassador Bennett had been messaging Washington so earnestly the day before, about food for the loyalists and other items.

The San Isidro dispatcher reported that "rations were delivered to troops" but then observed that FAD (the Spanish initials of the Dominican Air Force) "is limited in delivery capabilities."

He then went on to relay the message that "de los Santos

requests augmentation of supplies for the area" and apparently was requesting helicopters. Brigadier General de los Santos was the commander of the loyalist air force at San Isidro.

A few minutes later another message urged "rations for additional men. . . ."

San Isidro came back on the air to say that with the delivery of rations, "expect good psychological effect."

And then a little later this: "A significant morale boost is evident here since the arrival of rations."

As we were to discover later, the Wessin forces were at the end of their rope at that point. They were out of food and their power and water supply had been cut by the rebels. The arrival of American rations and U.S. support apparently was saving the day for the loyalists.

Shortly before 9 o'clock the Boxer requested details on the "type of equipment needed."

And at 9:25 A.M. Ambassador Bennett broadcast this personal message of encouragement to the junta chief, Colonel Benoit:

"Cannot phone or ride. Do you need more aid?"

And then: "Believe that with determination your plans will succeed."

A second message from Ambassador Bennett to the junta said: "Could you open Punta Caucedo [the International Airport] for traffic to bring in food and medicine? Uniformed Marines can operate there if civilians are not there."

Thus the radio waves carried the blow-by-blow account of mounting United States support for the forces of the junta.

Then someone tuned in to the San Isidro broadcasting station that addressed itself to the population of Santo Domingo. "Operation Clean Up is afoot and very soon the city will be free of the Communist mob," the station kept repeating.

Between announcements San Isidro continuously played Stars and Stripes Forever, perhaps because it was the only record of martial music available or, more likely, to identify for the Dominican people the Wessin command with the United States. As a matter of fact, while the Administration in Washington kept insisting publicly on its neutrality in the conflict, the Wessin propaganda tried just as hard to portray the United States as firmly on its side.

Indeed, there appeared to be little difference, at least in private, between the views of the San Isidro junta and those of the United States authorities in the area about the character of the rebellion they now seemed to be facing jointly. While the San Isidro radio kept talking about "Communist mobs" in the capital, a message from the U.S. Embassy to Colonel Benoit asked him at one point: "Do you have enough against the Castro forces facing you?" This, however, must have been a subconscious lapse, because 30 seconds later the dispatcher corrected himself, changing the word "Castro" to "rebel."

Shortly before 11 A.M. the Wood County came alongside the Boxer. We were to be transferred from the LST to the helicopter carrier on a highline, a much more formidable undertaking than it may sound. As the highline between the two ships was being rigged, we could see refugees from Santo Domingo—men, women and children—filling the lower decks and looking at us curiously. Marine helicopters were taking off and landing on the Boxer's deck with monotonous regularity and crewmen in multicolored overalls were rushing to and fro servicing the choppers.

Finally the highline was secured, thick but terribly unsafe looking. The distance between the two ships was only about 300 yards, but the churning water separating the Boxer and the Wood County looked from our deck like a mountain torrent at flood time.

Then the bosun's chair, an improbably flimsy affair with an equally improbable fringed top, slid down from the Boxer to the Wood County and the transfer of the newsmen began. In retrospect I think this was one of the most comical operations ever seen in the Caribbean. Reporters and photographers, clutching their typewriters or their cameras to their chests, were hoisted one by one from the Wood County to the Boxer by sailors cranking a cable winch. When one of the more corpulent newsmen was being sent over the cable slackened and he almost touched water. When my turn came I simply repeated for the hundredth time in my life that there must be a better way of earning a living. The trip took 50 long seconds.

Once aboard the Boxer we were handled with frightening efficiency. An officer awaited each of us and guided us to the commodore's stateroom for a sandwich, a quick cup of coffee and an even quicker briefing before we were to be coptered to Santo Domingo.

The briefing was held by Captain James A. Dare, the Commodore of the Navy's Task Force 44.9, also known in complicated naval parlance as the Navy-Marine Corps Deployment Group.

Commodore Dare told us that 520 Marines were already ashore. He said food and medicine for the Red Cross had also been landed, leaving the Boxer's own stores almost empty. In Santo Domingo, he informed us, dissident bands were roaming the streets, some wearing uniforms and some not and many armed with what he described as a "grease gun kind of weapon."

We asked the commodore whether the Marines were allowed to shoot at the rebels. He said they were authorized only to shoot back if fired upon. Then someone asked how long the Marines would remain in Santo Domingo and whether they would return to the ships once the evacuation of Americans and other foreigners had been completed.

The commodore said that in addition to protecting the evacuation the Marines would probably stay ashore as long as necessary to "keep this a non-Communist government." They would stay in the Dominican Republic, he said, until "their presence has produced the desired effect."

So here, aboard the flagship of the Navy's task force, we were told plainly and flatly that the previous evening's landing was not simply a matter of protecting lives, as Washington had been telling the world, but was intended in reality as a political operation.

Still confused by events—and the precise nature of what was going on in Santo Domingo—I made a point of reporting Commodore Dare's words in the first story I was to file from the Dominican capital a few hours later, though without using his name. From the Boxer each of us was allowed to file a 200-word story to the United States through the Navy's radio facilities. But the copy, it turned out, did not reach our papers until much after our deadlines that night.

Now we were whisked to the deck, led to helicopters in groups of six and flown the few miles over the Caribbean to the polo grounds at the Hotel Embajador. Suddenly we were in the Dominican Republic after almost five days of frustration and impatient waiting.

I hardly recognized the once-familiar polo grounds. On my last visit to Santo Domingo, about a year and a half ago, I had galloped many times across the wide field on one of the superb thoroughbreds that had belonged to Ramfis Trujillo and later were kept at the stables of the mounted police regiment down the hill from the hotel.

But now the polo grounds had become a military area. Helicopters were taking off and landing incessantly. Marine Corps tents were pitched around an improvised control tower, housing the command post, a first-aid station and other facilities. Around the field and the hotel gardens Marines were digging foxholes. Field telephone wires were strewn everywhere. Under the broiling sun we walked the 500 or 600 yards to the hotel, carrying our typewriters and luggage.

I had long known the hotel to be a luxurious but chronically empty monument to the tourism that never really came to the Dominican Republic. Now it too was beyond recognition. Its huge lobby was filled with refugees awaiting evacuation. Those who had already been processed formed long lines awaiting transportation to Haina, where Navy ships were to take them to San Juan. Others, including Dominicans who could not be evacuated, sat, squatted or sprawled on the floor, occupied sofas or simply stood about staring vacantly. The doors to the swanky casino were locked. There was a smell of sweat, unwashed bodies and half-eaten food in the air.

The first person I met in the lobby was a Mr. Lovatón, the Dominican president of the hotel corporation that managed the Embajador. We had known each other since the difficult days of the Trujillo dictatorship when early one morning I was visited by two secret policemen and ejected from the country after first being sentenced to two years in prison and a large fine for having written stories the old tyrant regarded as unfavorable. Now Lovatón greeted me as a long-lost friend. He told me that the hotel was terribly overcrowded and that it had no outside power supply and no fuel to make its own generator run. Therefore the elevators did not work and there was no light. There was also no running water because the pumps could not be activated. The place was a shambles. I asked about telephones and Lovatón told me the only phone that worked in the whole hotel was the private direct line from his own office. He led me there and invited me to go ahead and use the phone if I could reach anybody.

I did reach the embassy and told Malcolm McLean, the press attaché, of our arrival. I said I would be over before long and asked if there was any danger from snipers.

"Well, it is not too bad," he replied, "but be careful."

It was now mid-afternoon and my immediate concern was to get a story with a Santo Domingo dateline to The New York Times. It was then that our inferno of communications problems began. International telephones did work, I found out, but it was virtually impossible, at least for the time being, to get the long-distance operator to answer. His line simply was busy all the time. My next move was to call R.C.A. Communications, with which we had often worked before from Santo Domingo, and I managed to reach its local manager, Ray Anderson. The R.C.A. office was in the rebel-held zone downtown and it was apparently impossible to get there from the hotel because of heavy firing in that part of Santo Domingo. Ray said that except for an emergency circuit to New York, all his Telex and cable lines were out of order because some of the transmitting equipment had been damaged in the fighting. But he promised to try to rig up a voice line to New York over which we might be able to transmit copy. Here again it was a case of the absolute futility of having the greatest story in the world if one could not find a way to transmit it to one's newspaper.

Next I phoned All America Cables and Radio, with which we had also dealt in the past. There, to my intense pleasure, I was told that the Telex circuit to New York was in working condition. But again the All America office was in the middle of the fighting zone and it did not seem advisable to drive there to file copy, even assuming a vehicle could be found. However, one of the cable office's employes, a Dominican with a sketchy knowledge of

English, agreed to take my story over the phone. I spelled each word, pronouncing each letter in Spanish, and sweated it out for 40 minutes until I had completed the story. Then the circuit was taken over by my colleagues. We thought we had found a great solution for our communications problem until the man at the other end said "Hold on for a minute" and went away. That was the last we heard from All America Cables for several days as their phone went dead.

After I had filed my story I lugged my bags up the stairs to my third-floor room, which overlooked the hotel's swimming pool, the International Fair Grounds below it and the Caribbean, where the Boxer and the other Navy ships could be seen. The Marines had occupied the swimming pool area, set up water-purification tanks around it and were pumping the water out of the pool.

In the hotel lobby I ran into Benno Varon, the Israeli Ambassador to the Dominican Republic, who was at the Embajador saying good-by to his wife and two small children, who were being evacuated to the Boxer. After they left, Ambassador Varon sat with a few of us for our first detailed interview on the events of the last few days in Santo Domingo.

I still believe this was the most coherent and complete briefing I received at any time during my stay in the Dominican capital. In addition Mr. Varon had an odd story to tell. It concerned Donald Reid Cabral, the ousted President, who, as it turned out, had left the Presidential Palace secretly Monday and taken refuge in the house of his brother Charlie. Reid Cabral had been a friend of the Ambassador's since visiting Israel the year before as the Dominican Republic's Foreign Minister. It was during his stay in Tel Aviv that Reid Cabral was informed that he had been elevated to the presidency of what was then a three-man junta. Two nights before the April 24 revolution erupted, President Reid Cabral was a guest at an informal dinner at Ambassador Varon's house. Somehow they got on Biblical subjects and someone mentioned the Last Supper. Suddenly turning to his host, Reid Cabral said with a faint smile, "You know, I have a feeling that this, too, may be my last supper."

While some of us were filing early copy and beginning to interview people in the Hotel Embajador area, others in our group rushed downtown to see the fighting. Bert Quint of the Columbia Broadcasting System was one of the first to reach downtown Santo Domingo with a camera crew. He obtained what probably were the first television films of the downtown fighting. Harry Benson, the photographer for The Daily Express of London, immediately won the rare distinction of being arrested by both the loyalist and the rebel forces downtown. And he had a shattering story to tell on his return. First an armed mob had threatened to shoot him, or so he thought, and then he had been asked to drive a very pregnant woman to one of the downtown hospitals. Arriving there, Benson found a situation that was absolutely horrible. The hospital, like most of Santo Domingo, had no electric power and no running water. It was out of anesthetics and most medicines. The wounded, including women and children, sometimes underwent surgery on the dirty floors. Benson said he saw about a thousand people lying on the floor awaiting death. Doctors told him there was nothing they could give these people or do for them any more. Swarms of flies fed on the festering wounds of the injured. Benson told of a child with its belly ripped open, covered by flies. As soon as a person died his body was thrown into the back yard and burned. As we were to find out later, people were often buried where they died and frequently bodies were burned in big piles to prevent epidemics. Nobody had any idea what the toll of dead and injured was. But at this point, after five days of fighting, it obviously ran into the hundreds and hundreds.

Because of the late hour at which I had finished sending my story I decided to skip a trip downtown, feeling it would not be a good idea to be caught there after dark, what with all the sniping and firing. Instead I drove to the United States Embassy as a passenger in a U.S. Government vehicle that was going that way. It is not quite two miles to the embassy but, as dusk was falling, the trip seemed to take forever. Heavy gunfire could be heard from the downtown area and the dry crack of rifles seemed all around us. Sometimes there was a machine gun burst that sounded much closer than it really was.

Wessin's aircraft were no longer in the sky at this late hour, but earlier, from the hotel terrace, we had seen the jets and P-51's diving gracefully over Ciudad Nueva on their strafing and bombing runs. Columns of smoke rose after some of the passes but it was difficult to tell whether the hits were in the city itself or in the area of the Duarte bridge, where heavy fighting was continuing.

At the embassy we were waved into the garden by Marine sentries after they had checked our identities. The compound had come under heavy sniper fire earlier in the afternoon and the Marines were jumpy and watchful. They had already killed some snipers.

The chancery, a one-story white stucco building, was the scene of hectic agitation. The heavy wooden door was protected by an iron grille that was opened to let us in. Green wooden shutters were fastened tight over all the windows as a protection against gunfirer. Inside, embassy officials, secretaries, newsmen and unidentifiable characters were rushing back and forth across the small rotunda that served as the lobby.

The embassy, once a house belonging to Trujillo, had been rented by the United States Government to accommodate a fairly small diplomatic staff. But now it had to hold a great number of people, many of whom had turned the embassy into their home. Many officials and secretaries had worked and slept there without leaving for days. For one thing, their presence was required almost continuously because of the heavy burden of work. For another, it simply was not safe to go home at night, particularly if one lived some distance from the embassy or in an area where there was fighting or sporadic sniping. There were cots in some of the offices, and in other rooms officials and young women of the secretarial staff curled up on sofas and chairs for cat naps when they could.

I sat with other newsmen at first in one of the smaller offices talking to Ben Ruyle, chief of the political section, and L. Robert Satin, the Peace Corps Director for Santo Domingo.

Much of what we heard during that first embassy session consisted of Satin's accounts of the work of the Peace Corps volunteers in the embattled city. There were 33 volunteers and five Peace Corps staff members in Santo Domingo at the time. Seven of them were nurses who had worked in the downtown hospitals since the revolution began. Prior to the civil war they had been social workers and nurses in clinics in Santo Domingo's poorer districts. When the fighting began the seven girls moved into the hospitals to help the staffs. They worked under incredible conditions, assisting in surgery without electric light, water or medicine.

As I was to discover later, the Peace Corps girls were the real heroines of the civil war.

Satin, who visited them at least once every day, spoke of the esteem and friendship they enjoyed among the Dominicans because of their earlier Peace Corps work and particularly because of their dedication under the stresses of war. Satin and some of the other Peace Corps people often drove ambulances under fire, moving the wounded from one hospital to another and bringing in food and medicine. In fact, the Peace Corps volunteers and staff members were probably the only Americans associated with the U.S. Government who had continuous contact with the people downtown—both those who were rebels and those who were not. Their impression was very clearly that the rebel cause had much wider popular support than the official embassy view would lead one to believe.

This view was presently conveyed to us by Mr. Bennett himself.

We trooped into the Ambassador's office. He was in shirt sleeves, looked tired and drawn, but he welcomed us pleasantly and courteously. A tall and amiable redhead with a Southern drawl and from a traditional Georgia family, "Tap" Bennett was a classical State Department career ambassador with all this implies in both advantages and drawbacks. I had met him once before. He was a friend of an uncle of mine under whom he had served in Panama many years ago. "Tap" Bennett's ambassadorial appointment to Santo Domingo at the age of 48—his first chief of mission post—had come after 24 years of a Foreign Service career that had not been spectacular but had been, in State Department parlance, a "good one."

He had graduated from the University of Georgia, then spent a year at the University of Freiburg in Nazi Germany from 1937 to 1938 before obtaining his law degree from George Washington University. His first Foreign Service post, interestingly enough, was in the Dominican Republic in 1941. Afterward he specialized in Caribbean and Central American affairs and in 1951 became Deputy Director of the State Department's Office of South American Affairs.

This background had made Mr. Bennett something of a Latin American "old hand." In 1953 he was picked as personal assistant to Dr. Milton Eisenhower, who was then surveying Western Hemisphere problems on his brother's behalf. In his book Dr. Eisenhower described "Tap" Bennett as "an engaging, sensitive, tireless worker."

These, indeed, were the characteristics best known to Mr. Bennett's friends. He had married the daughter of a well-known former ambassador and the Bennetts carried a pleasant social cachet. In time he was sent on good assignments to Vienna and Athens and then President Johnson named him Ambassador to the Dominican Republic in 1964.

After his arrival in Santo Domingo the new Ambassador established close and cordial relations with President Reid Cabral. The President, who came into office in 1964, replacing a previous junta head who had succeeded the ousted Bosch, was a protégé of the United States. He concentrated on the Dominican Republic's economic problems and carried out the recommendations of the State Department and the International Monetary Fund for shoring up Dominican finances to such an extent that after a while he became known, somewhat derisively, as "el Americano."

Although the Reid Cabral Government by its very nature had to be authoritarian, the 41-year-old President was far from being the dictator Trujillo had been. In fact, Reid Cabral and his late brother, Roberto, had actively plotted against the old tyrant. When the Council of State, a transitional government set up after the eradication of the remnants of the Trujillo rule, was established, Reid Cabral had become its Second Vice President. In this capacity he was responsible for assuring that the Dominican Republic's first democratic elections in 38 years were actually held as planned in December, 1962. In that balloting Juan Bosch was elected President. It was ironical, then, that Reid Cabral should have become the head of a regime ruling after the brief life of the democratic Bosch Government.

In my own mind there is no question that Reid Cabral meant well. He went so far as to deprive the old-line military leaders, most of them one-time Trujillo henchmen, of their traditional privileges. But somehow he lacked popular appeal and Dominicans by and large turned their backs on him. Virtually his only friends were the Americans and a small group of right-of-center politicians, businessmen and landowners.

It was with this group in the Dominican social structure that "Tap" Bennett had his best personal contacts. The United States was again supplying economic aid to the Dominican Republic, the Reid Cabral Regime was a reliable ally in the O.A.S. and relations between Washington and Santo Domingo could not have been better.

Since nobody at the U.S. Embassy apparently believed that Dr. Bosch or his followers had any chance of ever ousting or even threatening the Reid Cabral Government, the Ambassador and his top aides seemingly saw no need for close connections with the opposition or any of the young officers. The junior members of the embassy's staff were supposed to maintain whatever limited contacts were required with those elements.

As a high Administration official in Washington was to say later, wondering aloud about the Ambassador's selectivity in his contacts, "Tap didn't seem to know anyone who was to the left of the Rotary Club." However, Mr. Bennett was conscientious in carrying out his ambassadorial functions and he traveled almost everywhere in the Dominican Republic, dutifully inspecting Agency for International Development projects and Peace Corps centers. But as one of his embassy associates remarked, "Tap seemed ill at ease with people who were not well dressed and to whom he had not been properly introduced."

When the revolt finally broke out in Santo Domingo on April 24, Mr. Bennett almost reflexively gave his full commitment to people he knew. And he subsequently found himself in a maelstrom set in motion by men he had never met and by powerful forces in the Dominican Republic he had never discovered.

By all accepted standards, his embassy was a good one. It was staffed by some 30 State Department and Agency for International Development officials, all of whom had good career records and most of whom had Latin American experience. Its only weakness was that the senior officials in the embassy had been in the Dominican Republic a relatively short time. This was because an entirely new team had been assigned to Santo Domingo after

President Johnson re-established early in 1964 the diplomatic relations that had been broken by President Kennedy following the anti-Bosch coup d'état. "Tap" Bennett had been in Santo Domingo for 13 months; Bill Connett, his deputy, for five and a half months. Ben Ruyle, the political section chief, had been in the Dominican capital a little over a year. Only the C.I.A. men had had a longer tenure in Santo Domingo as they had remained there after the embassy was downgraded to the level of a Consulate General during the break in diplomatic relations. Ed Terrell, the station chief, had come to Santo Domingo 10 days before Bosch was inaugurated in February, 1963. He arrived from La Paz, Bolivia, where he had had certain policy differences with the embassy there.

Now "Tap" Bennett and some of his associates began to brief us on the Dominican situation. Malcolm McLean, the press officer, and Ben Ruyle sat with us. The Ambassador was extremely frank. As it turned out later, most of the assessments he was giving us were being simultaneously sent to the State Department. And just as he had told Washington, he was now telling us that the rebellion downtown was highly infiltrated, if not altogether dominated, by Communists. Since this was our first day in Santo Domingo and we had had no direct access to the situation, none of us had any reason to doubt the validity of Mr. Bennett's judgment. Not surprisingly, then, our stories in the newspapers of the next day reflected strongly the line that a Communist situation was in the making in the Dominican Republic.

The Ambassador told us that the breakdown of order in Santo Domingo had made it necessary for him the day before to recommend the landing of the Marines. From the few things we had seen since arriving in the Dominican capital earlier in the day, none of us had any doubts about the wisdom of his recommendation.

"But," Mr. Bennett said, "I hope that never again will I have to make another such decision."

He went on to tell us of the junta's request for intervention. He actually showed us the written communication from Colonel Benoit asking for the American troops.

When one of us raised the question whether the United States was actively assisting the junta, "Tap" Bennett said this was not so. He said that basically the United States remained neutral in the conflict, even though he personally was concerned about the Communist inroads in the rebel movement. When a reporter mentioned to the Ambassador the radio conversations upon which we had eavesdropped in the morning aboard ship, the Ambassador looked embarrassed and changed the subject.

We went back to the matter of Communism in the rebel movement. The Ambassador then asked one of his aides to produce what he described as a list of Communists and their associates whom the embassy—and "our intelligence sources"—believed to be active in the revolution. The two typewritten sheets that were handed to each of us contained 53 names, including those of four women. This was the famous list of "53" that the United States Government subsequently used to support its contention that the pro-Bosch revolution was controlled or, at least, strongly infiltrated by Communists.

We asked the Ambassador and his aides which of the people on the list were actually active in the rebel command. The answer was that, as far as anyone knew, none of them had actually appeared in high positions but that, indubitably, they were hiding behind the first rank of leadership. The people on the embassy's list were identified as members of the P.S.P.D., which is the long-established Dominican Popular Socialist Party, the Soviet-oriented Communist group in the Dominican Republic; the M.P.D., which is the Dominican Popular Movement, a more recent Chinese-type splinter movement; and the A.P.C.J., which is the Popular Association 14th of June, a pro-Castro movement organized at the time of Trujillo's assassination.

The first two Communist organizations had negligible membership and an extremely limited popular following. A few army officers secretly belonged to the P.S.P.D. The 14th of June group, on the other hand, drew much of its strength from the university students and at different times had had not inconsiderable backing. But since the death of Trujillo these three organizations had been rather severely at odds with one another. The 14th of June Movement, for example, had once been a close ally of the right-of-center Civic Union Party, whose candidate, Dr. Viriato Fiallo, had been defeated by Dr. Bosch in the 1962 elections.

As a check of the names on the embassy's list disclosed later, a number of the persons listed had been allowed to travel freely between the Dominican Republic and Communist countries, including Cuba, first by the Council of State Government in 1962 and then by the Government of President Reid Cabral. One of the names on the list was that of Hector Homero Hernandez Vargas, identified as a member of the 14th of June Movement. The accompanying data said he had visited Cuba and China. However, Hector Homero Hernandez Vargas, who was active in the original pro-Bosch conspiracy and later was a rebel delegate in the peace negotiations, is a career diplomat who served as Trujillo's Ambassador to Ecuador. He had never been regarded as a Communist.

A well-known 14th of June leader, Fidelio Despradel Roque, was singled out by embassy officials as one of the "important Communists" in the rebellion. He had been seen by some people with the rebels downtown, but there were other interesting circumstances surrounding him. His wife openly worked for one of the pro-Western embassies in Santo Domingo. And, according to some people, Fidelio Despradel Roque had some "very special" connections with certain Americans.

Actually the list included virtually every well-known Communist and pro-Castro leader in the Dominican Republic. One, who actually had entered illegally from Cuba shortly before the rebellion erupted, was Pedro Julio Mir Valentin. As I found out later, Pedro Julio Mir Valentin did have a political function with the rebel command but it was arguable how important it was. Several of the Communists on the embassy's list were not even in the country during the revolution. In general, then, the list was more of a catalogue of the names of Communists and pro-Communists than a compilation of leftist extremists who might have been active among the rebels.

Another interesting episode illustrates the embassy's techniques in reporting to Washington. It concerned a rebel propaganda leaflet which said, among other things, that "it is necessary to defeat definitely the criminal band of Wessin." It went on to say that "Wessin is clamoring for massacre and dictatorship" while "Bosch is democracy and the defender of liberty." The leaflet proclaimed that "we will never accept any solution that is not the re-establishment of constitutionality with Juan Bosch as President of the Dominican Republic."

The leaflet was signed in the name of the "Constitutional Military Command" by Colonel Caamaño, Colonel Montes Arache and six lower-ranking military officers. The embassy transmitted the text of this leaflet to Washington—a copy was also given to us at this time—with the remark by Ambassador Bennett in his telegram that C.I.A. files showed that two of the eight signers of the leaflet were associated with "extremist groups." The Ambassador added that since neither the embassy nor the C.I.A. had ever heard of the other six officers, the total of Communists or pro-Communists in the rebel military command might actually be higher.

It was on the strength of this telegram, which in reality did little beyond emphasize once more the limited information the U. S. establishment in Santo Domingo possessed about the younger Dominican officers, that Administration officials in Washington began telling newsmen the next day that there might be as many as "six or seven Communists or pro-Communists" in the rebel movement. It might be added that none of the eight signers of the leaflet appeared on the embassy's own list of the 53 Communists. But it was of such stuff that policy was being made between Santo Domingo and Washington.

Next "Tap" Bennett went on to tell us of rebel atrocities. Again, having no reason at this point to disbelieve the embassy's information, we took copious notes. And again we filed most of this information to our newspapers just as the Ambassador had filed it to the State Department.

Mr. Bennett told us that rebels had severed the heads of Wessin's soldiers and policemen they had killed and had paraded the heads on pikes in downtown Santo Domingo. With indignation the Ambassador went on to tell us of mass executions by the rebels of their enemies. He said Colonel Caamaño had personally executed a Colonel Calderón, who had been aide-de-camp to ousted President Reid Cabral. He reminisced over his pleasant acquaintanceship with Colonel Calderón and expressed his revulsion over the alleged killing of Calderón in cold blood by the rebel chief.

In a telegram to the State Department during the day Ambassador Bennett reported that Caamaño had "personally killed" Colonel Calderón. He cabled that "Caamaño had gone berserk" and had committed numerous atrocities. He added in his telegram that it had to be remembered that "his father was one of Trujillo's generals."

I regret to say that I filed to The New York Times the information about Colonel Caamaño's allegedly having shot Colonel Calderón. I happened to have known Calderón for some time and a few weeks later I ran into him in a Santo Domingo hospital, where he was recovering from a slight neck wound. Calderón told me that he had been wounded by a shot fired during a fray on the first or second day of the revolution. A few days later Colonel Calderón was back on duty, again as aide-de-camp to the latest military government. A colleague of mine had a cold beer with him on that occasion. This whole episode, then, added up to the lesson that one never seems to learn well enough in journalism: do not ever trust anybody's word, no matter how high his position and how good his credentials.

But the effect of the Ambassador's reporting of atrocities (and, by the way, the tales of heads on pikes and of mass executions were never proved) and of our stories on the same subject, inspired by "Tap" Bennett, was to create an even more panicky atmosphere in Washington. The picture of the situation in Santo Domingo that was being drawn by the embassy doubtlessly helped justify the mounting extent of the U.S. intervention in the Dominican Republic.

Presumably working from the material cabled by the embassy in Santo Domingo, the United States Ambassador to the Council of the Organization of American States, Ellsworth Bunker, said in a speech to the Council during the evening that the United States was "faced with an immediate problem of how to restore law and order, in order to protect not only the citizens of foreign countries, private and official; not only to proceed with the evacuation in an orderly way; but also to stop the excessive personalized vandalism which many people are wreaking on their fellow Dominican citizens."

He mentioned that the U.S. Embassy had been "under heavy

fire throughout the day" and that, "according to our information, the diplomatic inviolability" of at least five Latin American Embassies had "been violated, one of them having been sacked and burned."

This account was apparently cabled by the U.S. Embassy. But although several Latin American Embassies were fired upon by snipers and, at least in one instance, a mob broke into one of them in search of some people in asylum there, no embassy was either sacked or burned.

However, this fiction subsequently became a myth of U.S. foreign policy. Many weeks later President Johnson himself referred to a sacked and burned embassy in an account of the events that led to his decision to intervene in the Dominican Republic.

The main purpose of Ambassador Bunker's speech to the O.A.S. Council was to press for a vote on an appeal for an immediate cease-fire in the Dominican Republic. But, he said, if the cease-fire appeal is made and goes unheeded, "the U.S. must . . . reserve its right to take the necessary measures to protect its own citizens and officials from violence in a situation of anarchy."

He said that "we are not now talking about intruding into the domestic affairs of other countries" but "we are talking about the elementary duty to save lives in a situation where there is no authority able to accept responsibility for primary law and order."

Mr. Bunker said that the United States "has no candidate for the government of the Dominican Republic; this is a matter for the Dominican people themselves."

Ambassador Bunker's speech foreshadowed, in effect, the next step in the U.S. military build-up in Santo Domingo. Even as Mr. Bunker spoke to the O.A.S. Council in Washington, "Tap" Bennett was telling us at his embassy in Santo Domingo that advance elements of the 82nd Airborne Division from Fort Bragg, N.C., would begin landing at the San Isidro Air Force Base at midnight.

The number of Marines in Santo Domingo had been increased from the original 405 landed Wednesday night to 1,700 by Thursday evening. Now the imminent presence of two battalions of the 82nd Airborne, totaling 2,500 paratroopers, seemed to be changing the character of the U.S. military action in the Dominican

Republic from a humanitarian expedition into something altogether different.

Writing from Washington, John Finney said in The New York Times the next day that "publicly, Administration spokesmen continue to emphasize that the Marine landing was a humanitarian move that did not represent political intervention."

"But in private briefings given to newsmen and members of Congress," Finney wrote, "there also were suggestions that the landings could have a precautionary political value in guarding against a Communist take-over of the insurrection."

In the same story Finney remarked that the Benoit junta's request for U.S. assistance, made on Wednesday, "may provide the public rationale for the next American step, for the Administration could then argue that the United States had moved in to help restore law and order at the request of Dominican authorities."

Finney then reported the view that "through a combination of hemispheric diplomacy and a military show of force, the Administration was helping to bring about a cease-fire and prevent a Communist take-over in the Caribbean country."

Despite official disclaimers, therefore, it was becoming amply clear by Thursday night that the Administration was setting in motion a full-fledged political intervention in the Dominican Republic—obviously in line with Ambassador Bennett's recommendations and his descriptions of the situation in Santo Domingo.

Also on the political front, the United States Embassy was taking steps that did not appear to be fully in accord with Ambassador Bunker's statement to the O.A.S. that the U.S. "has no candidate for the government of the Dominican Republic."

Having first set up the Benoit junta at San Isidro, the embassy now appeared to be making further efforts to try to hammer together some kind of government for the Dominican Republic that would be acceptable to Washington. Circumstantial evidence of such efforts had become available to some of us newsmen, quite by accident, the moment we landed at the polo grounds. As we alighted from helicopters a car pulled up to the landing pad. In it was a corpulent Dominican wearing a khaki uniform and a fatigue cap, a .45-caliber pistol strapped to his belt.

He was accompanied by a Dominican bishop and an American colonel. He quickly transferred to a helicopter that took off immediately, apparently for the Boxer.

Although neither the colonel nor the bishop wanted to disclose the identity of their companion, I recognized him as Brigadier General Antonio Imbert Barreras, a survivor of the Trujillo assassination plot and one of the most active proponents of Dr. Bosch's ouster in 1963. Since Imbert, a highly astute politician and a man of great ambition, had always been close to the U.S. Embassy, I surmised that his trip to the Boxer might represent the first step in a U.S. maneuver to turn power over to him. In fact, I took a chance on this and reported in The Times Imbert's trip to the Boxer and the possibility that he might be the chosen instrument of the U.S. Embassy in future Dominican developments.

I asked Ambassador Bennett about this as we talked at the embassy during the evening but he merely smiled and said that the embassy always kept in touch with "Tony" Imbert.

It was now close to midnight and in the darkness intermittent sniper fire was enveloping the embassy. Some of us decided to spend the night at the embassy's chancery rather than risk a drive back to the Hotel Embajador. We were still inexperienced in nighttime techniques of Santo Domingo. Malcolm McLean invited us to spend the night at his house, a few blocks away, assuring us that there was nothing to be feared from the snipers. However, exaggerated caution prevailed and several of us chose to stay at the embassy. "Tap" Bennett said we were welcome to remain and apologized for not inviting us over to his residence, across the garden from the chancery. The residence, he said, was already full of embassy officials and their families who were sleeping there. He himself had been sleeping on the floor, he said. But he offered me the use of the long green leather couch in his office.

Someone tuned in the Voice of America. Its news broadcast told of a resolution adopted by the O.A.S. Council in Washington calling for an immediate cease-fire in Santo Domingo and the establishment of an international security zone in which foreign embassies and foreign nationals could find protection.

Despite the lateness of the hour, embassy officials and secretaries kept working. The chancery quarters were crammed and we kept bumping into people who tried to work or take a cat nap on the sofa or even curl up on a chair. Two of us were chased away from the C.I.A. corner, where we had inadvertently wandered. We went back to the airless rotunda and chewed on some cold combat rations we found in a cardboard box on the floor. The embassy's power supply came from its own generator but every once in a while it was necessary to cut it off to replenish the fuel reserve. During those periods there were only lanterns, candles and flashlights to help one get about. With the doors and shutters closed because of the firing outside and the air conditioning not working, the heat in the building was almost intolerable. It was then that I discovered again the blessed taste of cold water. During the rest of the night the water cooler in the embassy's corridor became the focus of my attention until it ran dry. The embassy people also proved generous with their coffee and even their Scotch. For us it was the beginning of a rather extraordinary diet on which we were to live for days.

I went to sleep on the Ambassador's couch around 2 A.M. But I had hardly dozed off when violent firing outside almost made me fall to the floor. The snipers were at it again and the Marines in the garden were responding with .30-caliber machine guns, automatic rifles and even pistols. In addition, a grenade-launcher fired once with its characteristic thud.

I did not seem to be able to go back to sleep any more. But other people at the embassy—now veterans of several nights of firing—were more casual. It was an eerie night. Every hour or so Lieutenant Phil Tucker, the commander of the Marine platoon guarding the embassy, would walk into the rotunda to report on what was happening outside. If there is a real pro anywhere among the Marines, Tucker surely must be it. Strolling about with his targeting stake in his hand, Tucker spoke curtly and casually of snipers firing now from here, now from there. On one of his visits he told of eight snipers who had silently crawled over the tall wall surrounding the garden of the embassy's residence. The young Marines crouching in the darkness saw them get over the wall but held their fire—quite a display of discipline. Then the snipers suddenly found themselves face to face with the Marines. They stopped, turned around, went back over the wall and vanished in the night. Not a shot had been fired or a word exchanged.

Once Lieutenant Tucker removed his helmet and I saw that he was rather bald. I happened to mention this in a story a day or two later and subsequently I found out that it had had a shattering effect on my 8-year-old son. He is a great admirer of the Marines, my wife told me, and as he read that story at home in Washington he came upon the description of Phil Tucker and exclaimed: "I did not know that there were bald Marines."

But bald or not, Phil Tucker was as cool under fire as anyone I have ever met. About 5:30 A.M., as dawn was breaking over Santo Domingo, he sauntered into the embassy to say that a rebel tank was rumbling down the street and was now about a block from the embassy. We did not know, of course, what intentions the rebels or the tank might have had toward the embassy, but it did occur to us that a direct hit from the tank's cannon could have rather unpleasant effects. But Phil Tucker merely pointed with his targeting stake and said, "Well, the walls here are thick enough. And anyway we are now wheeling out our rocket launcher and we have a good chance of getting him if he starts firing."

A few minutes later the lieutenant returned with a big smile. The tank, he said, had swiped a car parked in the street, turned around and gone back to wherever it belonged.

It was now morning. The embassy's heavy doors were opened and we stood on the steps outside. An employe was sweeping the driveway. The sun was rising and out of the haze came two of General Wessin's jets. They swooped low over the city and seconds later we heard their bombs exploding. Another day had begun in the Dominican civil war.

Friday, April 30th.

United States forces went into action mid-morning Friday. Tank-led Marines fanned out of the Hotel Embajador staging area to secure the western, or residential, section of Santo Domingo. It became the International Safety Zone under the provisions of the O.A.S. resolution voted in the small hours of the morning.

This was the humanitarian mission that U.S. troops were carrying out under Presidential and O.A.S. directives.

But at the same time paratroopers of the 82nd Airborne Division moved out of the San Isidro Air Force Base, where they had begun to land after midnight. They pushed along the highway in the direction of the Ozama River. Their mission was to secure the road and the Duarte bridge, which leads into Santo Domingo. On the Santo Domingo side of the bridge the rebels were in control. The paratroopers were carrying out the very mission that had been explained to them Tuesday morning by General York at Fort Bragg, when he told them to stand by for a "parachute assault" on the Dominican Republic. Since there were no Americans or other foreigners to be evacuated from the rural and urban areas lying between San Isidro and the Ozama River, the move by the Airborne Division obviously was a military operation designed to serve a political purpose.

That political purpose was unquestionably to prevent the collapse of the Benoit junta. The rebels were steadily gaining in strength while the junta forces were disintegrating almost visibly. General Wessin's troops were no longer attempting to break into Santo Domingo over the Duarte bridge. The junta's concern, instead, was to prevent the rebels from smashing across the river and threatening San Isidro.

By mid-morning Colonel Caamaño's rebels, mostly army troops, had finally succeeded in capturing the ancient Ozama Fortress, the last junta enclave in rebel territory. The Spanish-built fortress on the bank of Ozama River was a major prize in the civil war. Defended by some 500 or 600 riot policemen—the "Cascos Blancos"—the fortress was a great repository of weapons. When the rebels finally took it after several days of fiery combat, they captured large quantities of light and heavy machine guns, bazookas and other arms and stores of ammunition.

With the junta's military situation deteriorating hour by hour, the troopers of the 82nd Airborne Division moved into the breach and for all practical purposes set up a wall that prevented the rebels from driving across the Duarte bridge to the other side of the river.

The paratroopers captured the bridge after hard fighting. Then they proceeded to secure an area of several blocks beyond it on the rebel side of the river. Using bazookas, 106-mm. recoilless rifles and machine guns, the troopers secured their new positions in a relatively short time.

This was the first instance in which United States troops had entered into direct combat with the organized forces of Colonel Caamaño. By any reasonable standard—or so it seemed to many of the American newsmen on the scene—this was also a direct intervention in the Dominican civil war, despite the continuing claims in Washington that the U.S. still remained neutral in the conflict.

Four paratroopers were wounded in the fighting in the area of the bridge, the first American casualties in the Dominican conflict. The extent of the casualties among the rebels and the civilian population of the densely inhabited downtown section of Santo Domingo is not known. But the American troops had superior and devastating firepower.

The paratroopers also established positions on the eastern bank of the Ozama River, occupying eight-story flour silos, from which their fire could cover the western bank of the river, including the Ozama Fortress and the entire downtown rebel stronghold. The paratroopers likewise moved on to the narrow tongue of land jutting into the Caribbean from the eastern side of the river. This tiny peninsula, known as Sans Souci, controls the entry to the Santo Domingo harbor. It also faces a section of George Washington Avenue along the seacoast. That section of the avenue was the southern flank of the downtown rebel stronghold. Thus the paratroopers entrenched across the river and at the entrance to the harbor held the rebel territory in a vise.

On the other side of Santo Domingo, in the area the Marines were securing for the International Safety Zone, the situation was different. There the Marines were not engaging regular rebel forces of Colonel Caamaño. Instead they had to cope with irregular snipers. And the first American serviceman to be killed in Santo Domingo was the victim of a sniper.

Preceded by tanks and huge armored personnel carriers, truckloads of Marines moved from the Hotel Embajador staging area on to Abraham Lincoln Avenue, one of the city's major north-south thoroughfares. Then they turned right into Nicolás Pensón Avenue where the U.S. Embassy is situated. Advancing in single file, platoons of Marines followed the armor. The men were deployed in columns on either side of the street, hugging garden walls and dashing from tree to tree and from telephone pole to telephone pole.

Newsmen and photographers who rode atop the tanks and in the armored personnel carriers thought at first that the Marines' precautions were exaggerated. But when the advancing columns were about three-quarters of a mile from the embassy, a sniper's shot rang out from somewhere in the thick clumps of bushes and matted grass to the left of Nicolás Pensón Avenue. A young Marine in the lead of his column fell dead. Later a Marine helicopter landed near the spot, bringing the black canvas bag in which the Marines usually place their dead. The bag with the body was put on a stretcher and flown by the copter to the Boxer.

All day long, as they attempted to secure the International Safety Zone, the Marines had to contend with the fire of hidden snipers.

The perimeter established by the Marines was roughly rectangular. It ran along the sea from below the Hotel Embajador to a point just past the Hotel Jaragua. Then it went north for less than two miles to a point above the U.S. Embassy, putting the embassy compound in the northeastern corner of the Safety Zone. From what was designated Checkpoint Charlie, about a block and a half north of the embassy and adjoining the National Police headquarters, the zone's perimeter ran west to Checkpoint Alpha Two on Abraham Lincoln Avenue. Then it swung south again to take in the Hotel Embajador area.

Checkpoints, some of them manned by tanks and the armored personnel carriers, were established at the main avenues and streets leading into the International Zone. At some of them the Marines came under considerable fire this first day and again on succeeding days. Dominican junta policemen helped the Americans at the checkpoints.

Company Item of the First Marine Battalion had some difficult hours in the late afternoon and evening of Friday as sharpshooters directed heavy fire at the company's position. This was the area of the old Santo Domingo airport, where low-income houses were now being built. The open stretches covered by grass, bushes, trees and half-built houses provided excellent cover for the snipers. The Marines were also receiving considerable fire from the industrial midtown area northeast of the embassy and above Checkpoint Charlie. At the end of the day, in addition to the Marine who had been killed, 12 were wounded. A Marine colonel told me late in the day that, given the terrain in the International Safety Zone and the intense sniper activity, not even the two battalions of Marines made available for securing the zone would be enough. The point that could never be established, at least to my own satisfaction, was the identity and purpose of the snipers in and around the zone. The rebel military command spokesmen said over and over again that sniping at foreign embassies and at the Marines in the International Zone was contrary to the interests of the revolution. They argued that the Constitutionalists were anxious to give the impression of being an orderly group and that this sniping served no purpose but to discredit them.

At the same time, however, the rebel commanders acknowledged that they had little if any control over the irregular bands. This, of course, was the price they were paying for the uncontrolled arming of civilians the past weekend. It was generally assumed that Communists and their allies were behind much of the sniping because their political interests would be served by as much bloodshed as possible between the rebels and the United States forces. The more bloodshed that occurred, they seemed to think, the easier it would be to weaken the democratic elements in the rebel command and drive an ever-deepening wedge between the Constitutionalists and the United States. Rebel leaders also spoke of the possibility that some of the sniping might have been the work of *agents provocateurs* of General Wessin in an effort to turn the Americans even more against the rebels. But perhaps the most plausible explanation of all was that many of the snipers were simply "*tigres*," young, thrill-seeking hoodlums who enjoyed the sense of power and adventure that came from carrying out their private guerrilla warfare in the city.

As if the confusion created by all this disorganized and irregular fighting were not enough, the junta's aircraft provided another touch of madness. Around 11 o'clock in the morning, as I was about to stop by the embassy to try to pick up some fresh information on my way downtown, I suddenly heard the scream of a jet plane diving almost directly at me. Instinctively I leaped for cover near a tree. Looking up, I saw for a fraction of a second the jet coming out of its dive. Then there was the thud of an explosion perhaps 600 yards from the embassy and a column of dust rose above the embassy's parking lot. Before I could make my way into the embassy the jet was at it again. Once more it flashed overhead and another rocket exploded 400 or 500 yards from me. The plane came back a third, a fourth, a fifth and a sixth time, spewing its rockets closer and closer in a semi-circle around the embassy. Inside the embassy a U.S. Air Force colonel grabbed the telephone and shouted: "Will somebody get hold of ground control at San Isidro and get this idiot out of the air before he kills all of us?"

The jet did not come back, either because San Isidro contacted it or because it had run out of fuel or rockets. We discovered later that it had been attacking a rebel tank a few blocks from the embassy.

About three blocks to the southeast, just outside the International Safety Zone border, there was a column of rebel soldiers with a tank and several vehicles, all of which had the word PUEBLO painted on their sides. When a few American newsmen walked past they were surrounded by rebel officers and soldiers who wanted to talk to them. Their first words were: "Can't you tell your Government that we are not Communists? We are not Communists, we are for constitution and democracy."

And this refrain was heard continuously whenever U.S. newsmen mingled with the revolutionaries or civilians in the downtown streets. The reporters were buttonholed by people who wanted to talk about the civil war and inevitably they kept saying: "Can't you tell them we are not Communists?"

As I began to find some of my old friends and acquaintances in Santo Domingo and to meet other people, the question of Communism dominated all conversations. Many of the businessmen, lawyers, doctors and other professional people kept insisting that the rebellion was not Communist in character. Everybody admitted that there were Communists in the rebel movement, but the point was made incessantly that the Dominican Republic was not a nation of Communists and that the problem of the Communists in the movement could be handled fairly easily as soon as a democratic system was re-established in Santo Domingo. The U.S. Embassy held, however, that this was a naive approach.

I asked a number of people why they did not try to establish contact with the embassy to present to Ambassador Bennett and his associates their view of the revolution. They told me the embassy did not seem to want any contact with them. "They all are for Wessin," a young Christian Democrat lawyer said.

And, indeed, "Tap" Bennett and his fellow diplomats at the embassy were so deeply committed to the notion that the rebel movement was Communist-controlled that they appeared unwilling to try to establish any contacts in the rebel area that might have contradicted their judgment.

Meanwhile, the Administration in Washington had become somewhat alarmed at the trend of events in Santo Domingo. Some influential aides at the White House began asking themselves whether, by any chance, the reporting from Ambassador Bennett was not too one-sided and whether the United States was not making a mistake in committing itself so totally to the side of the San Isidro junta.

Consequently, at midnight Friday, even as the paratroopers were about to land in the Dominican Republic, Bill Moyers of the White House staff telephoned John Bartlow Martin at his home in Connecticut and asked him to undertake a Presidential mission. Mr. Martin, a journalist and writer, had been pressed into service by President Kennedy and named Ambassador to the Dominican Republic after the establishment of the Council of State Government in 1962. He was a liberal with good connections among the anti-Trujillo elements in Santo Domingo. He also knew the Dominican Republic well. The White House idea was that Mr. Martin could take a fresh look at the Dominican situation and at the same time try to open contacts with the rebels, an endeavor that had been neglected by Mr. Bennett's embassy.

Mr. Martin was picked up in Connecticut by a White House plane and flown to Washington Friday morning for a quick briefing. Then a Presidential Jetstar flew him to the San Isidro base, where he arrived late in the afternoon. If all went well, the White House thought, Mr. Martin could play an important role in efforts to settle the Dominican conflict. As Ambassador to the

Dominican Republic during the seven-month tenure of President Bosch, Mr. Martin was held in high esteem by the former President, his associates and a great many other Dominicans.

Arriving at San Isidro, Mr. Martin discovered that a truce negotiation was already in progress there. Ambassador Bennett and Msgr. Clarizio, the Papal Nuncio, whom the Ambassador had at first tried to keep out of Santo Domingo, had flown by helicopter to San Isidro for cease-fire talks with Colonel Benoit and his junta.

Earlier the Papal Nuncio had driven to Colonel Caamaño's headquarters to discuss cease-fire possibilities with him and others of the rebel command. A slim and seemingly frail man, the Nuncio was turning out to be a veritable dynamo and a dauntless truce negotiator. Behind the wheel of his black sedan, in white robes and red skull cap, he had been driving up and down the streets of Santo Domingo, crossing back and forth between rebel territory and the International Safety Zone. He had placed a large yellow-and-white Vatican flag on the hood of his car and he quickly became one of the most familiar sights of the strife-torn city.

Now the Nuncio and Ambassador Bennett were discussing a truce with Colonel Benoit and his fellow officers. Alighting from the Presidential jet, Mr. Martin joined them at the junta headquarters at the San Isidro Air Force Base. Whereas a day earlier the junta might have been willing to talk cease-fire, the landing of the 82nd Airborne units, which had turned San Isidro into an armed camp of the paratroopers, seemed to change the junta's attitude. The paratroopers had sealed off the Duarte bridge and the United States was increasingly supporting the junta, so the San Isidro officers seemed much less concerned about the future than they had been 24 hours earlier.

When word came during the conference that the rebels were again attacking in force, Colonel Benoit argued against a truce. Describing his experiences in an article in Life magazine a few weeks later, Mr. Martin vividly sketched the scene at San Isidro.

"Colonel Benoit was speaking, his voice filled with passion," Mr. Martin wrote. "Everyone wanted a cease-fire, but how could he accept one when the rebels, he charged, had killed hundreds of

Dominican officers and men—a dozen captives shot down in cold blood—and beheaded an officer and paraded his head through the rebel area on a pole?"

Mr. Martin went on to describe how he approached General Wessin to persuade him to accept a truce. He wrote that he told the general that "President Johnson is deeply concerned about the senseless killing of the Dominican people. He has sent me here to try to help stop it. I ask you, General, to be the first to sign a cease-fire."

Mr. Martin reported that after a brief hesitation General Wessin signed the truce document. That he did so was revealing. He was not a member of the junta and the fact that he signed the cease-fire document seemed to indicate that the junta, set up two days earlier by the U.S. Embassy, was no more than a front for General Wessin, the real power of San Isidro, with whom the U.S. did not wish to be associated publicly as many Dominicans regarded him as a symbol of oppression and dictatorship.

The junta members followed General Wessin in signing the truce document at 5:45 P.M. The rebel liaison officer, Lieutenant Emilio Conde, who was present at the San Isidro negotiations, initialed the document for the Caamaño command.

In Washington President Johnson announced in a televised speech that a cease-fire plan, elaborated by the Papal Nuncio, had been accepted in principle in Santo Domingo. But on the basis of last-minute reports from the Dominican capital the President recognized that the cease-fire was not being observed. Actually it seemed as if no one had taken any cognizance of the truce and the firing continued with the same intensity as before. Therefore the President renewed his appeals for an end to hostilities and urged the O.A.S. to move rapidly to establish a permanent peace in the Dominican Republic.

It was only at this point, 48 hours after the first landing of the Marines, that the United States was willing to turn over to the Organization of American States some of the responsibility for Dominican events. Consequently the O.A.S. Secretary General, José A. Mora, a mild-mannered Uruguayan diplomat, left Washington for Santo Domingo to establish an O.A.S. presence in the embattled city. Some of the rebel spokesmen had insisted on the

O.A.S. presence before they would formally accept the Nuncio's peace plan.

Meanwhile, covering the Dominican civil war was becoming increasingly difficult for the newsmen on the scene. It was almost impossible to hire cars and when a taxi could be found the driver charged $50 a day for trips between the rebel zone and the Hotel Embajador. The fighting downtown and the sniping everywhere made coverage hazardous, but most of the newsmen and particularly the photographers would not be deterred and they ranged all over the war-torn city.

Communications remained the greatest problem. I had been able now and then to get a telephone call through to New York, but each call was limited to six minutes. This was hardly enough time to dictate a coherent story over what often was a bad radio-telephone circuit. In addition, Telex communications were at best sporadic and could not be depended upon any more than the telephone service. Therefore I concluded that the only way to assure that a comprehensive story would be transmitted every day to The Times in New York would be to set up a daily air shuttle of copy to Puerto Rico. As of Friday the military had established a twice-a-day press courier service between San Juan and the San Isidro base. Consequently I asked The Times to assign another reporter to cover the story with me so that we could take turns flying copy daily from the Dominican Republic to Puerto Rico. As my colleague was to arrive the next day, I decided to fly to San Juan on the return trip of the plane that was to bring him to the Dominican Republic.

Meanwhile I still had the problem of phoning in Friday's story. There was another power failure at the Hotel Embajador and we were in darkness. Sitting on the floor and working by candlelight—the Marines had warned us to keep candles away from the windows—I scribbled notes on a piece of paper while waiting for my call to come through. As soon as I had finished dictating my story over the phone there was an explosion outside the hotel, about 200 yards away. Suddenly a whole field of dry grass in front of the hotel was on fire, illuminating the entire area. Then rifle shots were heard. I found out later that a Dominican civilian had accidentally stepped on a trip-flare installed by the Marines and that the device had gone off, setting the dry grass aflame. It took the Marines 20 minutes to put out the blaze as snipers from the empty houses across the highway amused themselves by shooting at the firefighters.

Another step was already being taken by the United States to find a political solution favorable to Washington and its interests in the Dominican Republic. This was an attempt to see whether General Imbert, the man who had been flown to the Boxer the day before, could be made the head of a new regime that might be more acceptable to Dominicans than the paper junta at San Isidro. The negotiations were undertaken by Mr. Martin, who drove Friday night to General Imbert's home, a virtual fortress guarded by his private military detachment. The house was on Sarasota Avenue, almost directly across the street from the Hotel Embajador.

I heard later that one of the ideas that was considered by the U.S. Embassy about this time was the setting up of a government in Santiago de los Caballeros, the Dominican Republic's second largest city, in the agricultural Cibao Valley. But before this idea was pushed, Mr. Martin busied himself discussing the situation with Imbert. On his second visit to the Imbert house during the night, about 1 A.M., Martin found Imbert quite amenable to the idea of becoming the head of a new Dominican government.

This, of course, came as no surprise. Imbert once described himself as the Charles de Gaulle of the Dominican Republic and he was a man long hungry for power.

Born in Puerto Plata on the northern coast of the Dominican Republic, Imbert became the governor of his native province under Trujillo. After a falling out with the old dictator he began conspiring against him. On the night of May 30, 1961, he was one of the men who attacked Trujillo's car, killing Trujillo. Along with another Dominican politician, Luis Amiama Tio, Imbert survived the wave of revenge slayings ordered by Trujillo's son Ramfis. When the transitional Council of State Government was created with Washington's blessings early in 1962, Imbert was named one of its key members.

From that position of power he immediately started working for his own political future. But despite his role in Trujillo's murder,

Imbert was never accepted by the Dominicans as a liberating hero. Even those who had harbored deep hatred for Trujillo suspected that Imbert had entered the conspiracy against the dictator not so much out of an overwhelming love of democracy as out of the belief that the time had come for other persons in the Dominican Republic to share in the spoils.

Though the Trujillo family fled to Europe with their millions of dollars, they retained a certain influence in the Dominican Republic. Thus both Imbert and Amiama Tio—who were civilians, not military men, incidentally—feared for their lives. For this reason the Council of State Government named both of them brigadier generals in the army so that they could enjoy a military escort for life.

While on the Council of State, Imbert concentrated on enhancing his power and influence. To expand his power he proceeded to transform the Dominican National Police Force into a virtual private army. It was directly loyal to him through Colonel Belisário Peguero, whom he made police commandant. Before the year was out the police force had grown to an army of 12,000 men with modern equipment. Imbert even tried to obtain tanks for the police—just as the air arm at San Isidro had its own armor—but the military commanders flagged him down on that plan. Imbert also began flirting with Communists and the 14th of June Movement, an odd gesture for a man who was to be picked later by the United States as the champion of anti-Communism. Allegations have been made that during his tenure on the Council of State Imbert arranged for deliveries of arms to Communists and pro-Castro groups throughout the Dominican Republic. If these charges are true, Imbert was, as it often happened, playing both sides of the street.

To bolster his influence Imbert got several of his friends and relatives appointed to important Government posts. One was his cousin, Mocho Imbert, who was made administrator of the Haina sugar mills, which had formerly belonged to Trujillo and now was in the hands of the Government. Just before the 1962 elections Donald Reid Cabral, then Vice President of the Council of State regime, prepared documents to prove that under the Mocho Imbert administration the Haina mills had somehow lost between $6 million and $8 million. Reid Cabral, who became one of

Imbert's chief opponents, also charged privately that Imbert had opposed the plans for holding the December, 1962, elections that brought Juan Bosch to the presidency.

After Bosch's election Imbert quickly became involved in the conspiracies to bring about the constitutional President's downfall. When Bosch was finally ousted Imbert made the grand gesture of personally escorting him aboard a Dominican warship to the French island of Guadeloupe.

But because the military and Reid Cabral basically distrusted him, Imbert never rose to prominence in the regime that succeeded Bosch's. Yet he quietly maintained his power base in the police force and his influence elsewhere.

This, then, was the man whom "Tap" Bennett and John Martin now picked as the most appealing candidate to head a new government to be formed under United States auspices.

Even as Martin and Imbert were negotiating, we were awakened at the Hotel Embajador by the sound of firing. Snipers had come close to the Marines' lines around the hotel and were shooting at them and at the building itself. The Marines responded in kind and for nearly an hour heavy firing went on in and around the hotel gardens. A sniper crawled to within a few yards of a Marine sentry post, 50 yards from the hotel, and fired several shots. He missed, however, and was chased away by Marine fire.

The whole eastern wall of the hotel was peppered with bullet marks. Two or three bullets went through the window of the sitting room of the third-floor suite occupied by The Associated Press contingent. The bullets left neat holes in the windowpanes and embedded themselves in the ceiling. With the sound of firing in my ears I finally went to sleep.

Saturday, May 1st.

Saturday was May Day, an occasion when Communists parade and make speeches. In Cuba it was celebrated by Fidel Castro. In Santo Domingo it went unnoticed by everybody, including the rebels, whom both the military junta and the United States accused of Communist proclivities.

The day began with improbable quiet. After the night's firing peace reigned in the hotel's garden surrounding the swimming pool. The Marines were clearing away the debris, putting their foxholes and tents in order, cleaning their weapons and even engaging in morning calisthenics. A red-haired Frenchwoman, awaiting evacuation at the hotel, was walking her two black poodles around the pool area, oblivious of the stares of the Marines and of the empty cartridges littering the grounds. It was not yet 7 o'clock in the morning but the sun was already hot and another blistering day was in prospect. And the whole Dominican situation was to turn into an even more confusing multi-ring circus.

Although the truce worked out the day before by the Papal Nuncio was supposed to be in force, intermittent firing went on all over Santo Domingo. The United States flew into San Isidro two more battalions of the 82nd Airborne Division. The paratroopers then pushed a little farther into rebel territory in downtown Santo Domingo to consolidate their positions. When three jeeploads of paratroopers penetrated several blocks into rebel territory, possibly by mistake, they ran into an ambush. One trooper was killed and several were wounded.

With 6,200 Marines and paratroopers already in Santo Domingo and its environs and more arriving continuously, the United States was building up its military power in the Dominican Republic for reasons that no longer had any visible relationship to the evacuation of the few remaining Americans in town.

Writing from Washington on a Saturday, Max Frankel of The Times brought into the open the real motivations of the Administration's Dominican operation.

"The fear of 'another Cuba' has been the main inspiration for the Johnson Administration's responses to the rebellion in the Dominican Republic," he wrote.

"That motivation for United States military and diplomatic intervention is becoming increasingly evident in official comments and briefings here," he continued, "although in deference to Latin American sensibilities it has not been fully acknowledged in public.

"Officials report that they are getting more and more evidence of Communist and 'Castroite' activity among the rebels. They are not sure that left-wing extremists have actually gained control of the rebellion and they have been unable to measure the full extent of the leftists' strength or influence."

From the Dominicans' point of view, the United States was only beginning to admit publicly what had been evident in Santo Domingo for several days. The embassy was hardly disguising its pro-junta sympathies, policemen loyal to the junta were allowed to man checkpoints together with the U.S. Marines and paratroopers and, clearly, Washington had firmly chosen sides in the conflict.

Hoping to convey the Dominican reaction to these events, I wrote a story Saturday morning that appeared on the front page of Sunday's New York Times alongside Max Frankel's article reflecting the Administration's justification of its policy.

This was what I wrote: "In the eyes of a growing number of Dominicans, including those who accepted the need for the presence of American Marines and paratroopers to help halt the carnage, the United States has become identified with hard-line military elements here.

"There is no question that Washington is lined up with the three-man military junta, which operates from the San Isidro base across the Ozama River from this embattled capital but has no control in Santo Domingo. The junta thus is a paper government whose military forces have been badly mauled by the rampaging rebels. In this sense it owes its existence to the United States, which supplied it with food and medicine when San Isidro was at the point of collapse earlier this week."

I further wrote that "playing on a sensitive chord in the Dominican psychology," the Communists are emphasizing this alignment between the military junta and the U.S. I added that "the charge that Washington is leading the Dominican Republic back into a military dictatorship like that of the Trujillo era" is being increasingly heard.

"In the judgment of many Dominicans—and of some foreign diplomats—this may be the outcome of the situation, if the United States does not apply its overwhelming political and physical power here to correct it," I wrote. "It is because of the fear of a new dictatorship that so many non-Communist Dominicans are risking their lives."

I also remarked that "the point being stressed here is that unless the United States offers a democratic political alternative to the Dominicans, many may turn toward Communism. This is what the Johnson Administration hoped to avoid in risking an armed intervention here for the first time in 50 years."

Meanwhile Colonel Caamaño himself signed the truce document that his liaison officer had initialed the day before at San Isidro. All day long the rebel radio station kept urging observance of the cease-fire, ordering all rebels and sympathizers to respect the International Safety Zone and not to shoot at Americans even if fired upon.

Colonel Caamaño and his advisers evidently felt that in being asked to sign the truce document by the Nuncio they were being accorded for the first time at least a modicum of the status of a belligerent party. They hoped this would promptly lead to their being granted even further tacit recognition. Such would come about if they were to be invited to participate in political negotiations for a settlement of the crisis. Thus the rebels made an effort to be on their best behavior.

And the political negotiations were indeed starting. Dr. Mora, the O.A.S. Secretary General, had arrived at San Isidro and gone into conference with the Benoit junta. Then he announced that he expected to see Colonel Caamaño as soon as possible.

A meeting with Dr. Mora, the rebels reasoned, would give them new respectability and make it increasingly difficult for the United States to dismiss them as "Communist scum," as Ambassador Bennett had been referring to them in his private comments.

At San Isidro the Benoit junta was still struggling to portray the rebels as representing an imminent Communist danger. After meeting with Dr. Mora the junta issued a public statement emphasizing that nobody should "contemplate the moral aid of the United States as an intervention, but only as a measure to aid a people who are in a grave situation and who urgently need someone to mediate in the interest of restoring calm at the earliest moment."

In its statement the junta said that "at the same time we state, the same as the United States has done, that our country hopes to be aided by the other peoples of America, in view of the fact that only in the place where events are taking place can there really be felt the black shadow which constantly threatens to make of our country another satellite of Moscow."

Meanwhile the Dominican problem had already left the confines of the tortured republic to become a full-blown international crisis. The O.A.S. Council, which the day before had sent Dr. Mora to Santo Domingo, now voted to send a five-man ambassadorial commission, headed by Argentina's Ricardo M. Colombo, to reinforce mediation efforts. Although the United States had won a measure of O.A.S. support for its actions (it was in this manner that the Administration interpreted the O.A.S. votes on the cease-fire appeals and on the creation of the International Safety Zone), many highly influential Latin American governments were taking an increasingly dim view not only of the first step of landing Marines in Santo Domingo on Wednesday but also of the continuing American build-up and the now clear U.S. intervention in Dominican political affairs.

At the United Nations in New York the Soviet Union was forcing the Dominican Republic upon the attention of the whole world. The Soviet delegation, complaining that the U.S. actions constituted an intervention, formally requested a meeting of the U.N. Security Council. The Russians wanted an immediate meeting but most U.N. delegates were away for the weekend and the U.N. Secretary General, U Thant, was in Geneva. However, Mr. Thant agreed to return at once and the Security Council meeting was set for the following Monday. The Dominican crisis had indeed become a circus of many rings.

In the political ring in Santo Domingo Mr. Martin temporarily halted his incipient negotiations with General Imbert so that he could establish contact with Colonel Caamaño. The establishment of such contact with the rebels had been intended as his principal mission in Santo Domingo. The last contact between the United States and the rebels had come at the famous embassy interview between Ambassador Bennett and Mr. Molina Ureña and the rebel officers who had accompanied him. But since the rebels resumed their fighting on Wednesday the U.S. Embassy had acted as if the Caamaño forces were not one of two parties to a conflict but an enemy to be destroyed.

After a series of complicated arrangements Mr. Martin was

finally driven to the rebel zone by the Papal Nuncio to meet with Caamaño and his associates.

Until then Mr. Martin's presence in Santo Domingo had been kept secret both by the Administration in Washington and by the embassy. In fact, newsmen in Washington were erroneously informed by officials that Mr. Martin was flying to Santo Domingo on Saturday with Secretary General Mora of the O.A.S. Mr Martin, of course, had actually been in the Dominican capital since the previous day.

My own problem at this point was to get my copy to New York for Sunday's issue of The Times. After I had waited for an hour at the sun-baked landing pad at the polo grounds by the Hotel Embajador, the pilot of a Marine helicopter agreed to take me aboard on a flight to San Isidro. We flew low over Santo Domingo, which looked incredibly serene in the noontime sun. Only here and there could wisps of smoke be seen rising from the rebel area. A house was on fire somewhere and in the streets the rebels were burning garbage and automobile tires.

Landing at San Isidro, I found myself in the armed camp that had been established by the 82nd Airborne Division paratroopers. They had taken over one of the hangars for their headquarters. Military equipment was stashed all over the base, along the runways and on the grass plots between them. Jeeps carrying heavily armed paratroopers drove to and fro. Troop carriers were landing every few minutes, disgorging fresh troops and equipment and then taking off again. Not so oddly, the principal American military base in the Dominican Republic was also the headquarters of the junta forces.

Colonel Benoit and his associates were installed in the base headquarters building some distance from the main hangars. As I awaited the aircraft from San Juan I strolled over to see the colonel. This was my first visit to San Isidro since I had arrived in Santo Domingo. It had previously been impossible to get to the base because of the heavy fighting at the Duarte bridge. But this morning, even before my own flight, Marine helicopters had brought over several newsmen, and some photographers and reporters had driven to the bridge with the paratroopers from San

Isidro and penetrated into the narrow area held by the U.S. forces on the rebel side of the Ozama River.

A returning photographer told of rebels firing from roofs and windows at the paratroopers as the soldiers moved cautiously from house to house, seeking to consolidate their positions. But the photographer and his paratroop escorts found a bar open in the battle zone. It had bottles of cold beer for sale. The discovery was akin to that of finding an oasis in the desert.

Secretary General Mora had just arrived at the junta's headquarters and I only had a chance to exchange a few words with Colonel Benoit. He told me that the rebels were Communists, that he and his colleagues were grateful for the U.S. support and that unquestionably the junta forces would win in the end.

In front of the main hangar the U.S. Navy plane from San Juan had just taxied over. It brought the first contingent of newsmen from the outside since we had come off the Boxer two days earlier. To my intense pleasure, Peter Kihss, a reporter from the metropolitan staff of The Times was among the arrivals. He looked cool, clean and composed. His clothes were well pressed and he wore a Panama hat. I felt a little embarrassed in my soiled sport shirt and torn slacks, the result of two days and evenings of hitting the ground under fire. I was unwashed, unshaven and sunburned. There had been no water at the Embajador for several days, at least during the hours when I would have had time to shave or bathe, and now my innermost thoughts centered on getting a shower and shave in San Juan, buying some clean clothes there and having a decent meal, complete with a cold bottle of beer. It is striking how the little things of life that one normally takes for granted in an orderly society suddenly become vitally important when one finds himself deprived of them.

Peter and I shook hands and went into the hangar, where we could get out of the sun, to exchange information quickly. I gave Peter the key to my hotel room as it was impossible to get other rooms because of the mass of refugees staying at the Embajador. Then I tried to explain to him as rapidly as possible the arrangements under which we were working. And then I boarded the Navy plane.

It landed at the Isla Grande naval station in San Juan an hour later. Barnard Collier of The New York Herald Tribune and I rushed to the first hotel where we could find rooms, but our longing for showers and good food could not be assuaged at once. Both our papers had early deadlines on Saturday and we both spent the next several hours dictating stories to New York. Then there were calls to Santo Domingo, calls from New York and additional material to be dictated to New York. Finally we had only enough time left to go shopping for clean sport shirts and slacks. We also loaded up on cigarettes, toothpaste and razors—items not obtainable in the paralyzed city that was Santo Domingo.

One of my telephone conversations in San Juan was with Dr. Bosch. The former Dominican President, sounding deeply hurt, told me that there had been "absolutely no justification" for the U.S. intervention in the Dominican Republic.

"I have lost my homeland," he said. "My country is occupied."

We filed more copy to New York to meet our papers' insatiable appetite for Dominican news and, by the time we finished, it was late in the evening. But Collier and I were still determined to get a first-class meal. Tired as we were, we walked down the street in the hot night air. We were suddenly in another world, a world of busy hotels, of full bars, of automobiles driven for pleasure. Santo Domingo and its war could have been a million miles away. We savored the peace of San Juan. There was only one thing wrong with it. The good restaurants in the area where we were staying had already closed for the evening and all we could find was an all-night delicatessen-type establishment.

And the great meal about which we had talked for two days in Santo Domingo turned out to be a plate of scrambled eggs with lox and onions.

THE SECOND WEEK

Sunday, May 2nd.

By mid-morning I was on my way back to Santo Domingo. The aircraft that flew us from the naval air station in San Juan was a Coast Guard search-and-rescue plane, one of the many types of aircraft we used in the days and weeks to come in shuttling between Puerto Rico and the Dominican Republic.

Just before boarding the plane in San Juan I became aware of the extent of the U.S. military build-up in the Dominican Republic in the last 24 hours. We were, obviously, far past the stage of a "humanitarian" mission and now the Administration was pouring troops into the country for purposes that clearly were other than simply guaranteeing the evacuation of Americans.

A Navy briefing officer at the San Juan air station told me that 4,900 men, mainly additional brigades of the 82nd Airborne Division, had been rushed to the Dominican Republic in the last 24 or 30 hours. He said that 171 C-130 and C-124 troop carriers of the Tactical Air Command and the Military Air Transport Service had ferried the troops from bases in the United States to San Isidro in a dramatic airlift, the planes and their crews flying 24 hours a day. Each plane carried extra pilots and the crewmen took turns sleeping as they shuttled back and forth.

As of Sunday morning, the Navy officer said, we had 9,200 troops in the Santo Domingo area, including Marines, paratroopers and Navy personnel.

It was with a sense of uncertainty over what was to come next in Santo Domingo that we flew back to the Dominican Republic. We landed at San Isidro shortly after the arrival there of the five-man O.A.S. commission. The group was headed by Argentina's O.A.S. delegate, Ricardo M. Colombo. The other members were representatives of Guatemala, Brazil, Colombia and Panama. All were accompanied by their military advisers and by members of the O.A.S. Secretariat. It was quite a large diplomatic delegation. Secretary General Mora of the O.A.S. was, of course, already in Santo Domingo, engaged in mediation efforts.

San Isidro, meanwhile, had become a veritable U.S. military base. It had looked like one the day before when I was leaving for

Puerto Rico, but now it was filled with men from two brigades of the 82nd Airborne Division. The battalions which had landed earlier were in the front lines in the area of the Duarte bridge.

The paratroopers had strung barbed wire barricades at the entrance to the hangar which served as the division's temporary headquarters and office. Guards checked the identities of everybody allowed into the hangar. The officers and soldiers entering the enclosure had to put the safety catches on their sidearms and rifles.

Inside the hangar one of the Dominican civil war's many improbable scenes was unfolding. The O.A.S. diplomats, impeccably attired, sat on munitions boxes while learning the fine art of opening cans of C rations. It was a far cry from Washington luncheons.

Then another improbable scene occurred. A rifle shot was heard coming from the thick bushes behind the hangar—or someone thought he heard such a shot. There was a shout of "Watch out! Snipers!" and the cry was picked up and passed along in the hangar and on the runway bustling with paratroopers and newsmen. Everybody in sight—perhaps a hundred people—simultaneously hit the ground. I remember rolling under a parked jeep before I had even realized what was happening. One's reflexes become sharpened in such situations. If there had been snipers firing at the hangar, there might have been numerous casualties. Paratroopers in jeeps that had machine guns mounted on them rolled out from the runway toward the area in back of the hangar. Yet no snipers were ever found and, for all we know, the alarm may have been the result of taut nerves or somebody's strange sense of humor.

After a long wait at San Isidro I caught a helicopter ride back to the Hotel Embajador. The lobby was still full of refugees awaiting evacuation but by now they were mainly Dominicans who had American relatives. Under the evacuation policy the so-called "fireside cases"—Dominicans with American relatives—were being taken out by the Navy. But there were others who for a variety of reasons wanted to be evacuated and they pleaded with U.S. officials to be transported to Puerto Rico. However, the United States had to draw the line somewhere as it was obviously neither possible nor desirable to begin evacuating indiscriminate numbers of Dominicans from their own country.

I found Peter Kihss, my Times colleague, batting out his story for the Monday paper. Peter was no longer as elegant and fresh as he had been on his arrival the day before and in the intervening 24 hours he had turned into another news veteran of the civil war.

We took the crowded elevator to the hotel's spacious penthouse, where the O.A.S. commission had set up its headquarters. Peter's story carried the commission's first announcement. It had said that its task would be to do "everything possible to obtain the re-establishment of peace and normalcy in Santo Domingo" and that "it would be guided strictly by the principle of nonintervention and the free determination of peoples."

It was a tall order. The Latin American diplomats would have to work hard to arrive at a solid cease-fire—the truce signed two days earlier was at best tenuous and a good deal of shooting was still going on—and to reconcile the *de facto* situation of intervention in Santo Domingo with the inter-American "principle of nonintervention."

The commission had said further that it would "offer its good offices to the Dominican armed groups, political groups and the diplomatic representatives with the aim of obtaining urgently a cease-fire and orderly evacuation of persons in asylum in embassies and all foreign citizens who wished to leave the Dominican Republic." It also would undertake "an investigation of all aspects of the situation."

This was the beginning of a long, torturous and sometimes despairing process of mediation that was to go on for weeks with the cooperation—or interference in some cases—of other groups of mediators.

We attended the regular 4 P.M. U.S. military briefing at the hotel, a twice-a-day ritual. The briefings, conducted by Army and Marine officers, were designed to acquaint us with new military developments. The briefing officers gave us casualty lists and sometimes details of military actions. But soon these briefings developed into occasionally bitter and always frustrating contests between the newsmen who wanted to know what was really happening and the spokesmen who were not authorized to divulge this to them.

Most questions, whether about over-all military policy or individual situations, went unanswered. We were told either that there was no comment or that the briefing officers would try to get the answers for us the next day. There were also inaccuracies and often outright misrepresentations of fact. The briefing officers, to be sure, were merely carrying out orders from the headquarters of Lieutenant General Bruce Palmer, commander of the 18th Airborne Corps and of all the U.S. forces in Santo Domingo, and presumably from "Tap" Bennett's embassy. Thus no newsmen ever held the briefers personally responsible for what often was misguidance rather than guidance. But these military briefings were an important part of the whole picture of misleading newsmen and, through them, public opinion about what the United States was doing or planning to do in the Dominican Republic.

This Sunday afternoon we were told, for example, that the perimeter held by the 82nd Airborne troops around the approaches to the Duarte bridge on the rebel side of the Ozama River was unchanged from the time American positions were first established there Friday. The briefing officer said that while there had been paratroop patrols in the bridge area the day before, there was "no deep probe today" and there were no plans to extend the territory held by the 82nd Airborne. As it turned out the next day, however, such plans did in fact exist.

It also turned out that U.S. military men were getting ready for their own psychological warfare operations in regard to the presence of U.S. forces in Santo Domingo. The 82nd Airborne Division had brought along its psychological warfare teams as well as Special Forces men in the same field. I had run into several of them at San Isidro earlier in the day and they had told me of their plans to send helicopters equipped with specially adapted loudspeakers over Santo Domingo to explain the U.S. presence to the population. Air Force planes were also to fly over the city dropping propaganda leaflets and addressing Dominicans by loudspeaker.

Propaganda and information specialists from the United States Information Agency, the Government arm whose task it is to coordinate activities of this type, had not yet arrived in Santo

Domingo. Therefore the explanation of what the United States was doing in Santo Domingo and the psychological aspects of its operation were left entirely in military hands. One result was that later in the afternoon Army helicopters, hovering low over the city, not only blared President Johnson's official explanation of U.S. policy but also disseminated what in effect was the propaganda of the San Isidro junta. Thus Dominicans were told via the United States Army helicopters that the rebels in Santo Domingo were Communist conspirators.

Following the afternoon military briefing I got into a recently acquired Land Rover for a quick visit to the rebel zone before going to the U.S. Embassy, where I wanted to talk to Mr. Martin. The Land Rover was a rather peculiar vehicle that I had been able to rent from an American friend in Santo Domingo before I left for San Juan on Saturday. It had a green canvas roof and two rows of seats facing each other in the back in the fashion of a small bus. It had a Dominican license plate up front and Dominican and Ecuadorean plates in back. Its engine sounded like shots from a recoilless rifle, particularly when I drove at night through the deserted and silent streets of the capital.

I entered the rebel zone through the Marine checkpoint at Avenida Bolívar in the northeastern section of the International Safety Zone. Occasional firing could be heard from the northern part of the city but by and large things were quiet. Parque Independencia, the heart of the rebel district, had its normal warlike look. Rebel soldiers and armed civilians, many of them young boys, stood casually on the street corners, weapons in hand. One boy, who could not have been older than 11, wore a helmet three sizes too big for him and lugged an M-1 rifle. There were crude barricades here and there at the intersections leading to the square but there seemed to be no tension and some women and older people even strolled about the area. I drove into Calle Conde, the narrow street that is Santo Domingo's principal shopping thoroughfare. There were iron shutters over some of the store windows and grilles over others. Except for one jewelry store with broken windows and empty display cases, there were no signs of looting or violence in Calle Conde. Colonel Caamaño's official headquarters were at the Copello Building, a modernistic five-story structure housing business offices. I wanted to see the colonel but the frogmen sentries in camouflaged uniforms at the door told me he had just left for an inspection tour.

There was not much else to do in the rebel area so I drove back to the checkpoint to re-enter the International Safety Zone. There Marines, assisted by Dominican policemen loyal to the San Isidro junta, were checking cars and frisking their occupants. They searched for weapons inside the cars, in the trunks, under the hoods and, using mirrors, underneath each vehicle. Then the Dominican policemen asked the occupants to produce their identity cards while the Marines frisked them for weapons. This was the first time I had seen junta forces working directly with the Marines despite all the neutrality claims. However, U.S. officials subsequently insisted that this cooperation at the checkpoints did not represent a political action but simply a routine security operation.

I made a brief stop at the Hotel Embajador and met an embassy official who offered to drive me over to see Mr. Martin. While I was visiting the rebel area Martin had held a news conference. He had flatly told the newsmen present that the rebel movement had become Communist-dominated. He had said: "This was originally a P.R.D. [Dominican Revolutionary Party] attempt to restore Bosch's constitutional government, but I am now convinced after having talked to many people on the rebel side that this is Communist-dominated, and moderate elements of the P.R.D. are themselves aware of this fact."

"Bosch," he had added, "must feel as heartbroken as I do at what has happened to the movement in the last three or four days and at the loss of life."

I was a little surprised that Martin, after less than two days in Santo Domingo, with the situation chaotic, would have rushed to place on the record such definitive conclusions. I raised this point when I arrived at the embassy and found Martin in a small office off the rotunda drafting on a scratch pad a report to the President.

I had known John Bartlow Martin since the early days of his Ambassadorship in the Dominican Republic in 1962. I had admired him for years as a reporter and magazine writer. Because of this I felt I could not quite discard his conclusions, even though I had been taken aback by them. Some of the embassy officials privately expressed unhappiness over the fact that Martin had decided to announce publicly that the revolution had gone over completely to the Communists. They felt that in doing this Martin had weakened, instead of strengthening, the democratic elements in the revolutionary movement.

We started talking. Martin looked and was exhausted. His ulcer was bothering him. He repeated for me his conclusion that the rebel movement had been taken over entirely by Communists and he said that he was sending a report to that effect to President Johnson. He declared that his meeting with Colonel Caamaño and his aides at rebel headquarters the day before, as well as private conversations he had held with many of his former Dominican acquaintances, had led him to believe that the Communists were now indeed in full control of the pro-Bosch rebellion. He said it was as if a "great wave" had surged through a valley, destroying everything and drowning everyone in its path.

I asked Martin whether he did not think the United States should make new efforts to encourage whatever democratic elements were left in the rebel movement so that the Communists could be eradicated from it. But Martin said it was too late for that. He repeated that "all the democratic elements" had been pushed out of the rebel movement. All the P.R.D. people who counted, he said, had abandoned the rebel leadership and vanished or taken refuge in foreign embassies. Therefore, he declared, there wasn't really much to do.

Then we changed the subject. I told him that I had spoken by phone with Juan Bosch in Puerto Rico the night before and that the former Dominican President was extremely anxious to talk to Martin. I relayed Bosch's message that he would be very pleased to see Martin in San Juan. Martin replied that he would welcome the opportunity of seeing Bosch. He said he wanted to tell Bosch what had really happened in Santo Domingo because he believed the former President simply did not realize the truth of the situation. Martin said he had requested President Johnson's permission to fly to San Juan to see Bosch. The authorization came presently and Martin left immediately by helicopter for San Isidro, from where he was flown to San Juan.

That same evening he went to see Bosch in the company of Dr. Jaime Benítez, the Chancellor of the University of Puerto Rico and a long-time friend of Bosch's. Benítez, too, was later on to figure prominently in the attempts to unravel Dominican confusions.

Meeting with Bosch until 1 A.M., Martin told him essentially what he had told President Johnson and the newsmen in Santo Domingo. He indicated to Bosch that the democratic cause was lost in the Dominican Republic.

I think Martin's reporting to Washington during the weekend played an important role in subsequent developments in the Dominican situation. His assessment that the revolution had gone over to the Communists was the final element in convincing the Administration that this was the case and that there was no way out except to help the military leaders at San Isidro to liquidate the Communist danger in some manner.

But in retrospect I wonder whether Martin, in arriving at his conclusions, had not allowed himself to accept superficial signs and the testimony of people who were not in the rebel zone. I also wonder whether Martin's attitude was not the reaction of a sincere but deeply disturbed liberal to a situation of immense emotional importance to him. As Ambassador to the Dominican Republic during Bosch's regime, Martin had been deeply committed to turning the little Caribbean country into a "showcase of democracy" under the Alliance for Progress, as President Kennedy had so strongly desired. Martin was bitterly disappointed and, I think, personally offended when the military threw out Bosch. Finding chaos and bloodshed 19 months later in the country in which he had placed so many personal hopes, perhaps Martin had now let himself slide too easily into despair.

This same evening President Johnson again addressed the nation on the Dominican crisis. In a suddenly announced speech—only one network was able to carry it—Mr. Johnson formalized the charge that Communists had captured the Dominican revolution. Until now this accusation had been made by indirection through Administration spokesmen. But now it appeared that much of what Mr. Johnson had to say in his suddenly arranged speech was based on John Bartlow Martin's reporting. The original text of

Mr. Johnson's Wednesday announcement on the landing of the Marines had included a "surfacing" of the Communist angle, but it was cut out at the last moment and a reference to the O.A.S. put in.

Once more there seemed to be discrepancies between what the Administration was saying in Washington and what it was doing in Santo Domingo. And there were inaccuracies of fact.

Thus the President said that "Saturday, April 24, eight days ago, while Ambassador Bennett was conferring with the highest officials of your Government, revolution erupted in the Dominican Republic." Actually Mr. Bennett was in Georgia that day and, as pointed out earlier, he did not reach Washington until the following day.

The main thrust of the President's speech was to justify his decision to land Marines in Santo Domingo Wednesday night to help protect the United States citizens there—a decision that few people anywhere had seriously questioned.

Then the President hammered together what was in effect a bridge between the U.S. humanitarian mission in the Dominican Republic and what was rapidly becoming a military-political intervention.

"Meanwhile, the revolutionary movement took a tragic turn," the President said. "Communist leaders, many of them trained in Cuba, seeing a chance to increase disorder, to gain a foothold, joined the revolution. They took increasing control.

"And what began as a popular democratic revolution committed to democracy and social justice very shortly moved and was taken over and really seized and placed into the hands of a band of Communist conspirators."

Then the President went on to say that "the American nations cannot, must not and will not permit the establishment of another Communist government in the Western Hemisphere."

"We know that many who are now in revolt do not seek a Communist tyranny," he said. "We know it's tragic indeed that their high motives have been misused by a small band of conspirators who receive their directions from abroad."

Some of the passages in the President's speech underlined contradictions that existed from the moment the revolution erupted.

Thus, while the President said that at the outset the Dominican uprising "began as a popular democratic revolution committed to democracy and social justice," the telegrams from the U.S. Embassy in Santo Domingo in the opening days of the upheaval were already describing the movement as dominated by leftists or Communists.

But the crucial point at the heart of the entire Dominican controversy was whether the United States had, as President Johnson said this Sunday night, the "real evidence" that the revolution had indeed moved "into the hands of a band of Communist conspirators."

In his Life magazine article Mr. Martin mentions the names of 10 Communist leaders—all of whom were listed in an official U.S. document made available to newsmen on Wednesday, May 5—and says they had "joined the revolt."

Then he says that "during the present revolt, our intelligence agents saw many of these men at rebel headquarters and rebel strongpoints. Independently [Harry] Shlaudeman [the State Department's Dominican desk officer] and I were told by thoroughly trustworthy sources that they were there."

This is the only visible evidence adduced by Mr. Martin, or anybody else thus far in the U.S. Government, to establish that this was a Communist conspiracy and that the entire revolutionary movement had been taken over by the Reds.

While nobody has ever doubted that Communists and pro-Castro Dominicans were supporting the rebellion—and presumably were hanging around the rebel command and rebel strongpoints—it is at best arguable that their physical presence there, reported secondhand, meant that they were actually in control of the whole movement, as both Mr. Martin and the President have indicated. Yet this became the whole basis of the policy of intervention, which was put into effect while the U.S. was still claiming neutrality.

Another point on which there was a discrepancy between the President's words in Washington and the actions of his representatives in Santo Domingo was the question of what the United States hoped to accomplish in the Dominican Republic.

While the President said Sunday "that we support no single

man or any single group of men in the Dominican Republic," Mr. Martin and Ambassador Bennett were at that moment actively engaged in organizing a government to be headed by Brigadier General Imbert. In fact, Mr. Martin in his Life magazine article takes much of the credit for having placed Imbert in a position of power. He describes at considerable length the negotiations that led to the creation of the Imbert regime, a streamlined and only slightly more appetizing version of the San Isidro military junta of earlier days.

This Sunday night the President announced that earlier in the day he had ordered two additional battalions of troops—2,000 men—to proceed immediately to the Dominican Republic in the continuing build-up. He said that he had also directed the Secretary of Defense and the Chairman of the Joint Chiefs of Staff "to issue instructions to land an additional 4,500 men at the earliest possible moment."

This brought the U.S. military commitment in the Dominican Republic to a total of 14,000 troops ashore. A new phase was now beginning.

Monday, May 3rd.

The new phase began shortly after midnight when paratroopers of the 82nd Airborne Division moved out of their positions at the Santo Domingo end of the Duarte bridge and broke into the city to link up with the Marines on the other side of town.

This was done to open an east-west corridor connecting the International Safety Zone, garrisoned by the Marines, with the bridge over the Ozama River and beyond it the San Isidro Air Force Base.

This Security Corridor, in military parlance the Line of Communication, or LOC, made possible direct surface communication between the two main bodies of U.S. troops in Santo Domingo.

But it also bisected the city and thus split the rebel territory in two. Now Colonel Caamaño's main stronghold, in Ciudad Nueva and the capital's business district, was in effect surrounded by American forces. It was hemmed in by the Marines manning the border of the International Safety Zone to the west, by the new Security Corridor to the north and by the paratrooper positions across the Ozama River to the east and southeast.

North of the corridor, in the sprawling industrial area of Santo Domingo and adjoining neighborhoods, the rebels maintained a measure of control. But their forces there, mainly irregulars, were no longer in contact with the command area below the corridor.

The Security Corridor was one street wide in most places as it meandered from the Duarte bridge through the low-income residential sections and ended above the Marines' Checkpoint Charlie. This was almost directly above the Presidential Palace and six short blocks northeast of the U.S. Embassy.

To link up with the Marines the paratroopers advanced nearly three miles across the city in the post-midnight hours. The rebel resistance was sporadic, but here and there rebels fired at the paratroopers. There was sniping from windows and roofs. The troopers responded in kind as they advanced from house to house and street corner to street corner. They suffered several casualties, none fatal, in this nocturnal action.

However, a Marine was shot dead by a sniper near Checkpoint Charlie, bringing to six the number of U.S. servicemen killed in action since their arrival in Santo Domingo.

After securing the corridor the paratroopers began moving into some of the houses lining it and climbing to the roofs, searching for rebels. It was necessary to assign two battalions of paratroopers to secure the corridor and keep it open to traffic.

By late morning, almost as soon as the corridor had been secured, troops began distributing food and water to the inhabitants of the rebel area. Army trucks brought staples such as rice, flour and lard to certain points for distribution to Dominicans, who lined up in queues. Some troopers of the 82nd Airborne handed out their own combat rations to people who seemed to have a greater need for food.

Politically the United States was no longer pretending that its troops in Santo Domingo were there only to protect the remaining Americans and other foreigners. President Johnson's speech of the night before had made it clear that the Administration believed it was now acting to prevent a Communist take-over in the Dominican Republic.

A State Department spokesman, briefing newsmen in the crowded and impossibly hot conference room of the Hotel Embajador, explained late in the day that the mission of the U.S. troops now was not only to protect Americans and other foreign nationals but also "to help Dominicans to find a democratic solution to their problems."

On a background basis, it was explained later that this simply meant that the U.S. would maintain forces in the Dominican Republic until a viable government—removing any threat of Communism—could be established. Though nothing was mentioned by American spokesmen about the embassy's efforts to set up such a government, Mr. Martin, having apparently given up his contacts with the rebels, was now accelerating his negotiations to build a new regime around General Imbert. Martin, back from San Juan, held a long session with Imbert late Monday night.

At the United Nations Security Council in New York the latest U.S. policy line was explained by our U.N. delegate, the late Adlai E. Stevenson. In a speech to the Security Council he said the U.S. had summoned the resources of the entire Western Hemisphere to prevent Communism from gaining control of the Dominican Republic.

"The American nations will not permit the establishment of another Communist government in the Western Hemisphere," Mr. Stevenson said.

Simultaneously in Washington the United States urged in the Council of the O.A.S. the formation of an inter-American peace force for the Dominican Republic. In the face of Latin American and world criticism, the Johnson Administration had now resolved that it should no longer go on acting unilaterally but that it should bring the O.A.S. fully into the picture.

The idea was that the O.A.S. Council, which had been in session during the Dominican crisis with the special powers of a ministerial-level meeting of consultation, should adopt a resolution transforming the U.S. troops in the Dominican Republic into a hemispheric armed force and urging other nations to contribute contingents. This way, the Administration reasoned, subsequent moves in the Dominican Republic would no longer be purely American in character but instead would have an inter-American flavor.

More newsmen arrived from San Juan during the afternoon and one brought along Monday's New York Times. I quickly checked the news stories and then turned to the editorial page, curious about the position my paper was taking. The lead editorial said:

> The President's unwillingness to see another Communist state established in this hemisphere will command national support. But the question that needs a much clearer answer is whether a military dictatorship in Santo Domingo has not traded on United States fears of Communism to preserve its power in a country still scarred by three decades of brutal repression under Generalissimo Trujillo. . . .
>
> The massing of American Marines and paratroopers in ever increasing numbers already has stirred bitter recollections throughout Latin America and the world of the excesses of "gunboat diplomacy." A unilateral decision to assign these troops an active role in helping the Dominican military junta to put down the revolt would run counter to all the principles of "progress, democracy and social justice," for which Mr. Johnson appealed in his televised remarks Friday night.
>
> Such an abuse of our strength would do more to spread Communism in this hemisphere than the Castroite danger it was directed against. As the President repeatedly pointed out in the 1964 election campaign, the United States cannot bulldoze its way to security, nor should it try. The inter-American system, to which the President has pledged full support, is our best assurance—and the hemisphere's.

In Santo Domingo, too, concern that U.S. policy would play into the hands of the Communists, rather than against them, was beginning to spread. Rebel commanders and spokesmen were becoming increasingly outspoken in their resentment of the sweeping U.S. accusations that their entire movement was Communist. I telephoned Colonel Caamaño during the evening at his headquarters. He was the first to bring up the Communist question and he said: "We do not have a Communist problem."

However, he added: "Our problem, unfortunately, is not with the junta troops but with the American troops."

Elsewhere in the downtown area many responsible Dominicans—lawyers, doctors and merchants—were despondent over what they saw as the U.S. decision to tar the whole rebel movement with the Communist brush. In countless individual conversations they warned that the United States was committing the mistake of closing all doors to the supporters of the rebellion and thus forcing them toward the Communist alternative.

They insisted that the only likely result of the U.S. policy would be increasingly to radicalize the rebel movement and give the upper hand to those within it who were Communists or Communist-oriented.

Actually this fear was not limited to pro-Bosch Dominicans. It existed even within the confining walls of the United States Embassy. I had a long conversation with one of the embassy staff members and reported his words in a story to The Times: "It is one minute to midnight, and if we do not act at once in the political field the movement will really become Communist and we shall have to maintain a permanent military occupation in this country."

This view was obviously not shared by Ambassador Bennett. After Mr. Martin's visit to Colonel Caamaño on Saturday no further attempts had been made to maintain contact between the U.S. Embassy and rebel headquarters. Mr. Bennett, if not necessarily everyone in the Administration in Washington, had clearly given up on the possibility of salvaging anything from the revolution. He was thus determined to see the rebels liquidated, pure and simple. The officers of the Military Assistance Advisory Group at the embassy held the same view. One of them summed it up for some newsmen who were standing in the embassy rotunda. The way to deal with the problem, he said, "is to let us go downtown and finish them off."

In the face of the American refusal to have anything to do with the rebels, the five-man O.A.S. peace-making commission took it upon itself to establish contact with Colonel Caamaño. After all, someone had to work for a settlement. The commission and Secretary General Mora of the O.A.S. drove to Calle Conde in several black sedans with the big letters O.A.S. painted on the sides. Before and after the conference at the Copello Building and during the meeting itself the rebels and ordinary Dominicans buttonholed the O.A.S. delegates and the American newsmen in the street to insist again that they were not Communists.

Lieutenant Colonel Manuel Ramón Montes Arache, the rebels' "Minister of Defense," told the O.A.S. diplomats that "we are not Communist-inspired and we are in the front lines against Communism."

Peter Kihss of The Times had gone downtown with the O.A.S. commission and he wrote in his story that Colonel Montes Arache, in speaking of the anti-Communism of the revolutionaries, was echoing "what scores of workers and professionals and merchants kept asserting to newsmen."

A crowd had assembled at the door of the building housing Caamaño's headquarters and the throng clapped rhythmically and chanted Dr. Bosch's name. U.S. officials said later, however, that obviously this was a Communist maneuver to mislead the O.A.S. diplomats.

Colonel Caamaño, three of his military associates and his principal civilian adviser, Hector Aristy, received the O.A.S. delegation in a fourth-floor office. Ambassador Colombo, the chairman of the commission, and Dr. Mora sought to persuade the rebels that a lasting cease-fire should be established and that the rebels should enter into negotiations with the junta leaders.

But the rebels were opposed to any idea of negotiating with San Isidro. Colonel Caamaño complained that the opening of the Security Corridor by U.S. troops was a violation of the truce worked out Friday by the Papal Nuncio. He said that the U.S. was frankly collaborating with the junta against the rebels and that all the steps taken by the American forces in recent days had been aimed at destroying the revolutionary movement.

The conference ended inconclusively. The O.A.S. diplomats had mixed views about the Caamaño group and in fact were split in their opinions. None of them was prepared to share fully the U.S. estimate that the entire movement was Communist-dominated. In fact, several of the Latin American diplomats heatedly disputed this assertion. But at least one incident seemed to have disturbed most of them.

This was that an officer in the camouflage uniform of the frogmen, an officer who spoke Spanish with a "foreign accent," seemed to have been inordinately influential during the conference between the O.A.S. mission and the Caamaño command. Frequently the rebel commanders would look up at this man, though he was not participating in the actual talks, to ascertain his reactions before answering questions. The O.A.S diplomats mentioned this occurrence in private conversations at the Hotel Embajador and they reported it to their fellow O.A.S. ambassadors upon their return to Washington.

This foreigner turned out to be André Rivière, a French soldier of fortune who had become one of the leading rebel commanders.

I had met Rivière about two years earlier in Santo Domingo when he was conspiring with an underground Haitian group involved in efforts to overthrow François Duvalier, the dictator of neighboring Haiti. I had been working at the time on Haitian stories and became acquainted with Rivière during several trips to Santo Domingo.

A lean man in his late thirties, Rivière was born in French Morocco and served in the French Army in Indochina. He had the rank of lieutenant and was in charge of a disciplinary unit. After the Indochina campaign and during the Algerian revolt, when President de Gaulle decided to offer the Algerians independence, Rivière joined the Secret Army Organization, a terrorist group fighting to keep Algeria French. As a result he was cashiered from the French Army. Somehow he made his way to the Caribbean and wasted no time in engaging in new activities that seemed to suit his restless temperament.

In Port-au-Prince, the Haitian capital, he became involved with underground fighters but presently was discovered and expelled by the Duvalier regime. Then, moving on to Santo Domingo, he joined a movement known as Jeune Haiti, led by a young Haitian priest, Father Gerard Bissainthe. After the failure of numerous Haitian conspiracies, including those of Jeune Haiti, Rivière stayed on in Santo Domingo and somehow became friendly with the officers of the Dominican Navy's frogman corps. He attached himself to them and became a frogman instructor. In time he involved himself in the pro-Bosch conspiracy, presumably because his fellow frogmen officers were in it. At the outset of the revolution in April he became one of the rebel's key military experts.

It was contended at some point that Rivière was in fact a foreign Communist agent planted in the Dominican rebel movement. But nobody has ever proved this and the charge does not seem particularly plausible in light of his background.

Meanwhile the situation in Santo Domingo was deteriorating. There was heavy firing during the day and during the night—sometimes against American positions and sometimes in all directions and for no clearly discernible purpose. Food shortages were developing, the hospitals continued to have difficulty handling the injured and the dying and fear was spreading about the danger of an epidemic.

The O.A.S. commission, after meeting with the rebel command and many other people in Santo Domingo, sent a telegram to the O.A.S. Council in Washington. It said it wished to address to the Council "a most urgent call so that the dramatic situation existing in this country be known in the light of the armed struggle."

The committee asked the Council to appeal to all O.A.S. member nations to provide immediately food, medicine and medical personnel for the Dominican Republic.

Late in the day I flew again to Puerto Rico to file copy to The Times. Our staff in Santo Domingo had now been reinforced by the arrival of a third correspondent, Martin Arnold from our metropolitan staff, and I felt we had the flexibility to go on covering the civil war regardless of how bad the telephone or Telex communications might continue to be. The shuttling to Puerto Rico was a rather tiresome undertaking but at this point we had no real choice.

When I arrived by helicopter at San Isidro from the Hotel Embajador I was alarmed to discover that the U.S. Navy press courier plane had not arrived from San Juan and that nobody seemed to know if and when it would come. But a C-124 Hercules troop carrier was at the runway, revving up its engines. I asked a crewman standing by the huge ramp on which vehicles are driven in and out of the plane's belly where the Hercules was bound for. He replied that it was going to Ramey Air Force Base in Puerto Rico, less than 45 minutes away. This sounded fine. Using my special travel orders, I got aboard the huge aircraft. Two other newsmen came along. We were the only passengers on the troop carrier, which had just disgorged airborne forces and was now flying to Ramey to refuel before returning to North Carolina to pick up more troops.

At Ramey we were met by amiable Air Force personnel, for our pilot had radioed that he was bringing us along. We were driven at once to the base communications center. Breathlessly I telephoned Kihss's copy and my own to New York and then went to Base Operations. We had wanted to get to San Juan to spend the night there and catch the next morning's flight back to Santo Domingo. Now the only way to do this was to fly in a twin-engine Beechcraft of the Civil Air Patrol that had been taken over by the Air Force for the emergency.

Ramey is chiefly a Strategic Air Command base handling nuclear bombers, but one of the B-52 pilots was a Beechcraft buff and he offered to fly us to San Juan. Shortly after taking off we ran into severe thunderstorms and Major Dick Moyer, our pilot, decided to turn back. Presently the Air Force lent us a staff car and we drove to a resort hotel at Mayagüez across a chain of hills. We arrived there at midnight. Again we were out of luck when it came to decent food. Due to the lateness of the hour only soggy club sandwiches were available.

Tuesday, May 4th.

In the morning Dick Moyer picked us up at Mayagüez in his Beechcraft and flew us back to Ramey. From there we hitched a flight to Santo Domingo aboard the "Talking Bird," an immensely complex communications aircraft of the Oklahoma National Air Guard assigned to the Air Force.

I had been away from Santo Domingo for less than 24 hours but the whole picture was changing again.

While I was filing copy from the Ramey Air Force Base Monday night, Dr. Bosch had decided in San Juan to renounce his presidential rights in favor of another leader who could become the constitutional president. Some time during Monday the remnants of the Congress that had been elected with Bosch in December, 1962, and then ousted along with him held what I guess can best be described as a rump meeting attended by some 58 members. Colonel Caamaño, one of two officers suggested by Dr. Bosch as his successor, was chosen by an overwhelming majority to serve as the "Constitutional President" of the Dominican Republic until Bosch's term was to run out in February, 1967.

So, returning to Santo Domingo after my brief absence, I found there was a new "government," at least in the rebel area.

Cheering crowds of rebel sympathizers filled the Parque Independencia to see Colonel Caamaño take the oath of office as "Constitutional President."

Whether Caamaño was, or could be, a "Constitutional President" was, of course, a matter of controversy. Although the 1963 Dominican Constitution does provide for the election of a new President by Congress when all those in the line of succession are incapacitated or unavailable, it was far from clear where the Congress had met and what parliamentary procedures had been used in choosing the colonel. U.S. Embassy officials frankly doubted the legality of Caamaño's status as the new President. The San Isidro radio wasted no time in pointing out, rather startlingly, that under the 1963 Constitution no military officer could hold presidential office.

However, everything in Santo Domingo at this stage consisted of de facto situations. Legalism—whether relating to the rebels or the San Isidro commanders—seemed irrelevant in light of what was actually occurring.

As far as the rebels and their sympathizers were concerned, Colonel Caamaño was the legal ruler. But the Dominican countryside remained pointedly neutral and Colonel Caamaño controlled only his downtown stronghold and part of the northern section of the city above the Security Corridor.

Speaking through a portable loudspeaker, Colonel Caamaño was cheered by the crowds as he read his acceptance speech as "Constitutional President." He said that "we want United States troops to withdraw from our country as soon as possible" so that "the nationalism of the Dominican people may not be converted into anti-North Americanism."

After the ceremony American newsmen streamed to the colonel's headquarters for an interview. Sweating profusely in the afternoon heat, Caamaño was alternatively jovial and angry. He said he wanted to get along with Americans and did not desire any "conflict" with them. But he went on to say that U.S. troops were guilty of new penetrations into rebel territory, despite the cease-fire, and he warned that if these penetrations continued "we will be obliged to repel them to defend ourselves."

He also told the newsmen that "I will not tolerate dictatorships of left or right."

The news conference ended on a friendly note and Colonel Caamaño announced his first "Cabinet" nominations. He picked his friend Hector Aristy to be "Minister of the Presidency," Jottin Curi to be "Foreign Minister" and Lieutenant Colonel Montes Arache, the commander of the frogmen, to be "Secretary of Defense."

But hardly had the swearing-in celebrations ended downtown than new and dangerous friction developed.

It concerned a move Tuesday night by the Marines to extend the International Safety Zone by an area four blocks deep to encompass several foreign embassies. The continuous sniping along the original eastern line of the International Zone had made work virtually impossible at many of those embassies, notably the French, the German and the Ecuadorean. It was not uncommon for diplomats in these embassies to spend a good part of their time on the floor or under their desks as shooting by the Marines and the rebels or snipers kept the embassies in a crossfire. On occasion the diplomats had to spend the whole night at their embassies because it was not safe to leave the buildings after dark, when the sniping usually picked up in intensity.

Although the rebels had apparently agreed the day before to the extension of the Safety Zone, Colonel Caamaño was now protesting it as a violation of the cease-fire agreement. A spokesman for the colonel threatened that the rebels would fight if the Marines did not pull back. It was another of those daily misunderstandings, some accidental and some perhaps deliberate, that were turning all efforts at negotiations into a nightmare for the mediators. In the end, however, the matter was settled and the Marines took up their new positions, slicing four more blocks off rebel territory along the entire line running from the sea to Checkpoint Charlie in the north.

In the early evening we heard heavy gunfire at the eastern end of Santo Domingo. By now most of the newsmen were becoming experts in distinguishing at a distance the sound of a bazooka from that of a 106-mm. recoilless rifle, even at recognizing the difference between .30-caliber and .50-caliber machine-gun fire. Often, standing on the balconies of our rooms at the Hotel Embajador, we held learned discussions as to whether firing downtown was from 81-mm. mortors or bazookas. This time the sounds were unmistakably those of recoilless rifles. As we were told later, they were being fired by paratroopers from the Yacht Club at Sans Souci at a small trawler in the mouth of Ozama River which, according to U.S. spokesmen, had fired at the troopers' positions.

It was another of those situations in which nobody could really tell why firing had broken out, who had ordered it and with what intention if any. The most baffling thing about the civil war in Santo Domingo was this continuing firing and sniping, which served no visible purpose from the viewpoint of the rebel command but which was seemingly beyond the control of Colonel Caamaño or his associates to stop.

After six days of the presence of U.S. troops in Santo Domingo it was becoming clear that the sniper problem was extremely serious. By now we had more than 16,000 troops in Santo Domingo but the sniping went on, particularly at night, with frightening monotony. It kept the city paralyzed. The U.S. commanders in Santo Domingo were learning what their colleagues in Vietnam had learned a long time ago: that even a large, well-equipped modern military force has great difficulty in assuring peace in an area where even a handful of snipers choose to be active.

Almost every night snipers crept up to the Hotel Embajador and the Hotel Hispaniola, about a half-mile to the east, where the Marine Expeditionary Brigade had set up its headquarters. Despite all the checkpoints, sandbagged positions and patrols, the guerrilla fighters could and did sneak by undetected in the darkness. One night a single sniper bullet felled a Marine lieutenant at the corner of Abraham Lincoln Avenue, a few hundred yards from the Marine headquarters. Nobody ever found out where the shot came from.

In the International Safety Zone the terrain was ideal for snipers. There were half-constructed houses and wide stretches of empty land covered with vegetation and tangled underbrush. To find, let alone flush out, a determined sniper was nearly impossible. Occasionally, however, the Marine patrols found snipers' bodies.

Downtown the paratroopers in the Security Corridor were continuously exposed to sporadic firing from a roof here or a window there. Since the paratroopers could not occupy every room of every house along the corridor, they were vulnerable to the rebel technique of the "invisible sniper." It worked this way: an unarmed man or woman—or sometimes a youth—would casually stroll down the street, looking as innocent as could be. Then he would enter a house, walk up the stairs to the second or third floor, pick up a rifle or machine gun that had been hidden under a bed or in a closet and start firing from a window at the paratroopers. After a few rounds he would put his weapon back in its hiding place and just as casually return to the street. He would then walk to another house, go upstairs and repeat the procedure with another weapon secreted there.

Whenever I asked Colonel Caamaño why he did not prevent this pointless sniping, which further antagonized the United States, he would answer that the firing was either in response to "provocations" or was carried on by provocateurs deliberately seeking to embroil the United States with his movement. Again he spoke of the "Wessin provocateurs." He also admitted that some of the snipers might be Communists.

On one occasion the Marines at Checkpoint Charlie noticed a middle-aged woman leaning on her elbows at a third-floor window. She seemed to be idly watching the street. But then a youth with a rifle would appear behind her and fire at the Marines over her shoulder. She remained motionless, a human shield for the sniper.

The Marines held their fire several times, fearful of hitting the woman. But after a Marine was wounded by the youth the platoon commander decided that things had gone far enough. A Marine machine gunner fired a round alongside the window without injuring the woman. And that was the last that was seen of her and her sniper friend.

The same morning a Marine lieutenant commanding a position near Checkpoint Charlie was faced with a new kind of problem. A small mangy dog had attached himself to the lieutenant's unit. The dog would lie quietly by the .50-caliber machine gun. But when it began firing the dog would leap up, stand under the weapon's muzzle and begin barking furiously. This had a most unsettling effect on the machine gunner. "How can I aim properly with a damn dog barking at my bullets?" he asked half seriously.

To deal with the snipers in the International Safety Zone, particularly around the two hotels, the Marines often experimented with sniperscopes. These are "black light" devices, employing infrared rays, that detect human movement through the heat of the human body. But sniperscopes have a limited range and are therefore not foolproof devices. And a Marine intelligence officer told me one day that the rebels, too, had sniperscopes.

While the sniper fire went on day and night and the O.A.S. diplomats worked hard to arrange for a more effective cease-fire, United States diplomats were busy negotiating with General Imbert for the creation of the new government they had in mind as a political solution to the Dominican problem.

John Bartlow Martin, having held a long session with Imbert late Monday night, saw him again Tuesday. Mr. Martin has reported in his Life magazine article his conversations with General Imbert. After Imbert told him of his willingness to form a government, Martin asked him if he really wanted to do it. Imbert's reply, as quoted by Martin, was: "I do it. For my country. Not for myself. Whatta hell I want to get in this mess for? I can sit here quiet."

Some Dominicans who know "Tony" Imbert well have seriously questioned his alleged altruism in agreeing to become the head of a U.S.–supported government. They have made the point that

"Tony" Imbert, employing every conceivable expedient at his command, had tried for years to become the Dominican Republic's ruler. Therefore what was now being proposed to him, they said, was hardly a personal sacrifice.

As Mr. Martin reports it, the swearing-in of Colonel Caamaño as "Constitutional President" complicated the delicate negotiations for the formation of an Imbert government. In fact, several more days were to elapse before the U.S. Embassy and Imbert produced a regime.

It was well after midnight when I finally got back to my hotel room. It had been a long day that had included a conversation in mid-evening with a group of Peace Corps volunteers. These brave young Americans had refused to be evacuated from war-torn Santo Domingo and had gone on working in the hospitals and elsewhere despite the fighting and the mounting resentment in the rebel zone against the United States intervention.

Six nurses had come to the hotel with Bob Satin, the Peace Corps director in the Dominican Republic, for a decent meal and a rest. Although these were relative concepts at the Embajador, what we had available there was still a vast improvement over conditions downtown. Since only the auxiliary generator was working in the hotel, there were lights in the corridors but not in the rooms. So Bob, the nurses, other Peace Corps volunteers and I sat for well over an hour on the floor of the third-floor corridor, discussing the war. At one point a young Marine on security duty in the corridor joined us. He leaned his rifle against the wall, took off his helmet and all of a sudden seemed just a young boy playing at soldier.

"Hell, can anybody tell me what we're doing here anyway?" he asked. This was a question many of us had heard from Marines and paratroopers. In the haste in which the Dominican operation had been mounted someone had apparently forgotten to brief the troops, to explain to them coherently what had brought them to the Dominican Republic, why they were risking their own lives and shooting at Dominicans.

One day at the helicopter pad a young Marine had asked a few of us: "Maybe you newspaper men can tell me which are the good guys here and which are the bad guys?"

At the daily military briefings, the officers usually referred to the junta forces as the "Friendlies" and to the rebels as the "Unfriendlies." When a reporter questioned this rather black-and-white distinction the exasperated colonel replied, "What the hell, those who shoot at us are the enemy and those who don't are friends. What else can I tell you?"

The Peace Corps kids were disturbed, too. They had come to the Dominican Republic—most of them 18 months ago—to serve in the villages and in the slums of the capital as social workers and specialists in various fields. They had made friends among the Dominicans with whom they worked. Many of these friends lived in the rebel zone and had rebel sympathies and the Peace Corps volunteers inevitably accepted their viewpoint. Also, as young people, their instincts were against the military dictatorship they and their Dominican friends felt the Wessin forces represented. The volunteers were not supposed to discuss politics with newsmen but privately they could not hold back their fears that the current U.S. policy was undermining their efforts to "build bridges" to the Dominicans.

Perhaps the most impressive person in the whole group, in his quiet way, was a young man named Geer Wilcox from New Britain, Connecticut. As we sat on the floor he was facing me across the passageway and he participated in the conversation as freely and easily as the others. It was only later that I discovered that Geer was blind. He had come to Santo Domingo to teach Braille to children in the Home for the Blind and he had refused to leave his post when the fighting began. Now he was more concerned with his pupils downtown than with his own safety. He told me he planned to return to the Home for the Blind as soon as possible, shooting or no shooting.

Because of the heat we often slept with the doors to our rooms open. About 2 o'clock in the morning, as I was falling asleep, I heard a commotion in the corridor and decided to investigate. Secretary General Mora of the O.A.S., who occupied the suite two doors away, was leaving on a sudden mission. I stopped him and asked where he was going. He would say only that he and members of the O.A.S. peace commission were going to the helicopter pad near the hotel for a flight to San Isidro to meet with the junta there. "I'm sorry I cannot tell you more," he said.

The Santo Domingo story went on day and night without respite.

Wednesday, May 5th.

In the morning I found out what Dr. Mora and the O.A.S. commission had been doing at San Isidro. They had gone there by helicopter to negotiate with Colonel Benoit and his colleagues the signing of a detailed and—they hoped—permanent truce agreement drafted by the inter-American group with the Papal Nuncio's cooperation. The junta had been reluctant to accept the new cease-fire agreement, but U.S. officials had pressed Colonel Benoit to go along with it and in the end the document was signed at dawn. The United States was anxious for the fighting to stop so that a political settlement could be worked out, even though Washington had its own ideas on what it should be.

About 10 o'clock in the morning some reporters were alerted that Dr. Mora and the O.A.S. commissioners would be going to the rebel zone. As soon as the O.A.S. motorcade left the hotel I followed it in my Land Rover. Two other press cars went along. First we drove to the Papal Nuncio's residence, where a 15-minute conference took place. We were not allowed inside and waited in the garden.

Then the Nuncio came out and got behind the wheel of his black sedan with the Vatican flag to lead the way. We crossed the U.S. checkpoint into no man's land and then entered Parque Independencia in the rebel zone. Armed men watched us go by; some waved and smiled at the motorcade.

We came to a stop at the Copello Building, Colonel Caamaño's headquarters. A small crowd gathered as we got out of our cars. Crowds always seemed to be forming in front of the headquarters, presumably because there were a great many people in the area without anything special to do.

There was some applause and cheering for the O.A.S. mission and then the diplomats went into the building. We newsmen were stopped by the frogmen guarding the door. They said they had orders to keep everybody out but the O.A.S. delegation.

So we stood in the doorway and waited in the hot late-morning sun. Small groups, some of them armed rebels and some just ordinary people, began converging on us. They displayed no animosity or hostility, just a desire to talk to the American correspondents. Again the first words, now a theme downtown, were: "We are not Communists."

A middle-aged woman in a green dress, speaking loudly, began to criticize the Johnson Administration for its efforts to make "our constitutionalist revolution appear as some kind of Communist plot."

She became increasingly agitated, spoke heatedly of the "bad American propaganda," "of the lies of the Voice of America" and finally shot this inquiry at me: "And why is it that Hubert Humphrey is not saying anything about this question?" The other people surrounding us nodded approvingly. A youth, perhaps in his early twenties, said: "My God, all we want is the right to a democratic government and a chance to work."

Another youth, leaning on his rifle, said: "And I want to be able to go to the university but I cannot afford it because I have to work to support my parents. Is that Communism?"

Suddenly there was a commotion down Conde Street and a group of men in the camouflage uniforms of frogmen walked up to the building. At the head of the group was Lieutenant Colonel Montes Arache and a thin man with an aquiline nose. I recognized him as André Rivière, the Frenchman, and he spotted me at once. We shook hands warmly and I asked André why we could not be allowed to enter the building.

"Come right in," he said and made a sign to the frogmen sentries to let us pass. We walked up the four flights to the top landing, where Colonel Caamaño had his office. The sign on the frosted glass door read "Dominican College of Engineers, Architects and Surveyors." Inside, Colonel Caamaño and his colleagues were meeting with the O.A.S. group. Rivière told us that we surely could see Caamaño and the others as soon as the meeting broke up and that we should wait on the landing.

Two tall frogmen were guarding the entrance to the office but they were friendly and smiled proudly when some of us photographed them. A little old man, looking like a janitor, sat on a chair by the stairs, holding a submachine gun on his lap. A rather corpulent man in his forties sat on the floor next to me and struck up a conversation. He wore white duck trousers and a frogman's camouflage blouse. He put down his helmet and tommy-gun as he lit a cigarette. He told me he was a dealer in spare parts for tractors—"I have my own business"—and introduced a man who had just joined us as his younger brother. "We are businessmen," he said, "but we have joined the revolution . . . I am now in charge of Caamaño's personal guard."

We talked for a while about the civil war, about the fighting against the Wessin forces and about what had made the two brothers get into the rebel movement.

"It's very simple," the younger man said. "We in this country are just dead tired of dictatorships. We just don't want another one."

Everybody on that fourth-floor landing was at ease and the atmosphere was relaxed. Once Rivière appeared and handed me a blue plastic bottle full of ice-cold water. The rebels, it seemed, had refrigeration, at least for water, which we did not have at the Hotel Embajador. It was a pleasant surprise. I took a few gulps and passed the bottle to a very tall, thin man in a camouflage uniform who, like Rivière, did not look Dominican. I asked him what he was doing here and in heavily accented English he told me that he was an Italian and had served as a Foreign Legionnaire in Indochina. He was from Rome and his name was Elio Capizzi. He was one of Rivière's friends from Indochina and had come to the Caribbean to follow André. He had a gaunt, deeply lined face and quick, darting eyes. While Rivière was a highly articulate and sociable man, the Italian was almost silent, answering questions in monosyllables.

Presently there was considerable commotion downstairs and a large group of men climbed up to the fourth-floor landing. They were all in business suits, neatly dressed and visibly well off. The leader of the group, a middle-aged man in a gray suit, said this was a delegation of professionals and businessmen who wanted to submit a statement to the O.A.S. diplomats on the purposes of the revolution.

Firmly but politely the dealer in tractor parts asked the delegation to wait on the floor below, allowing only a few of its members to remain upstairs. Starting a conversation with some of them, I discovered that the group was composed of representatives of Santo Domingo associations of lawyers, doctors, dentists, engineers, merchants and storeowners. As so many others had done, they began telling me about the non-Communist character of the constitutionalist revolution.

An elderly lawyer repeated what I had already heard many times. "Of course there are Communists in our movement," he said. "But you find Communists associating themselves with every group in the world that is fighting for liberties. But we can get rid of them. Aren't there Communists associated with the Martin Luther King integration movement in the South of the United States?"

"That's right," said a man who introduced himself as the head of the Medical Association. "Why is it that the United States insists on painting all of us as Communists? Does President Johnson really want to create Communism in the Dominican Republic?"

Suddenly the door to Colonel Caamaño's office was thrown open. The delegation of professionals and businessmen was held back but the newsmen were allowed to enter. It was pleasantly air-conditioned inside and everybody in the room looked happy. The rebel command had agreed to sign the new cease-fire accord, one of the O.A.S. ambassadors told me. Now there was going to be a ceremony to mark the event. Caamaño's office looked like the site of a successful business negotiation, but rebel soldiers crouching at the windows with their rifles pointed downward—they were assigned to protect the office from any attack—were a reminder of the civil war outside.

From the office we stepped out onto a terrace under the brilliant sun. The soldiers took positions along the edges of the terrace, their rifles and submachine guns covering all the roofs and windows around us as well as the street below. Black smoke curled up into the sky from a vessel burning in the estuary of the Ozama

River. One of the rebel officers told me it was the freighter Santo Domingo, which American paratroopers had hit with their recoilless-rifle fire the night before. This was the vessel the American military had identified as a trawler but which turned out in reality to be a merchant ship.

Colonel Caamaño, smiling broadly, marched to the center of the terrace. At the age of 32 he was a slightly paunchy man in a khaki uniform, the blouse open at the throat. He was joined by several rebel officers and his civilian associates of the rebel command. Ricardo Colombo of Argentina, the chairman of the O.A.S. commission, and his four colleagues strolled toward the rebel commanders. So did Msgr. Clarizio, the Papal Nuncio.

At 11:50 A.M. Mr. Colombo cleared his throat and announced that there was a "feeling of relief" throughout the Americas "over this historical act."

Mr. Colombo, a rather formal man, went on to say that "today I have the honor to participate in the historical act of the signing of the Act of Santo Domingo, the fundamental basis for the cease-fire accord."

Colonel Caamaño responded, declaring that "the O.A.S. commission performed an extraordinary labor and made all the sacrifices to achieve this cease-fire."

"We are deeply thankful for this extraordinary work of the O.A.S. commission in our country," Colonel Caamaño said. Everybody applauded. Just then a single rifle shot somewhere in the street below shattered the solemn moment. The frogmen crouching at the edges of the terrace tensed visibly, fingers tightening on triggers.

But nothing further happened and the ceremony continued. Now the delegation of professionals and businessmen was allowed to join Colonel Caamaño and the O.A.S. commission on the terrace. Its spokesman urged that the U.S. military "intervention" should end as soon as possible after the cease-fire became effective. "There is no reason for the intervention to continue," he said.

We went back to the office and Jottin Curi, the rebels' "Foreign Minister," showed me a copy of a cablegram he had sent earlier in the day to most governments in Europe, the Americas and the Middle East explaining the position of the revolution. The first cablegram had been sent to the State Department in Washington. But none had been sent to any of the Communist governments in the world, including Cuba.

Hector Aristy, the "Minister of the Presidency," told me that he and Caamaño would like me and one or two other American newsmen to have lunch with them. I said that first I would like to get to a telephone to start dictating a story to New York on the cease-fire agreement. Aristy said that nothing would be easier, that we should go to the rebels' military headquarters, a few blocks away, where I would be able to get a call through to New York immediately.

On the terrace everybody was shaking hands and embracing each other. It truly seemed as if the civil war had come to an end.

A rebel soldier was assigned to guide us to the military headquarters and we went downstairs to my Land Rover. We drove from Conde Street across Parque Independencia and turned left into Peña Street, which leads to George Washington Avenue, bordering the sea. It was a narrow street littered with garbage, odds and ends of barricades and broken-down furniture. Several automobile tires were smoldering at one intersection. We left the Land Rover at a street corner and walked several steps to an ancient house that contained the rebels' military headquarters.

The dwelling, with a Spanish-like inner courtyard, housed lawyers' offices and a bookstore. The bookstore was on the second floor and that is where the rebels had their principal command offices. The walls were peeling and there was a smell of decay about the building.

I was greeted by a tall, pleasant-looking young man who introduced himself as secretary to Hector Aristy. His name was Bonaparte Gotreaux Piñero and he was the coolest and most efficient man I had met among the rebels. I told him that Aristy had suggested that I try to get a phone connection to New York from the military office and Gotreaux at once picked up the phone and asked the operator—the telephone exchange was still in the rebels' hands—for a priority call to New York.

As we chatted, waiting for the call to go through, rebel officers and soldiers kept coming in on various errands. Quickly and efficiently Gotreaux directed them to the proper offices. He seemed to enjoy considerable deference from his fellow rebels, but I could never discover what his background was.

There was intermittent firing outside but nobody seemed to pay the slightest attention to it. There were armed rebel soldiers at the windows and on the narrow old-fashioned balconies surrounding the house.

When my call came I could not resist the temptation of including in my story the fact that I was telephoning my account of the cease-fire agreement from Colonel Caamaño's own military command headquarters.

Then Gotreaux assigned a young rebel officer to take me to see Caamaño. My escort's name was Rafael and he was a lawyer associated with the Christian Social Party. He wore black trousers, a white sweatshirt and a beret at a jaunty angle. His submachine gun was cradled in his arms.

Rafael led me to a dingy two-story house on Peña Street. He told two tough frogmen at the door that Colonel Caamaño expected me. Then we stood and chatted for a few minutes. Rafael told me a now-familiar tale: how he had joined the pro-Bosch uprising and stayed on with the revolution after Colonel Caamaño had moved it downtown following the disastrous Tuesday of last week. Actually, Rafael said, he had voted not for Bosch in the 1962 elections but for a Christian Democratic candidate.

But the point now, he said, was that the Dominican Republic needed the restoration of a constitutional system so it could concentrate on solving its basic problems without fear of oppression and dictatorship.

"That's why we are all in this one to the end," he said.

I knocked on the door of the apartment on the first floor. It was opened by Elio Capizzi, the Italian. He was Colonel Caamaño's personal bodyguard. The colonel himself sat on a chintz-covered sofa in the narrow living room. As I arrived he was being interviewed by Lou Uchitelle of The Associated Press. Barnard Collier of The New York Herald Tribune arrived the same time I did. Letting Uchitelle complete his conversation with Caamaño, we went into a back bedroom with Hector Aristy.

Aristy was one of the most controversial figures in a very controversial revolution. A short and chunky man of 32, Aristy moves like quicksilver. He speaks erudite Spanish and colloquial English and these talents served him well in becoming Caamaño's most trusted adviser. As Hector told us the story in his tiny bedroom, he and Caamaño had been friends for many years. They were together in the conspiracy to overthrow Reid Cabral and they fought side by side on the Duarte bridge during the somber hours of the revolution's first days.

Aristy's friends regard him as a dedicated democratic revolutionary—a man who in a short time has gone the long distance from the easy life of an opportunist and playboy to a sudden awareness of patriotism. To his enemies and detractors Aristy is some kind of Caribbean Rasputin, an evil and sinister influence on the naive and trusting Caamaño.

Both U.S. aides like John Bartlow Martin and some of the O.A.S. delegates had long been suspicious of Aristy. They thought he was too glib, too fast-talking and entirely too much in control of his boss. Both Martin and O.A.S. diplomats have related how Aristy would interrupt or correct Caamaño during their meetings with the colonel. And when Aristy translated Spanish into English, they said, his version of what Caamaño had said was sometimes quite different from the original.

But no matter what influence he wields today, Aristy's past is rather unusual. I had met him several years ago in Santo Domingo. He was a habitué of the Embajador's casino and the city's nightclubs. He seemed to know everybody—which was not really too difficult in the Dominican capital—and he was frequently seen with beautiful women. He was engaged in business activities in both Santo Domingo and New York. In fact, he spent a few years in New York as an exile during the Trujillo regime.

Aristy's circle of Dominican and American friends is intriguing. He is a friend of Diego Bordas, a wealthy Dominican businessman who served as Minister of Industry and Commerce in the Bosch regime. But Bordas was also a friend of Bobby Baker, the former secretary of the Senate Democratic majority who was involved in a series of Washington scandals in recent years. According to their mutual friends, it was Aristy who arranged for an invitation to Bobby Baker to attend the 1963 inauguration of President Bosch.

Subsequently, it was reported, both Aristy and Baker were interested in gambling concessions in Santo Domingo. A business group with which some in Aristy's circle were connected obtained in 1964 a lease on the Hotel Hispaniola and took over its casino concession. This group also secured control of Aerovias Quisqueyanas, a small airline shuttling between Santo Domingo and San Juan, apparently in order to bring customers from the Puerto Rican capital. Reid Cabral's Government was opposed to this operation and when the revolution against him erupted it turned out that Aristy, Manolo Bordas (a brother of Diego) and an American pilot connected with the airline were all active in the rebel movement.

Telling us about his participation in the revolution, Aristy made no bones about his having opposed Bosch in the 1962 elections. Earlier he had been Under Secretary of Agriculture in the Council of State Government. After the elections he joined a small party headed by Luis Amiama Tio, a survivor with Imbert of the Trujillo assassination. It was known as the Liberal Evolutionist Party but it was little more than a personal group around Amiama Tio.

When the April 24 uprising began Aristy was on the side of the pro-Bosch conspirators. That day, for no discernible reason, a rebel crowd burned down the headquarters of the Evolutionist Party.

Smiling broadly, Aristy told me that "I have always loved politics."

He said airily that there had been few conspiracies in recent years in which he had not been involved or at least known about.

We chatted a bit more, discussing the Dominican situation and the position of Juan Bosch. Aristy said that in the circumstances it had been a sound move for Bosch to have stepped aside and let Colonel Caamaño be chosen "Constitutional President."

For Bosch to have attempted to resume the presidency after all that had happened in Santo Domingo in the last 10 days would have been very difficult, Aristy said. He added, however, that as soon as the "Constitutional Government" had been consolidated Bosch would be asked to come to Santo Domingo and act as the gray eminence of the new regime. Later, when elections were held in 1966, Aristy said, Bosch could again run for office and most likely would be elected. I had the feeling that Aristy was pleased at the way things had worked out with Bosch.

At this point Aristy and the rest of the rebel command were exultant. The fact that the O.A.S. commission had come to negotiate with them, they believed, meant in effect tacit recognition of their government. Caamaño and Aristy had actually insisted that the truce document, signed a couple of hours ago, refer to Caamaño as Constitutional President. Finally a compromise was reached and the title was placed in quotation marks: "Constitutional President."

We walked back to the living room just as Caamaño was completing his conversation with Lou Uchitelle. I had barely started talking to Caamaño when strong firing was heard from Parque Independencia, a few blocks away. Everybody in the room stiffened visibly.

Elio, the Italian ex-Foreign Legionnaire, grabbed his submachine gun and ran out to the little balcony overlooking the street. He stood there covering the apartment. Aristy, too, picked up his weapon and ran downstairs. Caamaño's hand went automatically to his pistol holster, but then he relaxed and, lighting an American cigarette, resumed talking to us. There was more heavy firing from the Parque—we could hear machine guns and rifles—but now Caamaño remained unperturbed. Somewhat improbably a rebel sergeant in the room passed around a paper bag full of yellow Dominican sweets.

As I look back, the scene was one of complete unreality. This tiny unkempt apartment on Peña Street in downtown Santo Domingo was the center of one of the most important news stories in the world at the time. But the actors somehow did not seem to fit their roles: the relaxed, slightly paunchy colonel, the sergeant passing around candy, the gaunt Italian paratrooper crouching on the balcony.

Between bursts of firing and single shots downstairs—they were now coming closer and closer—Caamaño answered our questions about his background. Yes, it was true that he was the son of General Fausto Caamaño and it was true that his father had been one of Trujillo's most brutal henchmen. How did the colonel feel about his father? Caamaño shrugged.

"What difference does it make now?" he asked. "The important thing is what we are doing now or trying to do for our country. The past, let us forget it."

He told us he had spent a year at a high school in Hollywood, Florida, returning to Santo Domingo to go to the military school. His last year as a military student was spent at the small Dominican Naval Academy and Caamaño actually graduated as a Dominican Marine Corps officer.

After graduation he was invited by the United States Government to complete his training on the mainland. He took a course at the Amphibious Operations School at Coronado, California, and another at Quantico, Virginia. Returning to the Dominican Republic, he served in its Marine Corps until Trujillo's assassination. In the military reorganization that followed, Caamaño was assigned to the growing police force that "Tony" Imbert had begun organizing. In fact, Caamaño and Imbert had become friends before they turned into the sworn enemies that they were now. And this is really a capsule appreciation of Dominican politics. At one time almost everybody is or has been someone's friend and ally or enemy and adversary.

In September, 1963, Caamaño passively participated in the military movement that overthrew Bosch. But now he said that privately he had never accepted this ouster of the democratic government. During the Reid Cabral regime he was put in charge of the U.S.-trained riot-control detachment, but later he was dismissed from the force because he tried to overthrow the police chief, a protégé of "Tony" Imbert's, as he believed his superior was given to considerable corruption. Reid Cabral then shifted Caamaño to the air force and it was there that he began plotting the revolution along with fellow officers and pro-Bosch civilians.

I asked Caamaño about his general political, economic and social ideas. He replied that he would rather not discuss them at this time. "This is the time to fight," he told me. "Politics and the broad plans for our country will come later."

He said, however, that he favored maintaining an effective but reduced military establishment after the old Trujillo-linked commanders had been eliminated once and for all. Answering a question, he said he also favored a form of land reform, but he was clearly not too well acquainted with the subject.

On the whole, Caamaño gave the impression of being a sincere and dedicated fighter for an idea in which he happened to believe. But, at least at this point, it was difficult to discern in "Francis" Caamaño mesmeric or charismatic leadership qualities. He was tough, all right, but he was not a Fidel Castro. He sounded like an idealist for democracy, but he was not a Rómulo Betancourt. He did not have the political sophistication of either the Cuban demagogue or the Venezuelan statesman. He was a figure whom fate had hurled to the center of the world's attention in this tragic hour of his country.

Now the firing downstairs and around Parque Independencia had become so intense that instinctively I sat behind a bookcase. It was one of those Dominican reflexes, I think. Hector Aristy burst into the room and told Caamaño that several jeeploads of U.S. Marines had invaded Parque Independencia.

"They have violated the truce," Caamaño cried in great agitation.

A rebel soldier arrived and reported that one of the jeeps had been captured and that there were American wounded. But, he said, other Americans were firing at the rebel positions. It was less than three hours since the truce had been signed at the Copello Building and the fighting had already resumed and tempers were flaring on all sides.

Caamaño grabbed the telephone and started calling his command posts. "Shoot with everything you have at the Americans if they cross again into our territory," he shouted.

Then, as an afterthought, he picked up the phone once more and ordered that a rebel tank be brought to Parque Independencia to act against the American forces.

Uchitelle, Collier and I were beginning to feel mighty uncomfortable. It looked as if we were caught in the middle of what could become a major shooting fray if the rebels really hit the Americans hard and our troops decided to respond in kind. We did not know, of course, what was really happening. But the firing was getting heavier and heavier and now it was coming from all sides. I said to Caamaño that perhaps we should grab my Land Rover and risk a dead-end run to the American lines before it got too late. It was already mid-afternoon and I had no overpowering desire to be caught in darkness in the middle of the rebel zone with a battle raging around us. But Caamaño looked out the window and said he thought it was not safe for us to go out.

Collier picked up the telephone and called the U.S. Embassy. He got hold of the military attaché there and told him that three American newsmen caught under fire at Caamaño headquarters would be most grateful if orders could be given to stop the firing, at least from the American side, long enough to let us make our getaway. The attaché did not seem to know what Collier was talking about and asked that we call him back in a few minutes. Collier did so, but the colonel at the embassy still was unclear about the situation and did not seem to be in a position to declare a private cease-fire for the benefit of the three of us.

Presently the firing diminished somewhat and Caamaño said he thought this might be a good moment for us to risk getting away. He sent one of his men to fetch the Land Rover, which I had left parked near Parque Independencia. There was quite a bit of firing at that corner and we were grateful to the rebel soldier for playing the parking lot attendant.

As we said good-by to Colonel Caamaño he suggested that we might be safer if he sent along an escort car as far as the limit of his lines. I got behind the wheel of the Land Rover and Collier and Uchitelle got in next to me. Four of the rebels got into a white sedan and we took off toward George Washington Avenue, along the sea, to where Caamaño thought we could find the safest passage to the American lines.

The rebel escort car led us as far as the big white obelisk in the center of a small park and traffic circle on George Washington Avenue. This was the edge of rebel-held territory. Ahead of us stretched 600 or 700 yards of an empty street—the no man's land—and beyond it we could see the silhouette of a U.S. Marine Corps Armored Personnel Vehicle, an Amtrack. The escort car turned around and vanished in the direction of rebel headquarters. The driver waved good-by to us. We were on our own.

I noticed a small blue sedan driving slowly ahead of us toward the American lines. I put the Land Rover in gear and followed just as slowly. My eyes were fastened on the Marine positions. I saw the Marines waving the little blue sedan away. It stopped and I stopped. The sedan, which apparently carried Dominicans, turned around and went back to the rebel-held territory. I looked at Collier and Uchitelle and said something to the effect that we had little choice but to try to get into the Marine lines without being fired at. I realized the Marines did not know who was in the car.

The word PRENSA—PRESS—was taped in orange on the windshield. On each side of the vehicle there were signs saying "The New York Times." However, I was not certain the Marines could see any of this at a distance. I drove at 10 or 15 miles an hour, but Collier kept saying, "Go slower, go slower."

Then I saw that the Marines were waving us away. It flashed through my mind that they thought we were a rebel vehicle, perhaps carrying armed soldiers. Simultaneously rebel snipers in the buildings behind us began shooting at Marine positions, maybe a quarter of a mile to our right. We heard the Marines firing back. The troops at the checkpoint facing us, now no more than 300 yards away, were still waving us off.

I stopped the car. I poked my head out of the window and began shouting, "We are American correspondents. . . . We are Americans. . . . Let us in. . . ."

I was getting ready to get out of the car and try to walk toward the Marines to identify myself. But before I could do this a tall figure in white trousers and a blue sport shirt burst out from behind the Amtrack, waving us in. I heard his voice calling out my name, telling me to drive on.

It was Ted Yates, a National Broadcasting Company producer from Washington and a friend of ours. He had recognized either my peculiar-looking Land Rover or my voice or my accent. In any event, Ted's presence may have well saved our lives.

As we drove the last few hundred yards to the checkpoint I saw that the Marines had their machine guns and rifles trained on us. Ted was there to identify us. But we still had to produce our Department of Defense accreditation cards to convince the Marine officer in command of the detachment that we were indeed American newsmen.

Later Ted told us how close we had come to what might have been a dire ending to our Dominican story. He said that when the Marines saw us approaching from the rebel side they assumed we were a hostile vehicle and, as he put it, "Safety catches began clicking all along the line."

The day before an old man and a youth, riding together on a bicycle, had approached that Marine checkpoint. Less than 100 yards from it the youth had jumped off the bicycle and begun firing at the Marines with a submachine gun he had concealed on him. It was one of those inexplicable acts of bravado and suicide because, as was inevitable, the Marines ripped him and the old man to pieces with .50-caliber machine-gun fire. Now the Marines were extra careful and extra jumpy.

A Marine jeep escorted us along a side street to the main checkpoint on Avenida Independencia through which traffic was allowed to flow in and out of the International Safety Zone.

To say the least, we were a bit shaken by our experience, particularly when it really began to dawn on us what a narrow escape we had had. If Yates had not been with the Marines, supervising his camera crew, chances are that we would not have escaped unharmed.

This episode, emphasizing the danger in driving around Santo Domingo in the middle of a civil war, reminds me of another incident that occurred the same week, involving Richard Valeriani. Dick, an N.B.C. correspondent who has been to Castro's Cuba and to Selma, Alabama, before winding up in Santo Domingo, was returning one evening with his camera crew from Caamaño's downtown headquarters. Like us, they had received an escort, but the rebel car left them at the entrance to Parque Independencia. The normal traffic pattern around the Parque is clockwise but, driving in pitch darkness, Dick cut across the plaza, heading toward Avenida Bolívar and the Marine checkpoint there. Suddenly, as Dick tells the story, his car was set upon by a band of armed rebels who had materialized out of the darkness. The leader of the group poked his head into the window on Dick's side and asked in English, "Do you speak English?"

Dick answered in a quivering voice that, yes, he did.

"Then," the rebel said, "I must warn you that you are driving in the wrong direction on a one-way street."

Indeed, the Santo Domingo civil war had its moments.

Back at the Hotel Embajador I was told by a military spokesman that several Marines' and paratroopers' jeeps had accidentally penetrated into rebel territory. This was the explanation for the late-afternoon fight in and around Parque Independencia. The military spokesman confirmed that one of the Marines had been captured and that three or four other U.S. servicemen had been wounded. The rebels had also captured one jeep.

After the incident was cleared up the fighting came to a virtual halt—except for the now normal sniper activity—and the truce seemed to be back on. Four of the five members of the O.A.S commission flew back to Washington during the evening to report to the O.A.S. Council. They left behind their Panamanian colleague, Frank Morrice Jr.

But the military cease-fire did not bring with it a political truce in the Dominican civil war. While the negotiations with "Tony" Imbert for the formation of a new junta were moving ahead, the Johnson Administration was back on the offensive, both in Santo Domingo and in Washington, to force across its point that the rebel regime was indeed Communist-dominated.

At an evening briefing at the Hotel Embajador a State Department spokesman told newsmen that the U.S. Embassy had new information according to which Colonel Caamaño had agreed to give Communists a "decisive voice" in the event of his ultimate victory.

The spokesman said it was his understanding that Colonel Caamaño had met the day before with five "prominent Communists" to discuss their participation in the revolutionary government.

He said that Caamaño had also committed himself, in the event the rebel movement was defeated, to negotiate with the O.A.S. for safe-conduct out of the Dominican Republic for the Communist leadership.

The spokesman was asked whether he could identify the five Communists. He said he thought Fidelio Despradel was one of them. But no other details were available.

In Washington the State Department and the C.I.A. made available to newsmen a list of 54 "Communists and Castroites" who were said to be conspicuously active among the rebels and to have infiltrated the rebel leadership.

This was a streamlined and more detailed version of the list of 53 names that Ambassador Bennett had made available to us in Santo Domingo six days earlier. It gave detailed information on the background of each person mentioned and was accompanied by additional data on the extent of what the Administration described as the Communist and Castroite infiltration in the rebel movement from the very outset.

The Administration briefers said these 54 Communist and Castroite leaders were playing an important role in organizing mobs among the rebels. It was said that of the 54 at least 18 were known or reliably reported to have been trained in subversive tactics by Cuban experts and that 36 had been clearly identified in recent years as Communist and Castroite subversives.

Named as the key man in directing the Communist activity among the rebels was Manuel Gonzales Gonzales, said to be a Spanish Communist.

Much of the information provided by the Administration emphasized that numerous members of the 14th of June Movement and of the Dominican Popular Movement, the pro-Chinese Communist faction, had traveled extensively in Communist countries before returning to the Dominican Republic, some secretly, in 1964 and 1965.

The Administration further said that the 14th of June members were active in the streets in the first hours of the revolt on April 24, urging popular demonstrations for the restoration of the Bosch Government. This, of course, had been known all along, but the rebels kept denying that it constituted evidence that these Castroites were in control of the whole rebel movement.

Another point made by the Administration was that Communist and Castroite leaders had obtained arms and ammunition from the Dominican Army arsenals held by the rebels. Again it had been common knowledge in Santo Domingo that Communists, along with non-Communists, were among those to whom weapons were made freely available on the second and third day of the revolution.

However, the Administration's information added that "party members" had been formed into separate armed teams that fanned out in the downtown and slum sections of Santo Domingo under the direction of Fidelio Despradel and Buenaventura Johnson.

The intelligence data went on to say that a separate Communist military headquarters had been established in Santo Domingo to collect arms from the police and the armed forces while at the same time Communist-manned strongpoints had been organized.

Rebel leaders and other informed Dominicans had acknowledged that Communists had indeed been active in gathering arms for their followers and that there unquestionably were Communists in the rebel strongholds. But they kept denying strongly that the presence of Communists within the rebel movement could be viewed as "decisively influencing the political leadership of the rebellion," as the Administration was charging in Washington.

This, of course, was the crux of the whole argument. There could be no question but that the Soviet-oriented and the pro-Chinese Communist groups and the 14th of June Movement were all actively distributing propaganda that sounded remarkably like Havana's output. They circulated leaflets signed by their movements attacking the United States and calling for "anti-American" and "anti-imperialist" warfare. This was the evidence adduced by the U.S. Embassy and by some newsmen in Santo Domingo to emphasize the importance of the Communist elements in the revolution.

However, official rebel pronouncements were rather free of the Communist-line tone found in the broadsides and leaflets of the Communist groups. It was then a matter of judgment whether, as the embassy was saying, the Caamaño leadership was deliberately misleading the world by trying to appear to be moderate and reasonable. But here again the burden of proof was placed not on the accusers but on the accused, and as far as some American quarters were concerned there was nothing Colonel Caamaño and his immediate associates could do to make it believable that they were free of Communist control.

The only major instance in which official rebel propaganda took a specifically outright anti-American line was in the barrage of truly savage personal attacks on Ambassador Bennett. Both in Spanish and in English—though more virulently in Spanish—the rebel-controlled Radio Santo Domingo constantly poured out invective against the Ambassador, accusing him of transmitting false reports on the character of the rebellion and thereby bringing the United States into conflict with what the rebels claimed were their democratic aims. La Patria, a small four-page newspaper published in the rebel zone, sometimes reflected the same line.

To some extent, at least, these outpourings were the result of personal animosity on the part of Colonel Caamaño toward "Tap" Bennett, an animosity going back to that session at the embassy April 27 at which, Caamaño charged, the Ambassador had insulted the rebel officers and demanded that they surrender. This charge, of course, has been strongly denied by Ambassador Bennett.

In a real sense the Administration list of Communists who had allegedly infiltrated the rebel movement added little to what was already known or suspected. But it kept alive the basic controversy over whether or not the rebels were really controlled by Communists.

Since John Bartlow Martin's meeting with the Caamaño command the previous Saturday—four days ago—there had been no new direct contacts between the U.S. Embassy and the rebel leadership. Whatever business the United States had to transact with the rebels—it was principally about security matters concerning the International Safety Zone and the corridor—was being handled through the O.A.S. Many of the U.S. newsmen on the scene, who were in touch with both the rebels and the embassy, felt that our country's interest in the Dominican Republic, which all of us also saw as being the elimination of any Communist danger, could have been better served by the re-establishment of some link between the Americans and the rebels. Since we knew that Communists were embedded in the rebel movement, many of us believed that the best way to handle them would be to encourage Colonel Caamaño and his associates to get rid of them rather than to force the "Constitutional Government" into accepting an intimate alliance with the Communists in the absence of any other workable alternative.

The point was not that the United States should recognize the Caamaño regime—I think none of us felt that this was justified at this stage—but that it should remain on speaking terms with the rebels, as it was with the San Isidro junta. Several of us brought this point up in private conversations with Ambassador Bennett and Mr. Martin. But in each instance we encountered a feeling of reluctance on the part of the embassy to do so.

On one occasion "Tap" Bennett remarked to a group of newsmen that probably the only solution for the Dominican Republic would be the establishment of some form of O.A.S. trusteeship for an indefinite time.

While we were trying to keep abreast of the military and political situation in Santo Domingo, another Times reporter was in San Juan, Puerto Rico, bringing to light the fascinating story of how an effort had been made early in the revolution to establish an understanding between the Johnson Administration and the democratic Bosch elements.

The reporter was Homer Bigart, who had twice won a Pulitzer prize for his distinguished international reporting, and he produced a story describing how Dr. Jaime Benítez, the Chancellor of the University of Puerto Rico, had attempted to act as an "honest broker" between the Johnson Administration and Dr. Bosch. To arrange a contact between the Administration and Bosch, Dr. Benítez got in touch several times with Abe Fortas, a Washington attorney and close personal friend of President Johnson. Dr. Benítez told Bigart that "Fortas was very much interested and talked to the President and then spoke several times with Bosch."

He said that "the sending of John Bartlow Martin as the President's emissary to the Dominican Republic was an extraordinary effort on the part of the President and Fortas toward gathering as broad and sympathetic a picture as possible of the Bosch cause."

As reported by Bigart, Dr. Benítez said that "I cleared the Martin mission with Bosch, and Bosch phoned Colonel Caamaño in Santo Domingo and told the colonel to give all information and aid to Martin."

"But Martin was almost destroyed by what he saw and experienced in Santo Domingo," Dr. Benítez told Bigart.

Bigart's story suggested that the White House request to Martin to go to Santo Domingo the previous week was the result of the secret talks involving President Johnson, Abe Fortas, Dr. Benítez and Bosch.

Although this particular attempt at establishing an understanding between the U.S. and the Bosch forces had failed, there were to be other efforts in the future through similarly secret channels.

Meanwhile, something was developing at the O.A.S. in Washington. There, late at night, the O.A.S. Council voted to create an Inter-American Armed Force to help restore peace and constitutional government in the Dominican Republic.

The United States, increasingly anxious to have maximum O.A.S. participation in the Dominican crisis, had pressed for several days for a decision to create such a force. The main point was that the U.S. troops in the Dominican Republic would now become part of the inter-American force under an inter-American command, hopefully working in cooperation with troops from Latin American nations.

But the U.S. obtained this diplomatic victory by a very narrow margin. With a two-thirds majority required, the vote was 14 to 5, with one abstention. Mexico, Uruguay, Chile, Ecuador and Peru voted against the establishment of the inter-American force, largely on the ground that they opposed multilateral as well as unilateral intervention in the affairs of another American state. This was one more illustration of how strongly many Latin American governments felt about the doctrine of non-intervention, no matter what the circumstances. The abstention came from Venezuela, whose Government was torn between its own concern about Castroite activities and its firm commitment to non-intervention and the preservation of representative democracy in the Western Hemisphere. Venezuelans were fearful that the creation of the inter-American force might in the end result in the strengthening of a military dictatorship in the Dominican Republic and thus remove for a long time any chance that constitutional democracy might return to the Caribbean nation.

The Latin American opponents of intervention were not alone in stating their case. The New York Times was even more outspoken in its views. In an editorial, "The Illusion of Omnipotence," written Wednesday for the Thursday paper, The Times said that President Johnson's explanations of American action in Santo Domingo was "the language of 1898, not 1965."

The Times editorial declared that "in its development if not in its origin, the Marine intervention in the Dominican Republic was reminiscent of 1916."

"At the beginning of the present crisis," it said, "no one questioned the need to protect American lives in Santo Domingo when law and order broke down. The practical reasons for intervening against an immediate Communist take-over would also have been understood. But American troops were used almost as soon as they had landed for political ends on the basis of reports that a few dozen Communists were involved in the rebellion and on the fear that they might gain control of it. And the Organization of American States was not consulted nor informed of the intervention until after it had been accomplished."

The Times editorial went on to say that "the result of an initially reasonable and acceptable maneuver was to engage American soldiers in an internal struggle, in which many thousands of non-Communist or even anti-Communist Dominicans were fighting, some of them no doubt because Americans—as they naturally saw it—were invading and occupying their country."

"Another and more serious result," the editorial added, "has been to glorify the previously weak Dominican Communists and make them seem such a power and such a menace that nearly 20,000 American troops—more than half the number now in Vietnam—have thus far had to be sent to insure order. Communism all over the world has been given new 'heroes' and some damaging propaganda against the United States."

The Times editorial concluded by saying that "ours is the most powerful nation on earth, but there are things that even the United States cannot do in this period of history. The sooner this country extricates itself from the Dominican Republic—if at all possible with the help of the O.A.S.—the better."

Thursday, May 6th.

But to become extricated, of course, was not so easy. And this morning's events proved it again.

Shortly after 8:30 A.M. seven Marines in a jeep and in a ¾-ton truck drove out of the International Safety Zone through the Security Corridor on their way to the San Isidro Air Force Base to get supplies. A few minutes later they made a wrong turn and drove from the corridor into rebel territory. The rebels opened up at them with automatic fire, killing two Marines on the spot and fatally wounding a third. Colonel Caamaño had obviously meant business the day before when we heard him order his forces to fire at any American serviceman crossing into the rebel zone.

The rebels also captured two Marines, who were unharmed, and took them to the revolution's military headquarters for interrogation.

The truce had been formally in effect since yesterday but it was far from a reality. The fighting between the rebels and the junta forces had died down but now the rebels were tangling with the American forces.

Earlier this morning Bob Satin, the Peace Corps director for the Dominican Republic, had made telephone arrangements with Hector Aristy, the rebels' "Minister of the Presidency," to discuss procedures for food distribution by the Peace Corps volunteers. It was Aristy who had approved the coming of the Peace Corps to the Dominican Republic in 1962 when he was Under Secretary of Agriculture.

Satin had telephoned Aristy from my hotel room, where he had spent the night on a mattress on the floor. Satin was a frequent visitor to Room 321, shared by The Times and The New York Herald Tribune, and we put him up for the night whenever he was caught after darkness in the hotel area.

Unaware of the early morning shooting fray involving the Marines, Bob drove to rebel headquarters for his food-distribution talks. He was the first American in any way connected with the U.S. Government to go into the rebel zone since Mr. Martin held his conference with the Caamaño leadership five days earlier. A former professor of geology, Bob Satin was now a familiar figure in Santo Domingo as he supervised his volunteers, including the nurses working in hospitals all over town. Often the 33-year-old Satin managed to find himself in dangerous situations. This morning, arriving at rebel headquarters, he found the two captured Marines—a private and a corporal—leaning against the wall in the courtyard.

His discovery immediately changed his mission in the rebel zone. As soon as he contacted Aristy, Satin persuaded him that the two captured Marines and the wounded Marine should be released as quickly as possible. The original rebel plan had been to hold them for release through the O.A.S.

But the rebels did not let the two captured Marines go free without first exposing them to an interrogation by Colonel Caamaño and Mr. Aristy, apparently largely for the benefit of American television cameras.

The two Marines had been treated fairly well by the rebels and now, as they underwent the interrogation, they seemed self-assured. Corporal Reuben Garcia of New York grunted out his answers. Private Darrell J. Southwell of Mason, Michigan, was downright defiant. With increasing exasperation he kept repeating that they had wandered into the rebel zone by mistake.

Presently the rebel commanders tired of the interrogation and turned the men over to Satin as promised.

Bob brought the men, including the wounded Marine, back to the International Zone. The wounded serviceman was flown to U.S.S. Boxer but died later.

Aside from the public interrogation of the two prisoners, the rebel leaders used the occasion to display their assurance and even cockiness. Talking to us after the interrogation, Colonel Caamaño claimed to have 10,000 armed men in the center of Santo Domingo and 37,000 men elsewhere in the city. My feeling, shared by many others, was that these figures were considerably exaggerated. But even if Caamaño had only a fraction of this force, there seemed to be little question but that the rebels were determined to resist the Wessin forces, or the Americans, at all costs and to the end.

They had demonstrated this in fighting the San Isidro forces and in skirmishing with the Americans. Now Caamaño and Aristy were telling us again that they would "die rather than surrender." To be sure, the entire rebel leadership was so deeply engaged in the situation they had created that there really was no way out for them. But in their peculiar Latin fashion they were not grim about it. Their attitude, instead, was a blend of romanticism and fatalism. In their state of mind courage and readiness to die were the order of the day. There was a quixotic touch to these rebels.

Back at the Hotel Embajador we found out that Dominican civilians had brought the bodies of the two Marines who were killed in the morning's firefight to the Marine checkpoint at the entrance to the International Safety Zone. One of the bodies was driven to the vicinity of the Hotel Embajador, where the Marines took it to the helicopter pad. This incident led one of the wire services to send out a story, widely published in the United States, that Dominican rebels had "dumped" the body of a dead Marine at the doorstep of the hotel in an act of defiance by Colonel Caamaño against the United States presence in the Dominican Republic. It was this kind of inaccurate and almost slanted reporting that contributed to creating misunderstandings in the United States about the Dominican situation, which was already difficult and complicated enough.

Also at the hotel we were informed by the military spokesmen that the United States military build-up was still on the increase. As of that morning, we had a total of 30,209 men involved in the Dominican operation. Of these there were ashore more than 14,000 paratroopers—almost the entire 82nd Airborne Division—and nearly 7,000 Marines. There were more than 8,000 Navy men manning the 30 ships participating in the Dominican operation and 275 aircraft were involved full-time in supplying the force ashore.

It was a vast undertaking and one of the officers remarked to us, "I bet there will be no tax cut this year."

We became involved in an argument with the military briefers as to whether or not the United States took rebel prisoners and what it did with them. Although several of us had been told by commanders in the field that prisoners were being taken and news cameramen had pictures of Dominicans in stockades guarded by

U.S. troops, the military spokesmen insisted they had no knowledge of rebel prisoners in our hands. There were some fairly reliable reports that the U.S. troops were turning the rebel prisoners over to the junta forces. Again the military spokesmen would not offer confirmation. But later we heard this practice was eventually abandoned.

Shortly after lunch at the hotel I heard a tragic report. Two American newsmen, Al Burt, a reporter for The Miami Herald, and Douglas Kennedy, his photographer, had been seriously wounded by Marine fire at one of the checkpoints.

When details became available I learned that Burt and Kennedy had been hit at the same checkpoint where Collier, Uchitelle and I had crossed the day before. Ted Yates and his N.B.C. camera crew were again at the checkpoint but in a confused situation Ted was unable to do for Burt and Kennedy what he had done for us. It appeared that the Dominican driver of the car carrying the two Miami newsmen had misunderstood instructions, panicked and thrown the vehicle into reverse just as rebels began firing at the Marine positions across the no-man's land. Marine fire riddled the car with .50-caliber machine-gun bullets, seriously wounding Kennedy and inflicting wounds on Burt.

In the briefing room of the military's Joint Information Bureau the numeral 2 was placed in the W.I.A. (Wounded in Action) column of the casualty list under the heading "The Press."

In the rebel zone the situation was getting back to normal after the morning's fighting. Many Dominicans seemed to be going about their business in a more or less ordinary fashion. Actually the people in the rebel zone, even those not actively participating in military actions, had a passion for remaining in the streets while firing went on. This unquestionably accounts for the high number of casualties. But this afternoon things were reasonably quiet and such basic services as garbage collection were resuming. There was again water and electricity in the rebel zone.

Colonel Caamaño completed the formation of his "constitutional government." In addition to the three Cabinet ministers appointed earlier—Colonel Montes Arache for Defense, Aristy as Minister of the Presidency and Curi for Foreign Affairs—Colonel Caamaño now named Rafael Avinader Vellarde as Minister of

Finance, Marcelino Velez Santana as Minister of Health, Ramón Ledesma Peréz as Minister Without Portfolio, Luis Scheker as Governor of the Central Bank and Antonio Rosario as Representative to the O.A.S.

This was a fairly moderate group. The Finance Minister was an apolitical specialist. Mr. Scheker, the new Governor of the Central Bank, was a monetary technician who had served as vice governor of the bank under the Reid Cabral regime. Mr. Ledesma was a member of Bosch's political party.

But now it was mid-afternoon and our problem once more was to get our copy to New York. So much had already happened during the day that Peter Kihss, Marty Arnold and I had at least three lengthy news stories in the works. Since we could not hope to transmit all that copy to New York over the telephone or the Telex, it was back again to the air shuttle to Puerto Rico. Peter had been to Puerto Rico the day before and today it was again my turn.

I got aboard a dilapidated green bus driven by an 82nd Airborne trooper, which was to proceed through the Security Corridor to the San Isidro base, where I hoped to catch a plane to Puerto Rico. But the bus broke down about a block from the U.S. Embassy. If I was to get to Puerto Rico in time to file copy for the next morning's paper, I would have to be in San Isidro in less than half an hour. My only alternative was to walk to the embassy and ask Ambassador Bennett to make his helicopter available to me for the hop to the base. There may have been differences in our appraisals of the situation but "Tap" Bennett was invariably courteous and within three minutes I was aboard his personal copter on my way to San Isidro. Chuck Rappoport of Magnum, a photographer, and Barney Collier of The Herald Tribune were with me.

By now the constant shuttling of newsmen between Santo Domingo and San Juan had become so institutionalized that a special radio code call had been invented for our benefit. It was, rather aptly, "301.6 Ulcer." The pilot of any aircraft flying newsmen to Puerto Rico was to radio the Ulcer code ahead to let the military public information people know that correspondents were arriving with copy.

Again the best available aircraft was a troop carrier bound for the Ramey Air Force Base. We got there within 45 minutes and a waiting Air Force car took us to the telephone. I made the first edition of The Times with our three stories by the skin of my teeth. And this time our friend Major Dick Moyer, the B-52 pilot, had no trouble flying us to San Juan in the Civil Air Patrol's twin-engine Beechcraft.

Since both Peter Kihss and Marty Arnold were in Santo Domingo, I decided to give myself a short "rest and recreation" vacation in San Juan. After almost two weeks of steady work it seemed like a good idea. In addition, we had a tremendous shopping list to contend with. Aside from cigarettes and all the other usual items, Collier and I had agreed to buy underclothes—brassières and panties and what-have-you—for the Peace Corps nurses who had lost most of their belongings in the downtown area.

In contrast to my first two flying visits to Puerto Rico, this time I did get a first-class meal. I found Homer Bigart, who had just finished another interview with Juan Bosch, and we went off to dinner at the Swiss Chalet, one of the best restaurants in San Juan. There were Bloody Marys, a fine steak, good French wine and, in the background, an excellent jazz pianist. For the first time in almost two weeks I was wearing a tie and a jacket. It was sort of odd to be back in civilization.

Friday, May 7th.

While I rested in San Juan—catching up on my newspaper reading and consulting with my office in New York—the situation in Santo Domingo was taking still another turn.

After nearly a week of secret negotiations Mr. Martin and Ambassador Bennett finally succeeded in creating the Imbert government in place of the highly discredited San Isidro junta.

About noon "Tap" Bennett sent an exultant telegram to the State Department announcing that after days of effort "it looks like we've got it now."

In the late afternoon the junta headed by Colonel Benoit obediently resigned and shortly afterward "Tony" Imbert was sworn in by Supreme Court President Julio Cuello as president of what was to be known henceforth as the "Government of National Reconstruction."

General Imbert, of course, had been groomed for the job for almost 10 days, ever since he had been flown to the Boxer the day after the Marines landed in Santo Domingo. Colonel Benoit was named the other military member of the new regime. The three civilian members were Alejandro Zeller Cocco, a civil engineer whom "Tap" Bennett greatly admired; Carlos Grisolía Poloney, a lawyer and former Civic Union Senator; and Julio D. Postigo.

As Dominican politics went, it was not a bad group of men who had been selected to be the civilian members of the "Government of National Reconstruction." Postigo, in particular, gave a special touch of respectability to the new regime. He was a well-known Santo Domingo book publisher and a friend of Juan Bosch. In fact, he had recently published Bosch's new book, the account of his brief period as President and of his downfall.

But, as it was to develop quickly, the real power in the new government was not the civilian members and not even Colonel Benoit but General Imbert and his military commanders. General Wessin was there, without a formal title but presumably in charge of the troops. Commodore Francisco J. Rivera Caminero, the officer who had brought the navy over to San Isidro's side, was the Minister of Armed Forces. And General Jesus de los Santos Cespedes remained in charge of the aircraft based at San Isidro.

The embassy—and the Administration back in Washington—evidently hoped that the new government would do away with the impression that the U.S.-supported forces opposing the rebels constituted a military dictatorship. Efforts were undertaken both in Santo Domingo and in Washington to make General Wessin appear unimportant and to play up General Imbert as a Dominican "popular national hero." Neither of these claims were accurate, however. Wessin was still quite important while "Tony" Imbert was nowhere the heroic figure in the eyes of Dominicans that the Administration spokesmen in Washington were making him out to be.

Actually I have sound reasons to believe that the embassy and the Administration did not expect the Imbert junta—as it was invariably called despite its formal title of "Government of National Reconstruction"—to be in business for a very long time. In fact, embassy officials privately made no bones about the fact that Imbert had been drafted to serve only a short-term function. The United States had wanted to balance Colonel Caamaño's "constitutional government" with a regime of its own that looked sufficiently respectable. The idea was that the O.A.S. mediators could then be used effectively to negotiate a more permanent solution.

At this point, there already were signs in Washington that the Johnson Administration was beginning to rethink some of its original policies.

The Latin American and other world reaction against what had been virtually acknowledged in Washington as a direct intervention in Dominican affairs was beginning to have its effect. With the creation of the inter-American force and the signing of the truce on May 5, the Administration was now anxious for the O.A.S. to take as much of a hand as possible in trying to settle the nearly two-week-old civil war. Besides, it was felt that the presence of nearly 22,000 troops ashore in the Santo Domingo area and the creation of the Imbert regime were protecting what the Administration regarded as the basic U.S. interests in the Dominican Republic.

There was also rising unhappiness in the United States over what was happening in Santo Domingo. Several leading newspapers, including The Times, were critical in their editorials of the Administration's position. There was a deepening split among officials in the State Department and in the White House over the wisdom of the course being followed by the Administration. And, significantly, Senator Robert F. Kennedy of New York, the brother of the late President, went out of his way in an interview with John D. Morris of the Washington Bureau of The New York Times to express his concern over President Johnson's intervention in the Dominican Republic.

In his first public criticism of the Johnson Administration Senator Kennedy said: "I think there should have been consultation prior to any action we would take in the Dominican situation.

I don't think we addressed ourselves to the implications of what we did in the Dominican Republic."

A new emphasis seemed necessary. On the one hand, Administration spokesmen in Washington began to tone down the Communist angle in the Caamaño movement after having played it for all it was worth. On the other hand, United States-sponsored soundings were made as to the possibility of having the O.A.S. send to the Dominican Republic a mediation team made up of three of the most distinguished Latin American elder statesmen: Luis Muñoz Marin, former Governor of Puerto Rico; Rómulo Betancourt, former Venezuelan President, and José Figueres, former Costa Rican President. All three were top exponents of what was known as the Latin American "Democratic Left" and all had been closely associated with the initial stages of President Kennedy's Alliance for Progress. In addition, all three were now in Washington, apparently ready to undertake the proposed mission.

It was assumed that Muñoz, Betancourt and Figueres, as widely respected liberals, would be welcome to the "constitutionalist" forces in Santo Domingo. It was also assumed that "Tony" Imbert would offer no opposition in dealing with this new team. He was, after all, something of a creature of the U.S. Embassy.

But even before the notion of this new mediation group really got off the ground, it turned out that "Tony" Imbert had other ideas. In his inaugural speech he announced that he had joined the Government of National Reconstruction "to save the Dominican people from Communist dictatorship."

At the inauguration ceremonies at the National Congress Palace, situated just behind the Marine-manned International Safety Zone, Imbert's military commanders made it clear in talking to newsmen that they were awaiting the first opportunity to resume their fight against the Caamaño forces. Thus it became immediately apparent that while the Administration was now hoping for a reasonable negotiated settlement, "Tony" Imbert and his commanders were thinking of winning the war, now that they felt themselves fully sponsored by the United States.

A spokesman for Colonel Caamaño described the Imbert regime as "a shady deal" against the interests of the Dominican people.

And for all practical purposes the lines in the civil war were drawn again. At a news conference earlier in the day Colonel Caamaño had said that the O.A.S. had not consulted him about the creation of the inter-American armed force to keep peace in Santo Domingo and that he would "prefer not to see the forces of any nation in our country."

Watching the new situation, the rebels were cautious and on their best behavior. The sniping activity had diminished considerably in the last 24 hours and in San Juan Dr. Bosch was making the point that the Caamaño command had proved to be very reasonable in the recent truce negotiations.

In his interview with Homer Bigart, the former Dominican President said he had encouraged his rebel friends to accept the new cease-fire. He also said it was his personal intervention that had led the rebels to accept the first cease-fire, worked out by the Papal Nuncio the week before. He told Bigart he had urged the rebels to accept that first truce, despite the opposition of Caamaño and Aristy to it, because he had feared that otherwise U.S. Marines would burst into the downtown section and try to capture the rebel headquarters.

United States officials have heatedly denied that there were any plans for the Marines or paratroopers to break into the rebels' downtown strongholds. But a study of the telegrams exchanged between Ambassador Bennett and Washington on April 28 and 29 does suggest the possibility that some strong action might have been undertaken against the rebels by U.S. forces if the San Isidro contingents had completely collapsed, as the Ambassador feared might happen. There were his recommendations for a full-scale intervention to prevent a Castro-type take-over and the State Department's reply that the U.S. would consider direct military intervention against the Caamaño forces only if "the outlook" were in doubt. In any event, the arrival of the 82nd Airborne troopers at San Isidro on April 30 sealed off the rebels and prevented them from moving out of Santo Domingo against San Isidro.

Now the military aspect of the civil war seemed to be stabilized. And in talking to Bigart in San Juan, Bosch sounded dispirited.

"This was a democratic revolution smashed by the leading democracy of the world, the United States," Bosch told Bigart. "That is why I think my term is over. I belong to a world that has ended politically."

Saturday, May 8th.

Homer Bigart flew to Santo Domingo Saturday morning to do a few stories on the Dominican situation after his interviews with Dr. Bosch in San Juan. I decided to give myself another day's vacation in Puerto Rico as long as we now had three men in Santo Domingo—Bigart, Kihss and Arnold—and to concentrate on writing a background story on the implications of the creation of the Imbert junta.

If there had been any doubt that the formation of the "Government of National Reconstruction" would only complicate matters in the Dominican Republic, the statements made during the day by both sides promptly removed it.

I telephoned Dr. Bosch at his San Juan home and he told me that Colonel Caamaño had called him a little while ago to express his opinion that Imbert's appointment could mean only that the "United States was now openly committed to the destruction of the rebel movement."

Dr. Bosch quoted Colonel Caamaño, with whom he was in constant telephone contact, as having said that he was convinced the Imbert forces would attack the rebels under the cover of United States troops.

As it developed later, Colonel Caamaño was not too far wrong in his estimate. Meanwhile he held a meeting of his military command, which took the decision to resist any attacks to the end. Bosch heartily approved of the decision, he told me. Bosch also said that, according to Caamaño, the rebel leadership had refused to entertain suggestions by Imbert that the rebels lay down their arms. In Colonel Caamaño's eyes, the Imbert group was merely a new front for the old military junta supported by the United States.

Both Caamaño and Aristy publicly asserted again the rebels'

determination to fight. Aristy told a cheering crowd: "We are not going to give up our arms or anything else until we get this country back on the right track."

In addition, Caamaño charged that the creation of the Imbert regime was in itself a violation of the cease-fire. The rebels seemed to be so exercised over the new junta that Secretary General Mora of the O.A.S. and the Papal Nuncio, Msgr. Clarizio, went downtown during the afternoon to pacify the Caamaño group.

Afterward Colonel Caamaño agreed to continue observing the truce. He said: "We will respect the cease-fire although the new junta puts its legal status in doubt."

The very location of the Imbert government seemed to be creating additional problems. In setting up his headquarters in the Trujillo-built ornate Congress building at the old International Fair Grounds, General Imbert had in effect installed himself behind the protection of the U.S. Marines. Technically the Fair Grounds were outside the International Safety Zone, but for all practical purposes the Imbert headquarters adjoined the zone and U.S. Marine patrols were as active around the Congress building as elsewhere in the area.

The fact that the U.S. authorities had allowed eight truckloads of Imbert troops to enter the Fair Grounds led to a protest from the rebels. They charged that the United States was being partial to the Imbert group.

This was the first time American newsmen had seen convoys of junta troops being waved through U.S. checkpoints. Soon this was to become the subject of a major controversy. Up to now we had seen Dominican policemen and soldiers working with U.S. Marines and paratroopers at the checkpoints, searching Dominicans entering or leaving the International Safety Zone. We had also occasionally seen junta troops riding up and down the Security Corridor in a truck or jeep.

Meanwhile "Tony" Imbert was wasting no time in trying to consolidate his position. In Santo Domingo his military control extended only over the Fair Grounds in the western part of town and over the Presidential Palace and the adjoining police headquarters in the midtown area. The U.S.–controlled International

Safety Zone lay between these two points and General Imbert was able to move his men from one to the other only with the acquiescence of the Americans.

He also controlled, of course, the San Isidro area, where the bulk of the Wessin troops and aircraft were stationed.

However, General Imbert announced that his government was in control of all 26 Dominican provinces and 99 per cent of the capital district. The first claim was arguable because, outside of the Santo Domingo area, the Dominican Republic still remained neutral after two weeks of the civil war. The second claim was obviously a vast exaggeration.

Nonetheless General Imbert announced that stores and factories would reopen on Monday and that his government would begin paying salaries to public employes in the zone under his control. To that the rebel radio station replied: "With what? Yankee money?"

But the rebels, too, urged a Monday back-to-work movement in their zone. In the political stalemate that had developed both sides were anxious to impress the population—and the rest of the world—with their ability to restore normalcy in the areas they controlled.

Because it was uncertain from the very beginning just what General Imbert proposed to do next, Secretary General Mora of the O.A.S. immediately requested the Imbert government to confirm in writing that it subscribed fully to the truce commitments signed May 5 by the Benoit junta at San Isidro. General Imbert complied at once.

But truce or no truce, the nocturnal gunfire continued. Snipers disregarded the cease-fire and kept attacking American positions.

Saturday night several snipers made their way into the Marine camp at the port of Haina, seven miles from Santo Domingo, opening fire at the Americans. In the ensuing confusion a Marine warrant officer was killed. At first he was believed a victim of sniper fire, but it later turned out that he had been accidentally shot by a fellow Marine.

Along the Security Corridor downtown, rebel guns blazed during the night and three paratroopers were wounded. Again an argument developed as to who had fired first.

Finally three Seabees—men from the Navy's Construction Battalions—celebrated Saturday night by getting lost in rebel territory. They were captured by the rebels and released unharmed the next day.

After two weeks of the civil war no real solution was yet in sight. People—Americans and Dominicans—were still getting killed every day and every night. If anything, the stalemate was growing harder.

THE THIRD WEEK

Sunday, May 9th.

The third week of the Dominican civil war was to witness some very extraordinary diplomatic performances by the United States, further adding to the vast confusion prevailing in Santo Domingo. It was a week that also provided a rather frightening lesson in how a puppet can suddenly acquire a life of its own and proceed to defy the puppeteer.

Having created the Imbert junta, the U.S. Embassy now faced the next problem: how to turn it into a bridge toward a reasonable political solution. To serve as such a bridge the junta, of course, had to become more acceptable to the uncommitted mass of Dominicans, to say nothing of Colonel Caamaño and his rebels.

Efforts in this direction began as soon as the Imbert government was constituted. Ambassador Bennett and Mr. Martin took it upon themselves to play the role of master puppeteers.

I flew back from my brief Puerto Rican vacation just in time to watch this beguiling operation. But while American diplomats in Santo Domingo were thus attempting to influence the course of political events, top Administration officials in Washington continued to contend that there was no U.S. interference in Dominican affairs.

As I was returning to Santo Domingo from San Juan aboard a Navy plane I read in the Sunday issue of The New York Times a lengthy interview by Max Frankel, our diplomatic correspondent in Washington, with Under Secretary of State Mann. Essentially Mr. Mann was defending United States policy in the last two weeks, but he made a point of saying: "The action of the United States was not for the purpose of intervening in the internal affairs of the Dominican Republic or for the purpose of occupying that country."

"The United States forces are not asserting any authority to govern any part of the Dominican Republic," Mr. Mann said.

But, of course, the reality of the situation was that the United States was very much asserting its authority in the Dominican Republic. This was evident as much in the streets of Santo

Domingo as in the behind-the-scenes diplomatic maneuvers conducted by "Tap" Bennett and John Bartlow Martin.

Landing at the San Isidro Air Force Base, I ran into Homer Bigart, who was returning to San Juan after two very full days in the Dominican Republic. He told me that the situation remained extremely confused but that Peter Kihss and Marty Arnold had it as well in hand from the viewpoint of The New York Times as was humanly possible under the circumstances.

I rode from San Isidro to the Hotel Embajador in the same broken-down green bus that had quit on me three days earlier. The highway from the base to the Duarte bridge across the Ozama River was full of U.S. military traffic. Vehicles carrying General Imbert's soldiers were also very much in evidence. The 82nd Airborne Division's Military Policemen guarded the bridge. Crossing into the old city, I found everything quiet, but signs of recent battles were all around. There were bullet-scarred houses with smashed windows. There was the burned-out shell of a gas station. Beside it lay the charred remains of an automobile.

The Security Corridor, manned by the paratroopers, began at the bridge. A sign fastened to a telephone pole and lettered in black said: "You Are Entering the American Sector." Another sign said: "All-American Express." M.P.'s were posted at intersections, directing traffic, so U.S. military vehicles would not stray from the corridor into the rebel zone. In the past such accidents had led to firefights and casualties. At some points the corridor was only one street wide. At others it extended an extra block in each direction. At many of the intersections the paratroopers had set up wooden and barbed-wire barricades.

Squads and individual troopers were stationed practically every few steps. But it was a quiet, sunny Sunday afternoon and everybody—the Dominican families still living in the houses along the corridor and the U.S. servicemen—seemed completely relaxed. Heavily armed soldiers chatted easily with Dominican girls, leaning on garden walls in front of the little houses. Some of the houses were pink, others were blue or green. Flowers were growing in many of the tiny front gardens. Here and there a paratrooper would relax in a rocking chair on a porch, talking to the family with whom he and his buddies had moved in for the duration. It was an idyllic picture.

But it could all change in a fraction of a second. Someone could start firing from somewhere—as usually happened several times a day—and the young paratroopers who had been sitting in the rocking chairs or flirting against the garden walls would grab their rifles, machine guns or bazookas. Then the peaceful street would turn again into an inferno of flying bullets and exploding shells. There would be curses through clenched teeth and, occasionally, cries of "Medic!" And sometimes the girl in the gay print dress or the fat mother who had just been serving coffee to her soldier guest would be cut down by a bullet coming from God only knows where. In a few minutes, or in a few hours, the fighting would die down and all would become tranquil again. This was life in the corridor.

Just before the bus I was riding in reached Checkpoint Charlie, where the corridor ends, several jeeploads of the Imbert junta's armed soldiers were waved past the Amtrack guarding the entry to the International Safety Zone. The jeeps were coming either from Imbert's headquarters at the far end of the zone or possibly from the National Police Palace two blocks down the street. In any event, the Imbert forces obviously enjoyed the right of free passage through American lines. One of the newsmen aboard the bus with me raised his eyebrows. "What are they doing here?" he asked. "Aren't we supposed to be neutral in this?"

As we reached the Embajador I saw that the Marines had dug emplacements in front of the hotel for six 105-mm. howitzers. The artillery pieces, covered by their camouflaged netting, were pointed east, toward the rebel-held part of Santo Domingo. The howitzers' range was sufficient for them to flatten Colonel Caamaño's stronghold if the U.S. ever chose to do this.

But if United States policy was to impress the rebels with a continuing show of force, it also included applying simultaneous pressure to the two-day-old Imbert government. The object, of course, was to make the junta sufficiently palatable to enough Dominicans so that a permanent solution could be achieved while safeguarding U.S. interests in the country.

Much of the imbroglio that was to ensue stemmed from the fact that "Tony" Imbert took himself with immense seriousness—and regarded himself as the permanent solution—while his sponsors at the embassy had assigned him only a temporary role.

Whereas the chief concern of "Tap" Bennett and John Bartlow Martin in the creation of the Imbert government had been simply to counterbalance the Caamaño regime downtown, General Imbert saw himself, at long last, as the providential man in the Dominican Republic. He had waited for this moment for almost four years, ever since the evening Generalissimo Trujillo had been assassinated.

The net effect of this state of affairs, then, was that the U.S. was hoping to use Imbert for its purposes while the general was trying to play the Americans for his own aims.

The task of ridding the Imbert junta of the appearance of being nothing more than an improved version of the earlier military group at San Isidro devolved upon "Tap" Bennett. The first man who had to go if the dictatorial symbolism of the new junta was to be removed was General Wessin. There was irony in this. Wessin was the man the United States had helped to hold the line against the rebels. But now he, too, had to be sacrificed in the interests of the intricate political game being played in Santo Domingo.

Ambassador Bennett and Lieutenant General Bruce Palmer, the commander of the U.S. forces in the Dominican Republic, flew by helicopter to the Military Academy, not far from San Isidro. They told Wessin that he had to go. It must have been an immensely difficult moment for Mr. Bennett.

After considerable argument General Wessin appeared to agree that his departure would be helpful. But he told Mr. Bennett and General Palmer that if he were to depart, 10 other top military commanders also must go. Obviously Wessin did not want to be singled out as the sole victim of this proposed American purge. Wessin then sat down and wrote a letter to Ambassador Bennett informing him that he would resign effective at 4 P.M. of Monday, May 10.

After their conference the whole matter also had to be taken up with "Tony" Imbert. It soon developed that Imbert, a rather foxy politician, and Wessin played the rest of this involved game together against "Tap" Bennett.

Thus Imbert agreed to the removal of eight of the military commanders on a list drawn up by Wessin. Among those he agreed to fire was his long-time protégé, General Belisário Peguero, the man who controlled the police. But he refused to send away two of his top military commanders, the air force's General de los Santos Cespedes and the navy's Commodore Rivera Caminero. Straightfacedly Imbert told Ambassador Bennett that he indeed felt that General Wessin should go.

It might have been a coincidence, but this same day the director of the U.S. Agency for International Development mission in Santo Domingo wrote a letter to the acting secretary of finance in the Imbert junta advising him that the United States would make available $750,000 from assistance funds earlier earmarked for the Dominican Republic so that the new government could start paying some of its public employes. Nobody had been paid in Santo Domingo since the civil war had broken out and naturally the government could not exist without paying its employes. This may have been intended in part as leverage in the embassy's dealings with Imbert, but "Tony" managed in the end to turn it, too, to his own advantage.

To expel the eight objectionable officers from the country, Imbert staged a maneuver of his own. He advised them Sunday morning that a crucial conference with the U.S. command would be held later in the day aboard a U.S. warship in the port of Haina. But when the eight arrived there, Imbert's soldiers surrounded and disarmed them. Then they were led aboard a Dominican frigate, which sailed at once. Each man received $1,000 in cash, presumably for pocket money abroad, and was told that his family and personal belongings would follow. According to one reliable report, the packets of cash came from the United States Government.

In addition to General Peguero, who must have been the most stunned of all in being thrown out by Imbert, the group included Brigadier General Salvador Augusto Montás Guerrero, the man who had led the San Cristobal regiment into Santo Domingo on that fateful Tuesday when the rebellion appeared to collapse; Brigadier General Atila Luna Peréz of the air force, who was a latecomer to the side of San Isidro; and Commodore Julio Rib Santamaria, one of the most active military politicians.

The embassy now felt that an important initial step had been taken in turning the Imbert government into something with which not only the United States and the O.A.S. but also Caamaño's rebels could negotiate. The eight notorious Trujillo commanders were now safely out of the country and General Wessin had promised to leave tomorrow.

At the embassy "Tap" Bennett quite candidly gave a visitor his version of how the Imbert government had been formed and what the United States really thought of its latest protégé.

According to Mr. Bennett, it was the previous Wednesday, May 5, the day the truce negotiated by the O.A.S. mission was signed, that an agreement in principle had been reached with Imbert for the formation of the new government.

According to the Ambassador, Imbert agreed not only to bring into the proposed government such respected civilians as Mr. Postigo and Mr. Zeller but also to remove those military leaders whom the United States considered to be politically harmful. On Friday the Imbert junta was finally unveiled with the blessings of the United States. Although "Tony" Imbert has said in official statements that the U.S. was not at all consulted on the formation of his government, Ambassador Bennett told the story in numerous conversations with visitors and Mr. Martin narrated it in considerable detail in his Life magazine article.

In any event, now that the Imbert junta had been brought into being, Mr. Bennett made it clear that it would be up to Imbert to prove whether he could rally national support. Mr. Bennett indicated that if "Tony" Imbert could indeed prove that he had a real following, perhaps in time he could work his way up to being acceptable as a permanent solution to the Dominican crisis. But the Ambassador was quite skeptical about General Imbert's chances of winning such support. Quite prophetically he remarked to his visitor that there was the danger that "Tony" Imbert might turn out to be too headstrong to be manageable. "Tap" Bennett thus foresaw that the bridge toward a solution—which it had been intended for Imbert to be—could well become a collapsible bridge. But this was a chance the United States had to take.

As far as the future was concerned, Ambassador Bennett suggested that the real solution might well be found in the person of Joaquin Balaguer. He was the man who held the nominal job of President before Generalissimo Trujillo was assassinated and who took over the job of running the country together with Ramfis Trujillo after the generalissimo's death.

Dr. Balaguer, a quiet and mild-mannered man but a superb politician, was not a hated figure in the Dominican Republic despite his long association with Trujillo. In fact, he gained rather considerable popularity, especially with the low-income groups, during his presidential tenure after Trujillo's murder. Balaguer was forced out of office by the military in 1962. But before his ouster there had been a curious episode that almost resulted in a U.S. military intervention in the Dominican Republic.

At that time Generalissimo Trujillo's two brothers, Hector Trujillo and Arismendi Trujillo—better known as the "Wicked Uncles"—were believed engaged in a conspiracy with their nephew Ramfis to restore dictatorial rule with the help of some of the military elements. However, the Kennedy Administration took the view that the incipient process of democratization of the Dominican Republic had to continue and that the return of the Trujillos to power would be fatal to it. So a fleet was assembled in front of Santo Domingo and the Marines were ready to land in the city if the Trujillo brothers carried out their planned coup. President Balaguer, for his part, was prepared to request U.S. intervention if the plot was actually set in motion. But the presence of the U.S. Navy scared away the Trujillos and the American willingness to land troops to protect Dominican democracy and to assure that free elections would be held gave the United States extraordinary popularity in the Dominican Republic. History, indeed, works in strange ways.

Mr. Bennett said he believed that in any free election at this juncture Balaguer would most likely win. This was unquestionably a very sound judgment. And the Ambassador added that the United States would not be unhappy if events turned out that way. He said that the State Department had been in touch with Balaguer, who was living in exile in New York, but that the former President had made it clear that he would return to the Dominican Republic only to be a presidential candidate and not to participate in any new juntas.

Later it turned out that the State Department's contact with Balaguer had been established through the good offices of Irving Davidson, a registered Washington lobbyist and agent for several foreign governments, whose clients included Haiti's dictator, François Duvalier. In any case, the idea that Balaguer might well become the solution to the Dominican problem was surfaced for the first time by "Tap" Bennett in this Sunday conversation with his visitor. As events were to show, this idea of Ambassador Bennett's became highly plausible before too long.

Mr. Bennett also offered some interesting new comments about the Caamaño group. Though the embassy's telegrams to Washington in the first week of the civil war had insisted that forces "identified with the Communist Party" were on the verge of winning power in the Dominican Republic, Mr. Bennett now told his visitor that the United States did not really have enough evidence to prove "in court" that Communists really controlled the rebel movement. But, he said, Colonel Caamaño had an "open set-up for clever Communists to infiltrate."

Musing about Caamaño, Mr. Bennett described him as unstable. This, he said, was largely because his father had been one of Trujillo's chief butchers. Therefore, he declared, Colonel Caamaño seemed to be trying to atone for his father's guilt. In a rather perceptive assessment of the psychological situation in the Dominican Republic, "Tap" Bennett remarked that many of the Dominican problems stemmed from a cleavage between the older and the younger generation, with the latter trying to atone for the guilt of their parents who had sold out to Trujillo.

In fact, Ambassador Bennett's comments focused on a point which has struck many other observers in the Dominican Republic. This point was that the savage explosion of the 1965 civil war was in reality a delayed reaction. The blood bath should have really taken place after Trujillo was murdered in May, 1961. But instead all the hatreds accumulated over the three decades of the Trujillo dictatorship were held back for four more years. The habits of a lifetime of tyranny are not shaken off easily.

Meanwhile, General Imbert, acting with great self-assurance, was renewing his demands that the rebels surrender. He said his government would be willing to deal with the Caamaño regime but only to negotiate its surrender and guarantees for its members' departure from the country.

The rebel chief, however, was not taking kindly to this idea. He commented that "we have defeated their best troops and the best from the national police force. Do they think that with reserves from the interior they would be able to defeat a people with its morale higher than it ever was?"

Asked about his reaction to General Imbert's removal of the eight commanders, Colonel Caamaño said: "They have killed the flies but left the beetles."

But the stalemate could not be allowed to go on indefinitely and all sides were aware of it. Thus the U.S. Embassy, Secretary General Mora of the O.A.S. and the Papal Nuncio, Msgr. Clarizio, launched a new series of efforts to get the situation off dead center. Their first objective was to bring the two opposing parties to the conference table. In fact, Dr. Mora and Msgr. Clarizio went to see Colonel Caamaño in the afternoon to open conversations that they hoped might lead to a meeting between the rival leaderships.

However, Colonel Caamaño remained convinced that in a short time the Imbert forces would attack him under the cover of U.S. troops. He voiced this conviction many times and presently he stepped up his defensive preparations. As for "Tony" Imbert, an attack was obviously just what the new junta chief had in mind. He realized that a quick military victory against the Caamaño forces was essential if he was to assert himself as the undisputed leader of the Dominican Republic.

Imbert's first step was to name a tough military commander, Brigadier General Jacinto Martinez Araña, to the post of army chief of staff. At the same time the Wessin troops at San Isidro, which were having a chance to rest and regroup under the cease-fire, began preparing for a major military movement. The United States must have been aware of these preparations. They were taking place in an area which for all practical purposes was controlled by American forces. But there are no signs that anything was done to discourage General Imbert. Instead, as Mr.

Martin relates it in his Life magazine article, "pressures began to mount for us to take the city."

"For the rebels," Mr. Martin wrote, "were using the cease-fire to move snipers and agitators and guns into the northern part of the city and on into the interior. And their radio station was promoting their cause powerfully. They began holding mass meetings. All of a sudden their battle cry became not Juan Bosch but 'constitutionality' and anti-Americanism."

Mr. Martin did not mention in his article that General Imbert, too, was moving his troops into offensive positions. A unit of his forces was quietly infiltrated—it is not quite clear how—into the building of the army transportation battalion in the northern part of Santo Domingo, an area of almost complete rebel control.

And, as Mr. Martin has further written, in the International Safety Zone the talk was increasingly that Americans might have to go downtown "to finish the rebels."

The word "Budapest" began to be used with increasing frequency by the rebels as they expressed their fears that the United States would use its own troops to liquidate the constitutionalist movement in much the same way as the Russians brought their tanks into the Hungarian capital in 1956 to do away with the freedom fighters there. Again the lines were being drawn and again new dangers loomed ahead.

Monday, May 10th.

This was another day of improbable events in Santo Domingo.

There was a U.S. military parade and a U.S. political defeat at the hands of the Imbert junta. American troops again fought with rebel snipers. One officer was killed and three paratroopers were wounded. The New York Times, too, suffered casualties. Peter Kihss injured his elbow badly when a defective chair collapsed under him. In the evening I walked into a plate-glass window separating my room from its balcony—we had had another power failure and were plunged in darkness—and I acquired a deep gash across the bridge of my nose.

At the Embajador things were getting more bizarre than usual.

A Marine helicopter pilot in orange overalls volunteered to run one of the hotel's elevators up and down for a while to relieve the exhausted lift operator. With more than 200 newsmen, scores of diplomats and military officers and indefinite numbers of indescribable people filling the hotel, the lone elevator on duty was continuously in service. Then the Chinese complicated matters even further. About a hundred of them, mainly farmers from the agricultural areas, moved in with all their belongings in the hope of being evacuated abroad. Since they apparently had nothing else to do, they spent their time riding up and down in the elevator, which presumably was as good a way as any to while away the long hours. At night they chatted loudly and incessantly in their rooms. A television cameraman who was awakened at 2 A.M. one night by unusually loud Chinese chatter decided to avenge himself in style. He tiptoed to the chatterers' door with his tape recorder and ran a half-hour tape of their conversations. The next night—at 4 A.M.—he placed the tape recorder at the door of the Chinese and turned it on. The Chinese woke up screaming.

In addition to the goings-on at the Embajador, we had the parade. It was never made clear who got the idea for it in the first place, but around noon the 30-piece brass band of the 82nd Airborne Division marched through the Security Corridor from the Duarte bridge to the U.S. Embassy, merrily playing away. Major General York, the division commander, marched at the head of the parade. All the musicians, including the tuba players, had their rifles or submachine guns strapped to their backs. At the embassy the band serenaded the Ambassador.

The whole performance, apparently, was a psychological-warfare gimmick but many people found it in somewhat poor taste. Rather bitterly a Dominican who had long lived in the United States asked, "Are they playing 'Marching Through Georgia' or 'We Shall Overcome'?"

But the parade was picturesque. Little boys ran ahead of the band carrying large leaflets with President Johnson's picture that had been printed by the local office of the United States Information Agency. Others followed the band shouting "Viva Bosch" or "Viva la Constitución." The musicians smiled but it was not clear whether they understood the slogans.

No sooner had Ambassador Bennett finished being serenaded than his complicated diplomatic maneuvering of the last few days ran straight into a wall.

Early in the afternoon he told a visiting newsman of the letter General Wessin had written to him in which the general had agreed to resign by 4 P.M. of this day. At the State Department briefing at the Hotel Embajador a spokesman was asked whether he could confirm officially that General Wessin had resigned after meeting with Ambassador Bennett and General Palmer. The spokesman said that this was correct and that his information had come from an official source. He added: "Because of the position Wessin has come to occupy in the minds of many people of the city, I would say that his resignation improves the political climate."

This apparent ouster of General Wessin, the symbol of a military dictatorship in the eyes of some Dominicans, loomed as the most encouraging event in the 16 days of the civil war. Since rebel spokesmen had insisted that they would not negotiate so long as Wessin was associated with the Imbert junta, it now seemed possible that serious talks between the two factions could be initiated.

I drove to the U.S. Embassy to try to get more details on the Wessin story. As I was parking my car in the driveway the Papal Nuncio arrived in a state of great agitation. He rushed into the chancery to see Ambassador Bennett. Lieutenant Conde, the rebel liaison officer with the O.A.S. commission, had arrived with the Nuncio. The lieutenant waited in the garden. A few minutes later the Nuncio came out and ran over to the helicopter landing pad next door with a Marine officer and the lieutenant. The three climbed into Mr. Bennett's helicopter and took off at once.

I found the Ambassador and asked him what had happened. He said the Nuncio had requested the loan of the helicopter to fly to San Isidro but he could not tell me for what purpose.

However, the full answer began to emerge almost immediately. My next stop was General Imbert's office at the National Congress building. With several other reporters I asked him what he knew about General Wessin's resignation. Peering innocently at us through his glasses with their black frames, "Tony" Imbert said this was the first he had heard about it. "As far as I know, there is nothing about Wessin resigning. This is the first I hear about it," he said.

At 2 o'clock the next morning, after we had been wondering for hours whether General Wessin was in or out, a State Department official made the rounds of the correspondents' rooms at the Hotel Embajador. Sheepishly he read us an official statement. It said: "We did understand from official sources that General Wessin was going to resign at 4 P.M. Monday. We now understand that he is reconsidering his decision. The question of General Wessin's resignation is a matter between General Imbert and General Wessin."

We set to work filing new leads for the late editions and trying to reconstruct what had happened. Apparently General Imbert and General Wessin had been willing to make a concession to the United States by getting rid of the eight officers whom they had deported on Sunday. But "Tony" Imbert, now planning his offensive against the rebels, was not about to deprive himself of General Wessin, his most experienced and forceful military commander. It was for the same reason that he would not give up General de los Santos Cespedes and Commodore Rivera Caminero. Imbert and Wessin had also made a point of informing junta troop commanders of the U.S. "plot" to ship out their chief. As expected, the officers protested, whereupon General Imbert and General Wessin advised the U.S. Embassy that it would not be possible to go through with Wessin's resignation.

As Mr. Martin put it in his magazine article, Wessin "welshed on his offer to go."

The Nuncio, who had heard in mid-afternoon what was happening, became so concerned that the promise of a "better political climate" was being compromised that he had borrowed Mr. Bennett's helicopter to rush to San Isidro in a final attempt to persuade General Wessin to keep his promise. He, too, failed.

So the stalemate persisted. Now the United States was not only facing the growing resentment of the rebels because of its obvious support for the Imbert junta but it was also at odds with its own protégés at San Isidro and at the National Congress building.

Predictably, Colonel Caamaño's reaction was along the lines of "I told you so." At the same time growing numbers of Dominicans, including those usually pro-United States, were becoming bitter and disenchanted with American policy. In a commentary I filed to The Times late this Monday afternoon I said that United States identification with the Imbert junta, "which functions behind the protection of American troops, had led to a surge of anti-United States feeling among many Dominicans who had welcomed those troops."

Feeling was rising in Santo Domingo that the United States support for the junta, combined with its refusal to deal directly with the rebels, could have catastrophic consequences. Reporting on my conversations with O.A.S. diplomats and influential Dominicans, I wrote that in their opinion "the United States should revise its inflexible attitude toward the Camaño group and explore the possibility of some relationship with them."

I went on to observe that "many diplomats and Dominicans say that American attitudes are aiding Communists' efforts because the State Department is eliminating all options from the rebels and their sympathizers other than to rely on Communists."

Then, using material made available to me by key diplomats, I wrote that "diplomats who are in touch with the Caamaño group report that in recent days the Communist elements have withdrawn into the background, on the theory that the United States is doing their work for them."

Mr. Martin was right in a sense in saying in his Life magazine article that "anti-Americanism" was rising in Santo Domingo. But I believe this was due more to the identification of the United States with the junta—the sight of truckloads and jeeploads of Imbert forces going through American checkpoints was becoming commonplace—than to any ideological or Communist-inspired basic opposition to the United States.

Dominicans, who have a talent for shifting sides quickly, were now making it evident that it was fashionable to be for Colonel Caamaño and against the Imbert junta. One heard remarks to that effect from wealthy people in the International Safety Zone, in the Hotel Embajador's lobby and almost everywhere one went. The magazine Ahora, published by a militant Catholic editor, came out with its first post-rebellion issue to charge the United States bitterly with the sin of intervention. The magazine was published in the rebel zone and since propaganda was being fired back and forth from both sides, it printed pictures of Marines with sarcastic, not to say inaccurate, captions depicting them as imperialist conquerors.

Radio Santo Domingo, the rebel broadcasting station, was pouring more and more invective on Ambassador Bennett. And its anti-American tone in general was also getting more strident.

The United States countered with efforts to jam the rebel broadcasts. The jamming was executed by the technicians who operated the radio station set up at the United States Information Agency offices—known as the "Voice of the Zone of Security"—and by Navy ships offshore. When Admiral John S. McCain Jr., commander of Amphibious Forces Atlantic, was asked at a news conference whether jamming of rebel broadcasts was being carried out from his ships, he replied: "I have no comment on this."

The junta's radio station, which had been interminably playing "Stars and Stripes Forever," now switched to "The Yellow Rose of Texas" as its theme music. I have reasons to believe that the embassy had requested General Imbert to stop appropriating for his purposes a tune so identified with the United States.

At the rebel headquarters downtown there was growing awareness that a new phase of danger was approaching. Colonel Caamaño and his advisers met with the Papal Nuncio and Dr. Mora to discuss the proposals of these mediators for a possible meeting between the rebels and the junta. Caamaño told them he would indeed negotiate, but first General Wessin had to be removed and the junta had to accept the basic concept of constitutional government. This meant in effect that General Imbert would have to accept the Caamaño regime's contention that it was the only legal government empowered to serve out Juan Bosch's term until February, 1967. These preconditions, of course, made the outlook for any talks extremely dim inasmuch as General Imbert saw his own regime as the legitimate Dominican government and was not about to offer such fundamental concessions.

Defending himself from U.S. criticism, Colonal Caamaño made

a point at his news conference in the afternoon of issuing his strongest anti-Communist declaration to date.

He said that "I am completely sure that a dictatorship of the left is infinitely worse than one of the right."

Hector Aristy, his principal adviser, elaborated. "The Dominican people are fighting for the principle of self-determination of the people," he said. "For this they will fight to the last man because they know if democracy is exterminated in the Dominican Republic, in less than five years the rest of Latin America will be under Communism. Democracy in America is fighting at this moment in the Dominican Republic."

This, naturally, coincided with the diplomatic reports that whatever Communists there were around the rebel leadership had now pulled out of sight. Although some U.S. Embassy officials insisted that this was no more than a tactical position, the diplomatic consensus in Santo Domingo was that even if this were true, here was a superb opportunity for the United States to isolate the Communists permanently from the top rebel leadership. Coincidentally, similar thoughts were beginning to germinate in the minds of some high White House officials in Washington, emphasizing again how far from unified the United States Government was on the Dominican problem.

There was, of course, complete consensus on the need for arriving at a negotiated settlement of the civil war. The question dividing officials in the Administration, however, was over the character of the settlement.

The Administration as a whole was anxious to set in motion a full-fledged negotiating procedure. During the night the United States joined with the majority in the Council of the Organization of American States to approve a resolution to send back the original five-man O.A.S. peace-making commission to Santo Domingo, this time with vastly expanded powers. The new mandate in effect gave the commission the power to restore governmental machinery in Santo Domingo and to lay the basis for the creation of a new government there.

With the Inter-American Armed Force already in existence, even if still only on paper, the O.A.S. commission was now to act as its political and diplomatic counterpart. Just as the Inter-

American Armed Force was an innovation in the history of the inter-American system, the commission's powers to rebuild a Dominican government were unprecedented in hemispheric annals.

Before sending the commission back to Santo Domingo, the Council rejected by a large majority a Mexican resolution demanding the withdrawal of U.S. forces from the Dominican Republic. Then the O.A.S. mediators prepared to fly back to Santo Domingo.

And time was already running out for mediation efforts. General Imbert and his commanders were saying openly that they would attack unless the rebels promptly agreed to surrender and turn in their weapons. Indications were also beginning to appear as to just how General Imbert porposed to carry out his threat.

The transportation battalion headquarters in the northern part of the city, the only enclave there now held by the junta forces, was being continually reinforced. It still was not clear to us how General Imbert was getting his men there through rebel territory. But some of our U.S. military friends were alerting us to pay maximum attention to the situation around the transportation building.

Colonel Caamaño, too, was paying increasing attention to it. Late Sunday night and again Monday rebel units tried to storm the transportation center. With a tank and heavy rifle fire the defenders succeeded in repelling these attacks. But this was only a foretaste of what was to come.

Tuesday, May 11th.

With General Wessin's refusal to resign, the Dominican deadlock was hardening. "Tony" Imbert, head of the U.S.-created "Government of National Reconstruction," was becoming increasingly intransigent as he claimed to control the entire country except for the rebels' stronghold in downtown Santo Domingo. His position was simply that any negotiation must lead to the surrender of Colonel Caamaño's forces.

At his downtown headquarters Caamaño, on the other hand, repeated to the Papal Nuncio and to Secretary General Mora of the O.A.S. that his side would not sit down with the Imbert government unless General Wessin resigned.

Now, however, the United States made up its mind that a coalition government, presumably composed of Caamaño and Imbert representatives, could be the best solution for the civil war. After two weeks of hurling accusations that the rebels were Communist-dominated, the Johnson Administration came around to the view that a coalition government could and should be set up to serve provisionally until new national elections could be held.

This was at least a partial shift in U.S. policy, although the United States remained at the same time actively sympathetic toward the Imbert junta, notwithstanding its annoyance over the Wessin incident.

Administration spokesmen in Washington began to tell newsmen, as reported by John W. Finney of The Times, that "despite the present military hostility between the two factions, it is believed completely possible to bring the Caamaño and Imbert forces into a coalition government."

But most of us in Santo Domingo felt this was a very unrealistic view unless the United States resolved to apply direct pressure to the Imbert junta to force it into concessions to the rebels. Not even "Tap" Bennett thought a coalition regime was feasible or desirable. The Administration, bogged down in its complicated and often contradictory maneuvers, did not yet appear ready to force Imbert into anything drastic. No further pressure was exerted on him, as far as is known, to bring about General Wessin's resignation despite the embassy's statement of the day before that such a move would "improve the political climate." And, finally, the U.S. military command in Santo Domingo must have been aware that "Tony" Imbert's commanders were preparing a new offensive against the rebels in the northern part of the city.

It was against this uncertain background that John Bartlow Martin met again with Colonel Caamaño, their first encounter in 10 days. Mr. Martin's own account in his Life magazine article is probably the best available public report on this meeting.

As he tells it, a telephone call from the Papal Nuncio to the embassy in the morning set in motion the new conference. It was to be the first serious contact between the rebels and the United States since Mr. Martin and Colonel Caamaño met on May 1.

The new meeting, according to Mr. Martin, was held at the colonel's request. Mr. Martin and Harry Shlaudeman, the State Department's Dominican desk officer and former head of the political section in the U.S. Embassy in Santo Domingo, were driven to the rebel zone by Msgr. Clarizio. At rebel headquarters the Americans and the Nuncio were received by Colonel Caamaño, Hector Aristy and Foreign Minister Curi. Colonel Caamaño, according to Mr. Martin, immediately said he would not meet with General Imbert so long as General Wessin, General de los Santos Cespedes and Commodore Rivera Caminero remained associated with the junta.

Then, Mr. Martin wrote, Colonel Caamaño and Mr. Aristy spent some time charging that the Imbert forces were breaking the truce and that American paratroopers were firing into the rebel area and had killed 22 people.

Mr. Martin reported that the Nuncio then broke in to stress the importance of peace negotiations. Msgr. Clarizio was said to have proposed to Colonel Caamaño that he meet with Imbert representatives at the Nunciatura, deep in the International Safety Zone.

But Colonel Caamaño would not go there. Mr. Martin asked him where he would consider going. He suggested that they look at a map together to find a place that would be acceptable to the colonel. Then Mr. Martin gave this account of what followed:*

"I wanted to get him alone—for the first time. I took him to the far end of the table and asked in a low voice, 'Are you a free agent?'

"He said, 'I am a free agent.'

" 'Can you leave here?'

"He hesitated, said, 'My people say that talking won't do any good as long as those three [Wessin, de los Santos Cespedes and Rivera Caminero] are there. If I did, I'd be out.'

" 'That's what I'm asking you—are you a free agent? Who would put you out? Who are your people?'

" 'My *militantes*. The Cabinet. Some Senators.'

* From an article in Life magazine to be included in Martin's forthcoming book, OVERTAKEN BY EVENTS, to be published by McGraw-Hill.

" '*Militantes*,' in this cloudy context, could mean either soldiers, like himself, who had defected, or Castro-Communists. I asked, 'Who are the *militantes?*'

"Caamaño hesitated again, then said, 'The officers.'

"I said, 'Not the Communists?'

"He said, 'There are no Communists.'

"I said, 'We know there are. What I am asking is whether you are free of them?'

"He said, looking away, speaking hesitantly, 'There may be individual Communists in my area. But they are not in the leadership. After we get this over, we get rid of them.'

"I was far from sure. And I think he was, too."

Mr. Martin then told Colonel Caamaño that Venezuela's former President Rómulo Betancourt, Costa Rica's former President José Figueres and Puerto Rico's former Governor Luis Muñoz Marin would not be coming to Santo Domingo. The idea that these three statesmen should undertake the mediation in the Dominican civil war had originated in the Johnson Administration. The Caamaño regime had heard about it and cabled a request to the O.A.S. that they indeed be appointed as mediators.

Mr. Martin's account does not say why the idea of this three-man committee was abandoned. But diplomats in Washington reported later that it was dropped by the Johnson Administration as a result of strong opposition from the Brazilian and Paraguayan foreign ministers, who were attending the meetings of the O.A.S. Council. There seemed to be some fear that Betancourt, Figueres and Muñoz Marin were too liberal and that their entry into the Dominican situation might tilt the balance in the rebels' direction. In one of its many vacillations, the Johnson Administration went along with these objections and that was the end of what already was being called in Washington the "supercommittee."

Mr. Martin wrote that after lengthy exchanges he and Colonel Caamaño agreed on three possible sites where a meeting might be held between the rebel chief and Imbert representatives. All three sites were within the rebel zone, but Colonel Caamaño was willing to come to a spot just inside the dividing line.

However, he told Mr. Martin that he would first have to consult his advisers and that he would call the Papal Nuncio at 3 P.M. to give his final answer.

From the rebel headquarters Mr. Martin drove to see General Imbert to fill him in on the morning conference with Colonel Caamaño. Imbert agreed to a meeting with the rebels at a spot acceptable to Caamaño.

Then Mr. Martin went back to the U.S. Embassy to wait for Caamaño's call. When word finally came, it was negative. Colonel Caamaño told the Nuncio, who conveyed the message to Mr. Martin, that the deal was off. He claimed Imbert troops had just attacked a point within the rebel zone, killing one rebel and wounding others. Then one of Colonel Caamaño's military advisers called Mr. Martin to complain that U.S. paratroopers stationed across the Ozama River were firing at "unarmed civilians" in the rebel area.

What happened between the time Colonel Caamaño met with Mr. Martin and Caamaño's call to the Nuncio canceling the conference is not known. The key factor may really have been this attack by Imbert troops. But Mr. Martin wrote that "suspicion grew that the rebels did not want to talk, that they were creating incidents in order to sabotage the talks—not Caamaño himself, but the Communists behind him."

There was no question in the minds of most of the newsmen reasonably familiar with the day's conversations that Mr. Martin was sincerely trying to arrange for direct negotiations between the rebels and the Imbert junta. We believed this even though only 10 days earlier he had despaired of any solution, claiming publicly that the rebel movement had been taken over entirely by the Communists and that all the democratic elements had been swept away.

On the other hand, we had no way of knowing what exactly were the pressures being applied to Colonel Caamaño by his own associates. Invariably the impression was that personally Caamaño was anxious to work with the U.S. and try for a compromise. But there was also an impression that Aristy was playing an "all or nothing" game and pushing for total rebel victory, excluding any form of compromise. If General Imbert was intractable in his own way, the rebels were not exactly overcooperative either. And, caught between the two sides, the United States was incessantly shifting its tactics, vulnerable as it was to internal pressures within the Johnson Administration and to international public opinion.

The latest tactical shift came after Mr. Martin's failure to bring Colonel Caamaño and General Imbert together. Again the United States decided to step aside briefly to let the O.A.S. come back into the picture. Armed with the new mandate from the O.A.S. Council, two members of the peace-making commission—Argentina's Ricardo Colombo, the chairman, and Guatemala's Carlos Garcia Bauer—returned to the Dominican capital from Washington and immediately contacted both sides.

But while everybody was trying to talk peace—at least on his own terms—war remained the grim reality of Santo Domingo.

At the Hotel Embajador U.S. military briefers gave an account of a furious firefight the night before along the paratrooper-manned Security Corridor. Again snipers in the rebel zone had fired on the paratroopers in the corridor. The standing orders of the unit commanders authorized them to enter the rebel zone in pursuit of snipers whenever this seemed necessary for the protection of American troops. In this instance the paratroopers penetrated a few hundred yards into the rebel area. Then they were pinned down by heavy machine-gun fire from at least one or possibly two roofs. One paratrooper was killed and others were wounded. To enable the medics to reach the wounded men, the paratroopers fired at the rebels' machine-gun positions with 106-mm. recoilless rifles. It was the first time the 82nd Airborne troops had used these powerful weapons inside the city. But, as the briefing officer explained to us, the unit commanders had discretionary power to do this in an emergency.

"What else would you do when it is a matter of saving your buddies?" the officer asked.

The shots from the recoilless rifles virtually sliced the penthouses off the roofs from which the machine-gun fire had come, presumably killing the machine gunners. But the rebels complained later that a number of civilians, too, had been killed in this action.

Also the night before, the military briefers told us, a paratrooper had shot a 17-year-old Dominican boy dead in a drugstore in the Security Corridor. It was one more senseless tragedy. Apparently the boy had offered the paratrooper an Alka-Seltzer, but the G.I. thought the boy was trying to poison him. So he drew his gun and shot him point-blank. General Palmer ordered an investigation and he and General York, the division commander, sent their personal apologies to the boy's family. The paratrooper was subsequently court-martialed.

Casualties and tragic incidents were, to be sure, inevitable in the situation in which the U.S. troops found themselves. But this fact did little to allay mutual suspicions and to bring about the desperately needed improvement in the political climate so that some solution could be found for the civil war, now in its third week.

A New York Times editorial, written for the next day's newspaper, again expressed concern over the situation.

"The United States is getting more and more deeply involved inside the Dominican Republic, politically as well as militarily," the editorial said. "What began as an uprising has become a civil war in a state of suspended animation. Whether there was or was not a genuine threat of a Communist coup . . . it is clear that Dominican and Latin American Communism has been strengthened in reaction against American intervention."

"The Dominican situation," the editorial said, "is proving that the best intentions mean little or nothing in the face of contrary realities." Then it added: "The fact is that the United States' intervention bolstered a right-wing military group against a movement that, while it had some Communists within it, was for the most part democratic in spirit and intention. The idea of supporting the Bosch element against the Communist minority in the rebel ranks was apparently never even entertained."

"In present circumstances the present stalemate can be broken in only two ways," The Times editorial said. "One is a clean-up by the American troops of the rebel enclave in Santo Domingo, with inevitable slaughter and destruction. The other is continued negotiation with the Caamaño-Bosch group. Of the two methods, it is a peaceful settlement that holds the best hope—we believe the only hope—of controlling ultimately the Dominican Communists."

During the evening, coincidentally, new indications appeared in Washington that the Johnson Administration was gradually reconsidering its position toward the Bosch elements, even despite the failure of Mr. Martin's encounter with Colonel Caamaño in the morning.

Returning from Santo Domingo, Anthony M. Solomon, Assistant Secretary of State for Economic Affairs, reported to President Johnson at the White House that the rebels' "consitutional" cause enjoyed more across-the-board support in the Dominican Republic than perhaps had been realized at the outset. According to White House officials, Mr. Solomon recommended to the President that this be taken into account in some way, now that the United States had explored so many avenues without success.

This was the beginning of another intriguing chapter in the continuing story of the Dominican civil war.

To us in Santo Domingo the Washington reports that the Administration had begun to discuss a coalition government—even if this particular approach seemed unrealistic—were a sign that the initial policy of writing off the rebels was being reconsidered. Mr. Martin's conference with Colonel Caamaño after 10 days of no U.S.–rebel contacts was another sign of this.

But we also had our own worries. Peter Kihss's elbow, hurt in the collapse of the defective chair the day before, had swollen badly and become quite painful. With the relative normalization of life in the Santo Domingo area, commercial airlines had resumed flights between the Dominican capital and New York. So we decided that Peter ought to fly home to receive proper medical attention. Besides, our communications had improved considerably with the installation of additional Telex channels. Marty Arnold and I no longer had to keep up the daily air shuttle to Puerto Rico and I felt we could handle the day-to-day situation by ourselves without too much strain.

Wednesday, May 12th.

The official truce in the Dominican civil war was one week old, but there were ominous signs that it was already at the breaking point.

Tensions were again rising seriously as neither the U.S. nor the O.A.S. diplomacy seemed to be making any progress despite the new tactical shifts in Washington's policy lines.

The Imbert junta, as most informed observers knew, was actively preparing an offensive against the rebels. In Colonel Caamaño's territory the more radical elements were again gaining ascendency. The rebel-controlled Radio Santo Domingo was describing the United States as an "occupying power" and incessantly hurling invective at Ambassador Bennett. In the morning the rebel radio station put on a skit in which a shrill-voiced woman described the invasion of her home by U.S. Marines and the "atrocities" that allegedly had taken place.

Clashes between U.S. forces and rebels were becoming increasingly frequent. In the early hours of Wednesday 20 rebels with a bazooka attacked Marine positions. In addition, a sniper penetrated the American lines during the night and peppered the Hotel Embajador's east wall with a fusillade of shots. One reporter counted 17 bullet holes in the windows at the hotel's northeastern corner. Secretary General Mora of the O.A.S., who occupied a corner suite, had a few bullets come in through the windowpanes. They embedded themselves in the ceiling.

During the morning Lieutenant General Bruce Palmer, the commander of the U.S. forces in the Dominican Republic, made a guest appearance at our regular 9 A.M. military briefing. Addressing a crowd of newsmen from a dozen countries, the General discussed the over-all military situation in vague terms, but he made one important point.

This was that the United States was not a signatory to the "Act of Santo Domingo," the formal truce document that both factions in the civil war had signed a week ago. General Palmer said that in the circumstances the United States retained its right of self-defense if its troops were fired upon by rebels or unidentified snipers, as happened every night and every day. He said that as a rule American troops never fired first at the rebels. But, General Palmer observed, "there are exceptions" to this rule.

Delivered at a news conference, this last statement may have sounded like an abstraction and presumably was susceptible to argument. Many reporters felt that so long as the United States proclaimed "strict neutrality," its troops should fire only if attacked first. But inevitably the reality in the field was different from news conference discussions.

To appreciate this fully, it was necessary to go out to the Marine checkpoints around the International Safety Zone or to the Security Corridor, where paratroopers often were sitting ducks for well-concealed sharpshooters.

As General Palmer remarked in talking to us, he could not very well tie the hands of his commanders by over-strict and literal orders. Unit commanders occasionally had to fire warning—or actual—shots as a protective measure. Thus on many occasions Marines or paratroopers would open fire if they noticed, for example, a rebel machine-gun position being set up on a roof or at a window. In one instance such preventive fire almost cost the life of an American news photographer. This was when the Marines manning a position near Checkpoint Charlie spotted a long black tubular object aimed at them from a window across the street. Instantly a warning shot from an M-16 rifle hit the wall next to the window. The tubular object turned out to be the long telephoto lens of a camera in the hands of the American photographer. When the photographer rushed downstairs protesting loudly that his own people were shooting at him, the Marine lieutenant in charge said coldly that "the next time you pull a gag like this, we'll shoot for the bullseye." He explained that the Marines could take no chances with menacing-looking objects aimed at them, what with all the sniping going on around the perimeter.

As for the paratroopers in the Security Corridor, there was nothing easier than for a sniper with a telescopic-sighted rifle or a machine gun, posted on some roof or at a window a block away from the corridor, to take dead aim at the American soldiers down below. So whenever shots were fired at the corridor the paratroopers blasted back with everything they had.

"We are not here to commit suicide," a paratroop major told me this Wednesday morning as we crouched behind a parked jeep and rebel bullets whizzed overhead. The paratroopers had spotted two rebel riflemen firing from the roof of a three-story building about two blocks away. When the paratroopers' rifle fire did not discourage the two snipers, the major gave orders to the recoilless-rifle squad to fire one shell at the building.

"I hate to do it," the major said, "but it's either us or them."

All these continuing incidents raised again the old question of just who were the snipers and why they so often fired at American positions. Colonel Caamaño and Hector Aristy kept assuring us that none of the sniping was ever ordered by the rebel command. Therefore we were faced once more with the question of whether the rebel leadership did indeed control its own men, not only in the outlying districts but even inside its own stronghold. The best answer, if there is an answer, was that many of the snipers firing at American troops were individuals acting entirely on their own, either because they had a political interest in doing so—if they were Communists, for example—or because they were thrill-seekers. And this thrill-seeking was not an inconsiderable factor in the over-all picture in Santo Domingo.

There was, for instance, a man who drove a yellow pickup truck around the rebel zone firing a .50-caliber machine gun at anything outside the area that caught his fancy. A sign painted on the side of his truck said "TIRO ALEGRE!" which, in free translation, means "Happy Shot." This "Happy Shot" probably had no ideological motivations. He simply enjoyed firing a machine gun.

In time the yellow pick-up truck became an obsession with the 82nd Airborne Division's sharpshooters installed on the top floor of the tall flour mill across the Ozama River facing rebel territory. The paratroopers in the silo were dying to have a go at "Happy Shot," but their orders were not to fire at him unless he fired at their positions.

While all this confused fighting went on around town, General Imbert's junta stepped up its preparations for an offensive against the rebels. In an unexplained manner more and more of Imbert's soldiers kept arriving at the transportation battalion headquarters building in the northern section of the city, quickly turning it into a major junta stronghold. In the early afternoon an estimated total of 300 junta soldiers were somehow allowed to move from the area of the National Congress Palace, where General Imbert had his headquarters, to the Presidential Palace, about four miles to the northeast. To reach the Presidential Palace, which was an enclave in rebel-held territory, the Imbert troops had to cross several U.S. checkpoints and the entire International Safety Zone. This move allowed the Imbert junta to relieve the exhausted troops who had been at the palace for more than a week with fresh and well-equipped units.

At his morning news conference General Palmer had told us that "there was no coordination" between United States forces and the junta troops. But a high U.S. official was to admit later that the Imbert relief force had been allowed to cross American-controlled territory as the result of "a mistake." Yet this official was at a loss to explain how such a "mistake" could have occurred while the U.S. was committed to an official policy of "neutrality."

A partial explanation of this "mistake" can perhaps be found in another statement that General Palmer made at the morinig press briefing. Answering questions from reporters, the general said that while the short-term mission of the U.S. forces had been humanitarian and designed to protect foreign nationals in Santo Domingo, their long-range mission was to assure that the Dominican Republic would not be taken over by the Communists or "any government inimical to United States interests."

So here again we were faced by the daily contradictions in U.S. policy. While the Administration in Washington was now talking of a coalition government and Mr. Martin had been to see Colonel Caamaño, U.S. military men were still thinking actively in terms of preventing the "Communist take-over." They were tolerating movements by the Imbert forces that, to say the least, were a violation of the proclaimed policy of neutrality.

But by now most of us had become accustomed to such confusion and contradictions. General Palmer had said that the situation continued to be "hairy" and indeed it was—in more ways than one.

I returned to the Hotel Embajador about noon from my daily morning expeditions to the U.S. Embassy, the United States Information Agency office, the rebel headquarters and two or three foreign embassies just in time to bid farewell to Peter Kihss, whom we were sending to New York to take care of his injured elbow. Our Dominican secretary, Ana Teresa Espaillat, joined me in saying good-by to Peter before he boarded the bus for the trip through the Security Corridor to the Punta Caucedo International Airport.

Late in the afternoon I took the elevator to the hotel's seventh-floor penthouse, where the O.A.S. peace-making commission had its headquarters. The inter-American team, now operating under a broad mandate, had met twice during the day with Colonel Caamaño's group and once with General Imbert. I wanted to find out what had happened. Upstairs I ran into one of my Latin American diplomatic friends from Washington. He was sitting dejectedly on the sofa, reading a magazine. I asked him to give me a fill-in on what the commission had accomplished during the day.

The big penthouse room, used in peacetime for cocktail parties and receptions, had been turned into the O.A.S. office. It was hot and stuffy so we went out to the terrace. Dusk was falling over Santo Domingo but it brought no tranquillity. We could hear heavy firing from the direction of the transportation battalion headquarters, some five or six miles northeast of the hotel, and occasionally puffs of smoke rose. The rebels were apparently again attacking the Imbert positions there and the junta forces were fighting back. Marine observers on the hotel's roof had their telescopes trained on the battle area.

I asked my friend what had happened at the O.A.S. commission's meeting with the Caamaño leadership.

"You know," he said, "we almost made it but then the whole thing collapsed in the end."

"What do you mean?" I inquired.

"Well, we had our first meeting with Caamaño earlier in the day," he said, "and we proposed that the 'constitutionalists' agree to sit down with the Imbert people. We told them that there were no preconditions, that we realized that the outcome of the talks was unpredictable, but that our immediate task was simply to get them to a table."

"The morning meeting was rather inconclusive and some of us had the impression that there was a split in the rebel leadership," my friend continued. "Jottin Curi [the rebels' foreign minister] came in at one point to say that the rebel leadership would prefer to negotiate directly with the United States rather than with the O.A.S. But then Caamaño and Aristy said that they wanted to keep up the talks with us. So we decided to let matters stand there for the time being and we drove back uptown to see Imbert. He told us that he was always ready to negotiate with the Caamaño crowd but that there must first be an agreement on their part to surrender their weapons. We tried to explain that all these points could be better discussed if we could get the two sides to sit down together. Imbert was not saying 'yes' but he was not saying 'no' to that. My own impression was that he was not closing the door at that point to a meeting with the rebels."

"Then, a little while ago," the Latin American diplomat added, "we drove back to see Caamaño. This time he appeared to be in better spirits and after a long series of exchanges we got him to the point where he nodded in agreement when we asked him for the thousandth time if he would agree to sit down with Imbert or his representatives. I felt thrilled. My God, it looked like we had it. But then Aristy and Curi whispered something to Caamaño and the colonel got up from the table and started pacing up and down the room. Then he turned to Colombo and said, no, there could be no conversations with the junta until Wessin and some of the others were thrown out and until Imbert accepted the principle of constitutional government. I almost felt like crying. For a second I had felt we had an agreement. But then I realized how completely in vain the whole effort had been and how terribly far apart Caamaño and the Imbert people really were."

Just then the Papal Nuncio entered the penthouse. He looked tired and discouraged. I asked him whether there were any prospects for an agreement between the two factions to start negotiating.

"I am still praying," Msgr. Clarizio replied.

Someone in the room said, "We are praying for you."

I went downstairs to the press room to file my story. I think my lead summarized reasonably well the situation at this point. I wrote: "Mediators from the Organization of American States met twice today with the rebel command and once with the United States–backed civilian-military junta, but the prospects for a prompt political settlement appeared dim."

As I was writing the main story for the day, Marty Arnold arrived. He had gone the day before to Santiago de los Caballeros. The conclusion he had drawn from his visit to the Dominican Republic's chief agricultural center was that the people there had adopted a mostly "wait-and-see" neutrality. I looked over his shoulder as he began writing his story. The neutrality in the Cibao Valley, Marty wrote, "means a desire for bread and peace no matter who is President." Marty's findings largely confirmed the reports we had been getting from the countryside for almost two weeks. These reports had said that while there was much latent sympathy for the rebels in the provinces, the military and police commands were carefully silent. Trujillo, the old dictator, had taught the Dominicans the art of fence-sitting and they had not quite forgotten it. The attitude, Marty said, was to let the people in the capital fight it out "and we will probably go with the winner."

While the Dominican Republic thus seethed with policy contradictions and uncertainties, still another act in this long drama was opening in Puerto Rico.

There Juan Bosch—no longer the constitutionalist claimant to the Dominican presidency but still the inspirational leader of the revolt—was considering his next move.

A few days earlier he had turned down an invitation from Harvard University to come and deliver a lecture on the Dominican situation. But now he received an invitation from a television network to come to New York for an appearance there. His inclination this Wednesday was to accept the invitation inasmuch as he was becoming increasingly perturbed that his—and the rebels'—viewpoint was not being understood or properly appreciated in the United States. He felt, therefore, that the network's invitation would give him a first-rate opportunity to plead the rebels' case before the American public.

When Dr. Bosch's wife, Carmen, had gone to Washington almost two weeks earlier to plead the revolution's cause, she had found her efforts largely blocked by subtle but persistent maneuvers on the part of the Administration. She was talked out of holding a news conference on her arrival and when she finally held it—a day after President Johnson had charged that the rebellion had fallen under Communist domination—its impact was virtually nil. So now Dr. Bosch felt, not without applying his sense of drama to the situation, that it was his turn to go to the United States to present adequately the rebels' case.

Before making a final decision, however, Dr. Bosch consulted with his close friend Jaime Benítez. Dr. Benítez, the Chancellor of the University of Puerto Rico, had been instrumental in arranging the first contact between Dr. Bosch and the Johnson Administration two weeks earlier through Abe Fortas, the Washington attorney and confidant of the President.

Dr. Benítez suggested that he phone Mr. Fortas in Washington before Dr. Bosch made his final decision whether to accept the network's invitation. Mr. Fortas's reaction was that Dr. Bosch should not come to the United States but that he would try to get down to Puerto Rico to talk to him.

Presumably Mr. Fortas consulted with President Johnson, as he had done when John Bartlow Martin's mission was organized at the end of the first week of the civil war. In a subsequent telephone call to San Juan Mr. Fortas confirmed that he would be arriving as soon as possible to reopen contacts with Dr. Bosch.

Although Mr. Fortas had been a frequent visitor to Puerto Rico for many years, this time he made his airline reservations under an assumed name. The Administration, whose policy line was now moving in still another direction, hoped that Mr. Fortas, as a friend of President Johnson's and a close associate of many Puerto Rican figures friendly to Dr. Bosch, could lay the foundations for a new understanding. Therefore it was essential that whatever moves were made by Mr. Fortas, the whole undertaking should remain completely secret.

Setting the tone for the new policy was a statement in Washington during the evening by a State Department spokesman that the objective of the United States in the Dominican Republic was one of "seeking to establish a broadly based interim government which would command wide popular support and get on with the job of reconstructing the country."

The White House, which had received the day before the report from Assistant Secretary of State Anthony Solomon on the Dominican situation, was thus embarking upon a new major diplomatic maneuver.

But in Santo Domingo peace seemed as far removed as it now had been for 18 days. As I went to bed—long after midnight to make sure I was not missing anything—the thud of mortars in the northern section of the city could be heard. Downstairs, past the Hotel Embajador's swimming pool, there were three rifle shots in quick succession and an immediate response from an automatic weapon. It was just another night.

Thursday, May 13th.

Suddenly Santo Domingo was again fully at war. The hostilities began in the morning with a nasty fight between U.S. troops and the rebels. And they resumed in the afternoon in wild confusion involving everybody.

Shortly after 9 o'clock in the morning, as I sat in my room working on my notes for a weekend roundup story, the telephone rang. Ana Teresa, our secretary, answered it. She said: "It's for you. It's Bill. He seems very upset."

Bill was an American of my acquaintance who was very close to some members of the rebel leadership downtown. He lived in the rebel zone and spent most of his time at the Caamaño headquarters or moving about the rebel area. This made him an extremely useful source of information, with which he was very generous. Unlike many Dominicans on the rebel side, Bill was also very accurate in his reporting.

Now Bill was saying that American troops had invaded a section of the rebel zone around the electric power plant on the bank of Ozama River. Bill said that the rebels were fighting back and that Colonel Caamaño had just issued an ultimatum that if the Americans did not withdraw within an hour, the rebel forces would attack on all fronts.

"Can't we stop this?" Bill asked in an agitated tone. "Can't you call somebody at the embassy and tell them what's happening?"

As soon as Bill hung up I put in a call to "Tap" Bennett. If something big was really going on downtown, I needed a quick assessment so that Marty Arnold and I could decide how best to cover the story.

Mr. Bennett said he was not aware that anything big was happening. But he suggested that if I had contacts at the rebel headquarters, it might be useful if I told them to "keep their shirts on" until the U.S. command could look into it.

About the time Bill had called me at the Hotel Embajador the rebel foreign minister, Jottin Curi, was calling John Bartlow Martin at the embassy residence. As Martin has described this conversation, Curi told him: "The North American troops have violated the cease-fire agreement. . . . Colonel Caamaño has given orders that if the North Americans do not return to their positions in half an hour, he will open fire on all North American troops."

Martin told Curi he wanted to talk to Caamaño personally. Curi replied that the colonel was out with his troops. But finally Caamaño got on the phone. Martin wrote that the colonel was "almost screaming." He told Martin: "We are men of honor. . . . We are tired of talking. We will fight to the death. . . . If they do not retire this is the final hour."

An extremely dangerous factor in the situation in Santo Domingo was that Colonel Caamaño and his associates could so easily be thrown into extraordinary agitation as a result of this or that incident. All their quixotic spirit would then surge to the surface. I had witnessed this the week before in talking with Colonel Caamaño when U.S. Marine jeeps strayed into Parque Independencia. But, on the other hand, Colonel Caamaño also seemed to know how to stop at the water's edge. His verbal explosions and fierce orders to his troops either helped to get his indignation out of his system or represented a concession to his more hot-headed colleagues. In any event—aside from his continuing inability to control individual snipers—Colonel Caamaño always knew how to display ultimate restraint and avoid a major showdown.

After checking with General Palmer, Mr. Martin telephoned Colonel Caamaño to tell him what the American understanding of the situation was. At the same time Ambassador Bennett called me at the Embajador with the same report.

According to this version, U.S. paratroopers had been under fire the night before from a tall building near the power station. Several days earlier the paratroopers had moved out of the Security Corridor near the Duarte bridge to occupy the area of the electric plant. Because they had been unable to return the fire effectively during the night, Ambassador Bennett told me, a paratroop unit penetrated a few more blocks into rebel territory at daybreak to wipe out the snipers' positions. Now, Mr. Bennett said, the paratroopers had withdrawn.

I called Bill at rebel headquarters just as Mr. Martin was making his report to Colonel Caamaño. Both Bill and Colonel Caamaño insisted separately that the fighting was still going on and that the paratroopers had not pulled back.

Later I found out that one of the paratrooper jeeps had run into heavy fire after it accidentally penetrated about eight blocks into rebel territory when it lost its way while returning from the morning's suppression mission. One American soldier was killed instantly in the action. A young paratroop officer was mortally wounded. The rebels placed the officer in one of their vehicles and immediately drove him to a hospital a few blocks away. Several Peace Corps nurses were still on duty there. A few minutes later the young officer died in the arms of an American girl.

No sooner had the morning incident in the rebel zone been settled than another battle erupted in the north. The fighting, heavier than at any time before, had resumed around the transportation battalion center. The Imbert garrison there had just been reinforced again. About 200 soldiers had arrived in trucks from behind the International Safety Zone, freely crossing the U.S. checkpoints. A television camera crew that happened to be at the Marines' Alpha-Two Checkpoint filmed the passage of the Imbert soldiers. Most of them wore their caps turned backward, apparently a sign that they were "friendly" forces and should be allowed to pass. As the Imbert convoy stopped for clearance at the checkpoint, the Dominican officers chatted pleasantly with the Americans. The network camera crew recorded it all on film.

Now the rebels were again attacking the transportation center, obviously aware that it was becoming the key point in "Tony" Imbert's plan to stage a big-scale offensive against them.

Another part of General Imbert's plan was to knock the rebel radio station off the air. What ensued after he issued an order for an attack on it was unquestionably the wildest scene of the whole Dominican civil war.

At 2:03 P.M., as Ambassador Bennett and Mr. Martin were

working in their respective offices at the U.S. Embassy, several planes swooped over it and the adjoining streets almost at treetop level, spraying the whole area with rocket and machine-gun fire. Lieutenant Colonel James Mullen, a paratroop officer in a jeep, said: "A plane came down for a pass and I saw smoke from its guns.

"It made the pass nearby, firing for about three minutes—really ripping the shots off—and banked and made another pass, firing for about 90 seconds."

In another jeep Lieutenant Richard J. Stack was riding with John W. King, a State Department official, and Matthew Kenny of United Press International. They were returning from a visit to San Isidro. As the attacking plane roared overhead, its machine guns blazing, the jeep swerved to get out of the field of fire. In trying to jump out of the vehicle Kenny fell and dislocated his shoulder. It was the Dominican war's third press casualty under fire.

In the embassy's garden and the adjoining field in front of General Palmer's headquarters, U.S. troops grabbed their weapons and began firing at the attacking planes. As an officer said later, "We let them have it with all we had." The American fire hit one of the Imbert planes and it crashed in flames about a mile to the north.

Inside the embassy people dived for cover. "Tap" Bennett and Deputy Assistant Secretary of State Richard J. Phillips were among those who dove under their desks. The Ambassador was quoted later by an embassy official as having shouted from under his desk, "I shall protest this."

What had occurred was that General Imbert had dispatched five P-51 fighters, equipped with rockets, to hit Radio Santo Domingo and get it off the air. His aim was to stop the rebels' propaganda, which obviously was doing the junta a great deal of harm. But the pilots apparently miscalculated because after they had knocked out the radio station they continued their firing runs throughout much of the midtown area, including the section of the International Safety Zone around the U.S. Embassy.

The attack was, of course, a definite breach of the truce by "Tony" Imbert. Livid with anger, "Tap" Bennett fired off a protest to the O.A.S. As John Martin was to write, "It was all upside down."

At a late-afternoon briefing at the Hotel Embajador a State Department spokesman confirmed all the details of the air attack. Under questioning he admitted that "the United States policy is not to let such attacks" take place. He said the fact that the air attack had occurred proved that there was no coordination between the U.S. and the Dominican commands. But he also said that steps were being taken immediately "to prevent a recurrence of such attacks."

These steps, as I found out later in the day, included placing U.S. Air Force fire trucks across the runway at the San Isidro Air Force Base from which the junta's Mustangs had taken off on the raid.

A paratroop platoon with bazookas was also stationed on the runway—just in case the Mustang pilots tried to take off from other runways for another attack.

General Imbert's action in ordering the air strike vastly embarrassed the United States, which only six days earlier had put him in power. The junta's planes had not only knocked the rebel radio station off the air but had also killed a woman and a 5-year-old boy. This brought angry crowds of Dominicans into the streets. Many shouted, "The barbarian Yankees are doing this!" And there were cries of "The Gringos are responsible" and "Let's declare war on America."

A group of armed civilian rebels forced an American television camera crew at gunpoint to go over to where the boy of 5 was lying. They forced the cameramen to shoot film of the dead child and his wailing parents. One rebel said, "Let the Americans see what their troops are doing here." The crowd's mood was so ugly that the men of the television crew feared for their safety. But providentially a rebel officer arrived and escorted them away. "It is not their fault," the officer told the crowd.

Meanwhile, it had become obvious that stern measures might be required to control "Tony" Imbert and his top commanders in their now clear determination to destroy the rebels. The junta's actions and the rising tension throughout Santo Domingo were having the effect of paralyzing the mediation efforts of the O.A.S.

group and the Papal Nuncio. Whatever tenuous hope there had been of bringing the rival factions together was fast vanishing. Though at the previous day's talks with Colonel Caamaño the O.A.S. mission had obtained his promise that a rebel delegate would attend a meeting with a junta representative at the Nuncio's house Thursday, nobody materialized in the end from the Caamaño side.

Some reporters recalled that this very morning "Tony" Imbert had told them that the pressures on him were so great that he could not resist indefinitely the demands from his own people that the cease-fire be done away with and a full-scale attack on the rebels be launched.

Late in the day General Imbert was making no bones about the fact that his aircraft had hit the rebel radio station. He alleged that the "incendiary" propaganda of the rebels in itself constituted a violation of the cease-fire since the Caamaño spokesmen were appealing for general violence. And he asserted that in sending out his planes he had done no more than to counteract this claimed violation.

With everything in Santo Domingo so confused, contradictory and ironical, this was the day the State Department's spokesman chose to confirm in detail that the United States was making $750,000 available to the Imbert junta. He read to us the exchange of letters between the U.S. Agency for International Development mission director and the junta's acting secretary of finance through which the transfer of the funds was arranged. The spokesman explained that it was necessary to make this money available to the junta—though he underlined that it did not imply any formal recognition of the Imbert government—because the continued failure to pay government employes outside Santo Domingo could lead to widespread unemployment and hardship.

It was an utterly insane situation. The United States was financing a government of its own creation that was intent on breaking the cease-fire and resuming the war at a time when the Administration's efforts—and those of the O.A.S.—were directed at winning a political settlement. And while with one hand the United States was blocking the Imbert aircraft at San Isidro, with the other it was allowing the junta to continue its military buildup for an offensive against Colonel Caamaño's forces.

At dinner this evening Marty Arnold, my Times colleague, offered what may have been the best explanation of the Santo Domingo events. "You know," he said suddenly, "I think that none of this is really happening. I think that all this is one great insane asylum and all of us are the inmates here."

But whether we were insane or not, the continued tension was beginning to tell on all of us. By now everybody's nerves were frayed and tempers were short. Embassy officials and newsmen had been operating for weeks on nervous energy, with rarely more than a few hours' sleep at night and with irregular meals that often were simply cold combat rations. On our side, we waged our daily battles for decent communications and for scraps of information from the military and from the embassy's spokesmen. Frequently, instead of information, we got misinformation or, at best, the "no comment" treatment.

At the embassy officials from "Tap" Bennett down to the lowest-ranking secretary were just as exhausted as we were. And on top of that they were increasingly sensitive to the newsmen's reporting.

Not only policies but careers and reputations were now at stake and many officials took personal umbrage at some of our articles. They denied our contentions that the U.S. was not observing the "strict neutrality" that was being claimed in Washington. They denied that Imbert forces were allowed to pass through American checkpoints while the Caamaño rebels were being regarded as the "unfriendlies."

The embassy was now receiving from Puerto Rico a special daily shipment of copies of The New York Times and other American newspapers. Our stories were read and analyzed at the embassy from the moment the papers were delivered. And at the first opportunity reporters were criticized for having said this or that, for having questioned the opinions or assessments of the embassy and the Administration or for having exposed what we regarded as untruths put out by U.S. officials.

Under the stress of the Dominican civil war relations among the newsmen were breaking down, too. A split was becoming painfully evident within the American press corps. There were reporters among us who completely approved of everything the United States was doing in Santo Domingo and who regretted only that U.S. forces were not ordered to go downtown and "clean up the Communists." To these men the reporters who took a different view—and that included perhaps more than half of us—were the nearest thing to traitors. Newsmen who had known each other for years now hardly exchanged greetings. And when they did speak it was much too often to hurl poisoned darts at each other. Words like "dupe of Communists" or "reactionary" were being increasingly heard behind the backs of reporters, spoken by other reporters.

To me this was the saddest part of what was happening to human relations in general in the Dominican Republic. I had heard of similar difficulties involving American reporters in Vietnam. But as one of my colleagues who had been in Saigon remarked one day, "This is Vietnam in spades." I had always felt, perhaps innocently or perhaps because of my Times training, that reporters were reporters in the first place and in the last place. I thought that newsmen should not be partisan in politics when covering stories. But the world was changing, a new dimension of pressures was rising, and maybe it was inevitable that one should take sides—whatever the sides were—to be able to live with oneself. For those of us working for The Times in Santo Domingo the only guideline was to report what we saw. I remembered that before my departure on my first foreign assignment for The Times 10 years ago my editor gave me this parting bit of advice: "You do the reporting and let the chips fall where they may." I still thought, even in Santo Domingo, that this was our primary function.

And, of course, the story went on. As night fell the rebels still fought the junta forces at the uptown transportation building. Along the Security Corridor and around the edges of the International Safety Zone guns blazed between Americans and Dominicans.

And in Puerto Rico still another aspect of the story was taking shape. Abe Fortas, the President's official emissary, had arrived in San Juan under an assumed name. He met at once with Jaime Benítez, the Chancellor of the University of Puerto Rico, who took him to see Juan Bosch. Former Governor Muñoz Marin was also back in San Juan and also active in this new round of secret conversations.

Both the Johnson Administration and, apparently, Dr. Bosch were now anxious for an honorable compromise that would permit a reasonable settlement. Ideas were discussed back and forth with the emphasis on the need for a compromise government in Santo Domingo since it was becoming amply clear that a real coalition between "Tony" Imbert and Colonel Caamaño was no longer possible. As someone remarked during one of the very few light moments in the conversations, "It looks as if we will never get a Camembert Government—the government of Caamaño and Imbert."

Then Dr. Bosch came up with his proposal for the compromise. He suggested that his former Minister of Agriculture, Silvestre Antonio Guzmán, be appointed constitutional president to serve out the Bosch term until 1967.

Dr. Bosch explained that Mr. Guzmán was a wealthy rice planter from the Cibao Valley—and therefore could never be accused of "Communist sympathies"—but that he had been a member of Dr. Bosch's Dominican Revolutionary Party. This, of course, made him acceptable to Bosch and presumably to Colonel Caamaño and his people. As to whether General Imbert would accept Mr. Guzmán as president under the constitutional concept, Dr. Bosch said, this was up to the Americans, who had set him up in power in the first place.

Mr. Guzmán, the same man to whom the second secretary of the U.S. Embassy in Santo Domingo had read the riot act on the first Sunday of the revolution, was a highly respected citizen of the Dominican Republic. Dr. Bosch felt that Mr. Guzmán could provide the answer for which everyone had been looking for so long while people went on dying.

Mr. Fortas could make no commitments but he communicated the gist of this conversation to the White House. Now a new diplomatic phase of the Dominican crisis was to be pitted against the hostilities which, for all practical purposes, had already resumed in Santo Domingo earlier in the day.

Friday, May 14th.

The truce was now completely shattered. It had been so tenuous that inevitably it had to break down sooner or later.

The last pretense that a truce existed had been removed the day before when the Imbert junta had defied both the United States and the O.A.S. by staging the air attack against the rebel-held Radio Santo Domingo, knocking it off the air. Early this morning, however, rebel technicians had succeeded in putting the station back in operation. Ana Teresa tuned it in shortly after breakfast. But I had no doubt that the junta would go after Radio Santo Domingo again at the first opportunity.

At the Imbert headquarters in the Congress building the junta commanders were increasingly bellicose and cocky. In the morning Commodore Rivera Caminero, the Secretary of the Armed Forces, told newsmen: "I personally ordered the air attack yesterday and it will be done again if necessary. The air force will take whatever steps are necessary."

A reporter asked him whether the air attack had been carried out with the knowledge and approval of General Imbert. Commodore Rivera Caminero replied: "As Secretary of the Armed Forces I may have and I may not have consulted Imbert."

Shortly afterward Secretary General Mora of the O.A.S., members of the organization's peace-making commission and the Papal Nuncio arrived at junta headquarters. They presented General Imbert with official protests from both the United States and the rebel command over yesterday's air raid. They again asked for guarantees that the junta would not reopen hostilities. But "Tony" Imbert was being extremely vague about his plans as he talked to the mediators. His offensive was about to start and he did not wish to have his hands tied when he felt that victory might be near.

During the night the junta's troops had begun moving out of San Isidro in preparation for an attack against the rebels in the northern section of Santo Domingo. To avoid the United States corridor running through the city, the junta's tanks and infantry units made a broad swing to the north over the Mella highway, crossing the Ozama River over a small bridge above the city. Skirting Villa Mella, a suburban area well to the north of Santo Domingo, the column then turned south and entered the city over the Villa Mella bridge, also known as the President Peynado bridge, on the Isabela River, which flows into the Ozama a few miles to the east. Thus by this morning the junta troops were poised for an attack against the rebel-held industrial district of Santo Domingo.

In contrast to the situation in their downtown stronghold, south of the Security Corridor, the rebels in the north did not have an organized defense plan. Most of the rebel forces in the north were irregulars and they lacked the intricate system of defenses and roadblocks that existed in the downtown area. As we began receiving reports of the junta's moves "Tony" Imbert's strategy became obvious.

He already had a strong force at the transportation battalion headquarters in the middle of the industrial zone. Now his units began infiltrating into the surrounding areas between the Quisqueya baseball stadium in the west and the peanut oil factory and the cemetery to the east. Clearly the junta's strategy was to oust the rebels from the industrial zone in a sweeping movement south to the edge of the International Safety Zone and Security Corridor. This would give General Imbert control of the northwestern part of the city, consisting mainly of factories and workers' housing, west of Máximo Gómez Avenue, which ran south from the Villa Mella bridge to the border of the Safety Zone. Then General Imbert could swing his forces east to clean up the rest of the rebel-held area in the rough rectangle formed by Máximo Gómez Avenue, the Security Corridor and the Ozama River. If successful this maneuver would confine Colonel Caamaño to nothing but his downtown stronghold, which was in turn surrounded by the American troops.

It is difficult to believe that U.S. military commanders were not aware that the junta forces had moved out of San Isidro, where U.S. troops were stationed, and had embarked upon this flanking maneuver. There may not have been any operational coordination between the U.S. and the junta command, but the Americans clearly kept track of all military movements around the city.

Nevertheless, there were no indications that the U.S. either tried to block this Imbert advance, which obviously presaged the resumption of a full-scale war, or that Ambassador Bennett or General Palmer took it upon themselves at any time to talk "Tony" Imbert out of the offensive. The U.S. was preventing junta aircraft from taking off from San Isidro for new air attacks on Santo Domingo, but it did not interfere with the launching of the ground assault.

However, the rebels were aware of the danger facing them. Thursday night, after the air attack on Radio Santo Domingo, the rebels' foreign minister, Jottin Curi, cabled the United Nations Secretary General, U Thant, urging his "immediate personal intervention" to prevent the destruction of Santo Domingo and "the slaughter of its inhabitants."

Mr. Curi cabled that the O.A.S. had shown it was "incapable of resolving the Dominican situation and of opposing the wishes of the United States."

He asked for an emergency meeting of the U.N. Security Council to "avoid a catastrophe" and the Security Council moved at once to call a session.

In retrospect it seems odd that John Bartlow Martin found it proper to blame the Caamaño command for creating "incidents" in order to avoid peace talks with the junta when it was obvious that it was General Imbert who not only was provoking dangerous situations himself but also was actively engaged in preparing the full-scale resumption of the war. I remember Colonel Caamaño's warning, passed on to Juan Bosch in Puerto Rico, the day after the United States formed the Imbert government. Caamaño said on that Saturday that he was certain the Imbert forces, acting under the cover of the United States troops, would launch an attack against the rebels. Colonel Caamaño obviously knew his old friend "Tony" Imbert and his warning—dismissed at the time by U.S. officials as "nonsense"—was turning out to have been rather prophetic.

Now the gunfire in the north was gaining in intensity. There was fighting in the whole area of the transportation building, the baseball stadium, the peanut oil factory and the cemetery. Mortars, bazookas and automatic weapons were being used by both sides. In the early afternoon the O.A.S. mediators made a second visit to the Imbert headquarters, apparently to express their concern over what was happening in the north. "Tony" Imbert again was noncommittal. Then the Latin American diplomats went to the U.S. Embassy to talk to Mr. Martin. A reporter trailed behind them and later chatted with him.

Seemingly ignoring the developing new military situation, Mr. Martin told the newsman that the obstacle in arranging for peace negotiations lay with the rebels. He said that every time the attempt neared success "a small Communist faction within the Caamaño group causes an incident that makes negotiations impossible." He added that he did not blame Colonel Caamaño personally for these incidents, but he saw them as an "indication that there is much political in-fighting" in the rebel movement. He also volunteered the opinion that yesterday's air attack on the city would have no greater long-range effects on a possible solution of the Dominican crisis than any other cease-fire violation in the past.

So here we were again in a situation of utter unreality. Either the embassy did not know what its protégé "Tony" Imbert was doing at that moment or it had given its blessings for the offensive just as high-level negotiations for a settlement were getting under way in Puerto Rico. The United States Government was either so divided on the whole Dominican issue that one hand did not know what the other was doing or else a double game was being deliberately played. In our mounting confusion, we, the reporters, argued interminably over which was the right answer.

In mid-afternoon Dr. Mora and the O.A.S. commissioners drove downtown for a new meeting with Colonel Caamaño in another attempt to persuade him to agree to negotiate with the Imbert junta. In the circumstances this, too, seemed a bit unrealistic, if not downright unreasonable.

And it did not take long for the O.A.S. commissioners to discover for themselves the unrealistic position they were in at that moment. At 4:56 P.M., as the diplomats sat across the table from Colonel Caamaño and his associates in the fourth-floor office at the Copello Building on Conde Street, heavy firing was suddenly heard coming from above the Presidential Palace to the north.

The burst of automatic gunfire and the explosions of bazooka shells went on for four or five minutes. White with fury, Colonel Caamaño jumped up from his chair.

"If this is another junta attack on us," he shouted, "I am breaking off all the talks and we will attack, too."

He rushed out of the room with his aides to find out what had happened.

I was at my room in the Hotel Embajador adding the finishing touches to a long story—what we call a "blockbuster"—when the phone rang. It was Bill, my American friend at rebel headquarters, reporting that there had been a new junta attack on Radio Santo Domingo. He was not certain, though, whether it had been another air attack or some other type of assault. He told me he had been listening to a rebel broadcast and suddenly had heard sounds of gunfire and then the station went off the air. The junta was now shedding the last vestiges of its pretense that it was willing to negotiate for a settlement. "Tony" Imbert was obviously determined to win the upper hand before being forced into negotiations and at this point he was prepared to risk U.S. displeasure.

Back at rebel headquarters, Colonel Caamaño burst into the room. He told the O.A.S. delegation that a truckload or two of Imbert troops armed with bazookas had driven up to Radio Santo Domingo and blasted it. The bazookas and a burst of automatic fire had destroyed or damaged the transmitting equipment.

His fury rising, Colonel Caamaño pronounced all negotiations broken and the truce ended. He then accused the O.A.S. commission of acting in collusion with the United States and the Imbert junta to destroy his movement. Dr. Mora and Ambassador Colombo, the Argentine chairman of the O.A.S. commission, protested heatedly that this was not so. Colonel Caamaño and Hector Aristy shouted back that there must have been collusion because how otherwise could the O.A.S. have been trying to negotiate a get-together between the rebel command and General Imbert when the "constitutionalists" were being simultaneously attacked by U.S.–supported junta forces.

The meeting broke up in anger with no further plans to reconvene. Dr. Mora and the O.A.S. commissioners walked downstairs to get into their cars for the trip back to the Hotel Embajador. Night was falling and a hostile crowd had assembled at the door to the Copello Building. Men and women shouted: "Down with the O.A.S." They banged angrily on the cars of the departing O.A.S. group.

The question immediately arose as to how the junta commandos could have succeeded in reaching Radio Santo Domingo, which was situated in the rebel zone north of the Security Corridor, without either the knowledge or the approval of the United States. They might have come from the Presidential Palace, where the junta kept a strong garrison, but this would have necessitated their crossing the paratrooper-manned Security Corridor. Or they could have made a long foray south from the junta positions in the area of the transportation battalion headquarters in the north. In any event, the United States forces were either unwilling or incapable of controlling "Tony" Imbert.

Almost at the same time the U.N. Security Council in New York was voting to authorize Secretary General Thant to send a personal representative to report on the deteriorating situation in Santo Domingo. Although the United States kept insisting that the peace efforts in the Dominican Republic should remain in the hands of the O.A.S., it joined in the unanimous vote on the resolution, which also urged a "strict cease-fire" and asked that all concerned cooperate with Mr. Thant's representative.

At once Mr. Thant announced that he would send a representative to the Dominican Republic as soon as he could select one. But, he said, an advance party would leave during the night. It was to be headed by Major General Indar Jit Rikhye of the Indian Army, who was the military adviser to the Secretary General and who had organized the U.N. peace-keeping forces in both the Congo and Cyprus.

The Dominican crisis was again in full swing and it had once more gained the status of a world emergency with the entry of the U.N. into the picture. After almost three weeks of contradictory maneuvers by the United States, there was no solution in sight and the crisis was being propelled into the arena of the East-West cold war rivalry.

In the Dominican Republic 150 Honduran troops and 20 Costa

Rican military policemen arrived to help give the huge United States contingent the inter-American flavor prescribed under the recent O.A.S. resolution setting up the hemispheric armed force. But since no inter-American command had as yet been created, nobody quite knew what to do with the Hondurans and Costa Ricans. So they were bivouacked near the San Isidro base, where they had landed.

The situation in Santo Domingo was again nearing the point of collapse. But in San Juan, Puerto Rico, the secret talks between Dr. Bosch and the United States were moving into high gear. But again it all seemed so unreal. Those in Santo Domingo did not know what was developing in San Juan. And the San Juan conferees did not know or did not fully appreciate what was occurring in the Dominican Republic.

By now Dr. Bosch's proposal that Mr. Guzmán be selected as constitutional president had evoked considerable interest in the White House. President Johnson and his advisers felt that the Guzmán formula should be explored further and that a high-ranking Administration official should fly to San Juan to open formal negotiations with Dr. Bosch and meet Mr. Guzmán. And while the war was erupting again in Santo Domingo a secret high-level meeting was being held at the White House to consider the next diplomatic step in connection with the Bosch proposal.

The decision was made that Mr. Guzmán should be contacted in Santo Domingo and flown to San Juan as soon as possible to be available for meetings with Administration officials.

I was unaware, of course, of all that was happening in Washington and San Juan. But the dangers of the situation in Santo Domingo, including the quickening erosion of the U.S. political position there, were evident. I had finished sending to New York more than 3,000 words of a dispatch wrapping up the whole situation from the first day of the civil war until now. I had no way of knowing that we had reached a radical turning point in Dominican policy, but as it developed this long article did mark the end of a phase.

My conclusions were to be displayed the next morning on the front page of The New York Times. The story said:

"Two weeks after the first American troop landings in Santo

Domingo, the United States is facing a surge of anti-American sentiment here. Virtually no such hostility existed here before the landings."

This was the principal conclusion I had reached as a result of extensive reporting throughout Santo Domingo. The second conclusion of my story was that enough evidence was already available to show that the U.S. decision to land in the Dominican Republic had been motivated by the fear of a Communist take-over. Subsequently, I pointed out, the United States had created and supported the Imbert junta. I wrote:

"As a result of the decision, the United States finds itself identified with a military junta that is widely hated, and it may be standing on the threshold of a violent showdown with the highly popular rebel movement. Since April 24, when the revolution erupted here, the United States has in effect closed all options to even non-Communist members of the rebellion." I added:

"A growing consensus among Dominicans and Americans here is that the United States may now be forced to keep occupation troops here for long months, if not for years, and face the rising hatred of the Dominicans, who greatly admired the United States until recently."

This may have been a pessimistic assessment. But the way things were developing at that point—what with the U.S. tolerance of the new Imbert offensive—matters seemed to be moving precisely in that direction. As a friend of mine at the embassy had remarked earlier in the day, there seemed to be no light at the end of the tunnel in which we were stuck.

It had been one of the toughest days of covering the Dominican story since I arrived in Santo Domingo just over two weeks ago. Marty Arnold had written the news story for Saturday's paper but, in addition to my "blockbuster," I had to get to New York another lengthy piece trying to portray a typical rebel and to explain why he was a rebel. To move all that copy Marty and I kept the Telex channel to New York open continuously for more than seven hours. While Marty and I wrote furiously, Ana Teresa shuttled the copy, page by page, to the exhausted Telex operators. A statistical note: this Telex call cost The New York Times more than $1,100.

Upstairs I found visitors. Bob Satin, the Peace Corps director in Santo Domingo, was in my room with Frank Mankiewicz, the organization's director for Latin America, who had just arrived from Washington. Bob had been uptown earlier in the evening, checking on his volunteer nurses at the Luis E. Aybar Hospital in the rebel zone, and he impressed on me the seriousness of the new fighting in the north. The wounded were again arriving at the hospitals in large numbers, he told me.

Because it was already after nightfall it did not seem safe for Bob and Frank to drive from the Hotel Embajador to Colegio Santo Domingo, the school building where the Peace Corps volunteers were now billeted, so we decided they should spend the night in my room. As we stretched out to go to sleep, the crackle of rifle fire broke out in the garden.

"What is it?" Frank asked.

"Oh, nothing," Bob said sleepily.

Saturday, May 15th.

The situation was deteriorating rapidly in Santo Domingo, but in Washington and San Juan new and complicated political efforts were under way.

Since Marty Arnold and I did not know what the Administration was attempting to do elsewhere, our attentions were riveted to the military situation in the Dominican capital. Since early morning heavy fighting had been raging in the northern industrial area. The junta forces were attacking the rebel positions around the transportation battalion headquarters and the peanut oil factory, seeking to break out into the area below, toward the International Safety Zone.

I went up to the Hotel Embajador penthouse to check on the activities of the O.A.S. group. The Latin American ambassadors were not concealing their concern over the situation. I ran into Ambassador Colombo, the chairman of the O.A.S. commission, and he told me that his group had just sent formal notes to both the Imbert junta and the rebel command exhorting them not to break the cease-fire. I ventured the observation that the cease-fire had obviously already been broken and that the problem now seemed to be how to get a new one, if possible. Mr. Colombo shrugged and walked away, his face gray with concern.

From the terrace of the penthouse we had a panoramic view of the fighting going on almost directly to the north of us, some five miles away. It was the heaviest firing I had heard in Santo Domingo since the truce negotiated by the O.A.S. mission was signed on May 5. Tanks, bazookas, machine guns and rifles were being employed in the furious combat between the rebels and the junta forces. Watching from the terrace, we could see every few minutes bluish smoke curling up into the sky from the explosions of artillery and tank shells. One of the Latin American ambassadors joined me on the terrace. I asked him whether the O.A.S. commission would make any efforts today to talk to either side.

"What for?" he asked. "Caamaño broke off the talks last night, and when we saw Imbert he told us that he would attack Radio Santo Domingo as often as necessary to keep it off the air. The best we can do is to send notes to both of them and hope for the best. But only you Americans can stop the war, if this is what you want to do."

Then Homero Hernandez, the rebel liaison officer with the O.A.S. commission, arrived at the penthouse. He delivered a note from Colonel Caamaño to Ambassador Colombo and came out on the terrace to join our little group in watching the fighting.

We shook hands and I asked Homero whether the rebels had really broken off all talks with the O.A.S.

"Well," he said, "if they have not been broken off completely, they are just hanging by a thread. But maybe we can keep this thread from breaking completely. The important thing is to stop Imbert and Wessin from continuing the war."

He pointed toward the fighting just as a wind from the north brought the sounds of explosions closer.

"But if *they* persist in attacking us, let me tell you that we are going to fight to the last man," he added.

Meanwhile tensions were rising everywhere. The junta radio station broke off its continuous playing of "The Yellow Rose of Texas" and announced that "Operation Clean-Up" was under way. It warned the population of the northern zone to stay off the streets and not to hide or protect the rebels. The storekeepers in the Safety Zone, who had timidly begun to reopen their businesses earlier in the week, now closed them again and rushed home.

And the rebels somehow got Radio Santo Domingo back on the air once more. Colonel Caamaño spoke briefly to his followers and told them that "we are very close to victory." But the way matters were developing in the north, this sounded like wishful thinking. The well-rested and well-equipped Imbert forces were slowly but steadily advancing against the rebels.

Downtown things were again "hairy," as the Army colonel in charge of the press briefings put it this morning. In the 24-hour period that had ended last midnight there had been 41 incidents involving rebels firing on American positions, a new record. Twenty-three of the incidents had occurred in the Security Corridor. In one instance paratroopers had had to use their recoilless rifles to silence a .50-caliber machine gun firing on them from a roof. As always happened in periods of tension, the hotheads in the rebel area were getting out of hand and their attacks on the Americans were increasing in frequency.

I went downstairs to the press room to write my story. On the way I ran into General Rikhye, the chief of the U.N. advance party, who had just arrived from New York with a group of assistants. He was wearing his Indian Army uniform and I could not avoid the impression that our Caribbean war was quickly becoming internationalized.

Then I drove a few blocks to the home of the Counselor of the French Embassy for lunch. Four French correspondents were already there and the tone of the conversation was highly critical of the U.S. attitude in the Dominican conflict. The Frenchmen were persuaded that the U.S. was deliberately allowing Imbert to proceed with his offensive, if not encouraging him to do so. Their sympathies were clearly with Colonel Caamaño's rebels and to them the American policies in Santo Domingo were a miniature replay of Vietnam.

Even as we were eating lunch against the background of the bombardment in the north of the city, President Johnson was issuing a sudden statement in Washington on the Dominican situation. We did not know whether it had been prompted by the news of resumed fighting in Santo Domingo and we were, of course, not yet aware of the simultaneous political developments at the White House and in Puerto Rico.

In his statement the President expressed his hope that a coalition government would soon be formed.

"I continue to hope that the O.A.S. mission presently in the Dominican Republic will rapidly find a solution that will at the same time assure for the Dominican people the principles of a democratic constitution and a government of national unity able to maintain economic and political stability," the President said.

"If the good offices of the O.A.S. succeed in achieving this solution, the United States Government will render all available assistance to assure rapid economic development," he added.

Although we did not know it then, Mr. Johnson was setting the stage for his Administration's latest diplomatic maneuver. We also were unaware of the intense secret activity going on at the White House. The President was meeting with his top aides in a series of unusual weekend conferences. Then an announcement was made, without further explanation, that McGeorge Bundy, the President's Special Assistant for National Security Affairs, had canceled his planned participation later in the day in a "teach-in" debate on Vietnam policy. Mr. Bundy, the White House said, had "other duties."

These duties, as it turned out, were a secret trip to San Juan to meet with Dr. Bosch and Mr. Guzmán. A rumor spread in the White House that Mr. Bundy had already flown to Santo Domingo but George E. Reedy, then the Presidential press secretary, would not confirm it.

Actually, Mr. Bundy and three top Administration officials were by then aboard a Presidential jet en route to Ramey Air Force Base in Puerto Rico. Accompanying Mr. Bundy were Deputy Secretary of Defense Cyrus R. Vance, Under Secretary of State Mann and Assistant Secretary of State Vaughn.

They landed at Ramey late in the afternoon. Mr. Vance remained at the base to confer with Air Force commanders while Mr. Bundy, Mr. Mann and Mr. Vaughn flew to San Juan. For reasons that are still not clear Mr. Mann and Mr. Vaughn immediately transferred to still another plane and flew at once to

Santo Domingo. Mr. Bundy, on the other hand, was driven to the home of Dr. Jaime Benítez to meet Dr. Bosch and Mr. Guzmán.

Earlier in the day a U.S. military aircraft had flown Mr. Guzmán from Santo Domingo to San Juan for this conference. The ironical aspect was that Mr. Guzmán had been taken by helicopter to the San Isidro base, headquarters of the junta forces, in complete secrecy and placed aboard an Air Force plane for the flight to Puerto Rico.

The meeting involving Dr. Bosch, Mr. Guzmán, Mr. Bundy and Dr. Benítez went on late into the night. At one point the former Governor of Puerto Rico, Luis Muñoz Marin, joined them. At another point Senators Henry Jackson of Washington and Jacob Javits of New York came calling on Dr. Bosch to learn more about the Dominican situation. They were not aware that Mr. Bundy was in another room.

In this cloak-and-dagger atmosphere a few basic decisions were made at once. Mr. Bundy, apparently acting with the full authority of President Johnson, expressed his willingness to fly to Santo Domingo in order to enter into formal negotiations with Mr. Guzmán and the rebels for the creation of a compromise government. Mr. Mann, Mr. Vaughn and Ambassador Bennett would have the task of dealing with General Imbert.

Because of the secrecy surrounding this operation it was considered unwise for Dr. Bosch to telephone Colonel Caamaño to advise him of what was happening. Therefore it was agreed that Lieutenant Colonel Rafael Fernandez Dominguez, former Dominican military attaché in Chile and one of the leading moderate rebel leaders, would fly to Santo Domingo with a personal message from Dr. Bosch to Colonel Caamaño. He was to be accompanied by Colonel Enrique Herrera, a retired officer of the Spanish Army who had been the commander of the Domican Military Academy in Trujillo's days. Colonel Herrera was now in San Juan, acting in his personal capacity as something of an adviser to the rebels. He had flown in from Spain when the Dominican revolution broke out but his precise role could never be clearly established.

Meanwhile in Santo Domingo we were advised that U.N. Secretary General Thant had just named José Antonio Mayobre of Venezuela—the executive director of the U.N. Economic Commission for Latin America—as his chief representative in the Dominican Republic. He was to arrive Monday. General Rikhye had already set up temporary offices for the U.N. mission at the Hotel Embajador and had established contact with the O.A.S. representatives.

In the evening Ambassador Colombo called a sudden news conference in the briefing room. Looking glum, he acknowledged that conditions were rapidly "deteriorating." He announced that the O.A.S. commission had maintained contact until today with both sides in the conflict and that it had sent notes this morning to both commands exhorting them to keep the peace.

"We are doing the impossible to maintain the cease-fire," Mr. Colombo said.

He added in a tired voice that "so long as there is one possibility of peace, we will keep trying."

I received a message that the Foreign Desk of The Times was telephoning me from New York. I took the call in my room and was told that Max Frankel of our Washington Bureau had wanted to pass along the tip that Mr. Bundy had gone to the Dominican Republic. Immediately I telephoned the embassy to inquire about this. I was told that Ambassador Bennett was busy but I succeeded in talking to Bill Connett, the deputy chief of misson, and to Dick Phillips, the Deputy Assistant Secretary of State for Public Affairs. Both disclaimed any knowledge of an impending visit by Mr. Bundy or anybody else from Washington.

By then, of course, Tom Mann and Jack Vaughn had already arrived in Santo Domingo and were conferring at the embassy with "Tap" Bennett. But everything was being kept under wraps and, as I discovered later, only Ambassador Bennett had been informed that evening that Mr. Bundy was indeed on his way to the Dominican Republic. He was not allowed to mention it to any of his embassy associates that night.

I stepped out on the terrace of my room for a breath of fresh air. Standing there in the cool evening breeze I had a front-row view of the fighting that now was going on all over town. Along the perimeter of the International Safety Zone heavy firing was in progress. The city was dark and the red and white machine-gun tracer bullets flying up and down the Marine line looked like fireworks. Farther in the distance, where the paratroopers and the rebels faced each other across the Ozama River, other strings of tracer bullets kept slashing the night.

I took the elevator to the penthouse terrace to find the O.A.S. diplomats watching the fighting from there. In the north the Imbert forces and the rebels were fighting with everything they had. Then I heard the whistling of artillery shells high overhead. One of the O.A.S. military advisers told me Imbert's howitzers were firing at the rebels from positions near the port of Haina to the west of us. The war was raging all around us and above us.

And, mysteriously, high over the city the air became filled with the whir of helicopters. They were obviously Marine choppers and they were flying back and forth between San Isidro and what appeared to us to be the battle area in the north. The rebels had charged earlier that U.S. helicopters were being used to ferry supplies for the Imbert offensive and even to carry junta soldiers into battle. This could never be confirmed, but neither were we ever given an explanation for the strange nocturnal helicopter activity over the battle zone.

The fighting went on throughout the night all over Santo Domingo.

THE FOURTH WEEK

Sunday, May 16th.

Three weeks had now elapsed since the outbreak of the Dominican civil war. Two truce agreements had been signed and both had been broken. There had possibly been as many as 1,500 killed in this vicious conflict and now the fighting had resumed in all its fury. The outlook for a settlement seemed dimmer than ever before.

Not only was the Imbert junta fighting Colonel Caamaño's rebels for control of the northern section of Santo Domingo but U.S. troops were being engaged by the snipers with growing intensity. This morning the pink slips of paper—given out daily at the military briefing—listing the incidents for the previous 24-hour period showed that there had been 85 of them. It was still another record, but considering the fighting we had observed the evening before this was not particularly surprising.

After the briefing I ran into General Rikhye, the U.N. military observer, in the hotel lobby. He told me he was about to begin an inspection tour of the city. He planned to visit the rebel zone, the International Safety Zone and the battlefield in the north. The general said that all sides had been advised of his planned tour and that he hoped that an informal truce would prevail while it was in progress.

General Rikhye left the hotel in a black sedan flying the white and blue U.N. flag. The car was driven by the local U.N. representative. Several press cars trailed behind. I drove my Land Rover, taking along five fellow reporters and "B.J." Warren, Bob Satin's administrative assistant in the Peace Corps in Santo Domingo. "B.J.," as she was known to the volunteers, had had her share of driving ambulances under fire throughout Santo Domingo and now she seemed to be looking forward to a more peaceful tour of the city.

Our little motorcade was waved through the U.S. checkpoint on Avenida Independencia after we found out that the seaside boulevard was blocked by the barricades of the Marines. Crossing the checkpoint, we skirted a long line of cars being searched by

Marines and junta policemen as they lined up to enter the International Safety Zone.

Parque Independencia, the heart of the rebel zone, was almost deserted this Sunday morning. Only a few rebel soldiers and armed civilians stood at street corners and they stared at us with friendly curiosity. We knew, of course, that at a signal hundreds of armed men could materialize in the park within minutes to defend their stronghold.

We drove up narrow Padre Billini Street, then turned left into an intersection and again left into Conde Street. There General Rikhye's car came to a stop in front of the Copello Building, Colonel Caamaño's headquarters. This was a prearranged stop and a crowd was awaiting us there. The rebels' foreign minister, Jottin Curi, was also on hand to greet the U.N. mission.

We were immediately surrounded by the crowd. There was applause and cries of "Viva Naciones Unidas"—Long Live the United Nations. A man on the sidewalk opposite the headquarters building began shouting "Out with the O.A.S.," but several rebels in the crowd, who appeared to be cheerleaders, signaled to him to be quiet. As one of my colleagues remarked, "This guy pulled out the wrong script at the wrong time."

General Rikhye and Mr. Curi shook hands and the foreign minister promised the U.N. mission all the aid and cooperation that might be required.

Except for the distant sound of firing in the north, all was quiet in the city. The informal truce for the U.N.'s benefit was being carefully observed.

We drove again around Parque Independencia and turned back into Padre Billini Street, which led us deep into the maze of the downtown streets of the old city. Except for piles of garbage smoldering here and there and for small groups of armed civilians, including as always the teen-agers lugging their big rifles, the rebel zone could not have been more normal on this Sunday morning. In true Latin American fashion people had brought chairs out to the sidewalks in front of their houses and sat there relaxing. An old woman emptied a bucket of water on the sidewalk at her door and busily worked her broom.

We reached a double intersection and it turned out that the

local U.N. representative, who was driving the general's car, had lost his way. Because we were so close to the Security Corridor it seemed reasonable to proceed with caution. As we debated which way to turn, a black Mercedes Benz drove up from a side street. A rebel major in a neatly pressed air force uniform jumped out and came over to greet the general. He produced a map and spread it on the hood of the U.N. car. The Dominican major and the Indian general gravely studied the map, working out the rest of our itinerary. By now a crowd had gathered around us. There was no place like the rebel zone in Santo Domingo for a crowd to materialize suddenly out of nowhere. The armed men and boys—and the women in their Sunday dresses, carrying parasols—were curious and friendly. They kept asking us whether the U.N. would not bring peace to their city and give Dominicans the constitutional government they had been fighting for. They wanted to know when the O.A.S. would be thrown out of Santo Domingo. Obviously the rebels had spread the word in the area that the U.N. was their friend and the O.A.S. their enemy.

After General Rikhye and the Dominican major had completed their study of the map we doubled back a few blocks and drove out to the harbor. At the gate to the port area a boy who could not have been older than 10 or 11 stopped us. He was wearing a helmet and carrying a submachine gun. After it was explained to him who we were, he waved us through. We drove several hundred yards and stopped at the end of a pier. Behind us was the battle-scarred Ozama Fortress. I saw two gray helmets and a policeman's cap lying on the ground. This was where one of the hottest battles of the civil war had been fought two weeks ago with the rebels succeeding in capturing the fortress and inflicting heavy casualties on the opposing forces.

We saw across the Ozama River the tall flour mill where the 82nd Airborne Division had assigned its most accomplished marksmen. We got out of the cars, aware that we were being closely watched by the paratroopers.

Marty Arnold had visited the silo the day before and written a long story for The Times on the activities of the paratroopers there. Behind a .50-caliber machine gun on the eighth story of the flour mill Marty had discovered Sergeant Douglas Lucas, a 21-year-old Kentucky-born paratrooper. In his story Marty described his interview with Sergeant Lucas.

"Man, you don't know what fun this is, ducking bullets and firing back," Lucas told Marty. "Thank God, the rebels are such lousy shots. But if we're here long enough they'll soon learn."

Sergeant Lucas, according to Marty, was the leading American sharpshooter at the silo. He had killed eight rebels.

Marty also found a frustrated soldier, Pfc. David Williams of Philadelphia.

"What kind of a war is this that we can't shoot unless they shoot at us?" Williams asked Marty.

Now we left the pier and the burning drums containing paint. The paratroopers had been firing at the warehouses the night before and had set the drums on fire.

Crossing the rebel zone again, we reached the Security Corridor at Avenida Duarte, a major thoroughfare.

At this point the corridor ran along Henriquez y Carvajal Street. At the intersection with Avenida Duarte the paratroopers had erected barbed-wire barricades and they eyed our little motorcade suspiciously as we entered the corridor. Traffic was extremely heavy. Cars, trying to cross the corridor or to drive along it, were being stopped by grim-faced paratroopers and carefully searched for arms. After lengthy explanations the sergeant in charge of the roadblock let General Rikhye's car go through but ordered a search of the press car behind it. We protested that we were American newsmen, but only after showing our Department of Defense accreditation cards were we allowed to follow the general.

Other paratroopers at the intersection were frisking pedestrians. They checked the pockets of mens' suits and shirts, ran their hands down trouser legs and opened packages and handbags carried by women. The Dominicans submitted silently and sullenly to the search. No words were exchanged between them and the paratroopers. But as we drove slowly along the curb a young man leaned toward us and whispered loudly through his clenched teeth, "Go home, Yankees."

We followed the Security Corridor all the way to Checkpoint Charlie. Everything was quiet there. Farther north, however, there was some firing, presumably in the transportation headquarters area, where fighting had been going on continuously for two days and two nights.

Making a sharp left turn, the U.N. car drove toward the National Police Palace, held by junta troops, and proceeded toward the Presidential Palace, a few blocks east.

At this point I had an inspiration. We were just two blocks from the U.S. Embassy and I still felt uncomfortable about the official denials concerning the reports about McGeorge Bundy's arrival. Only this morning Dick Phillips, the State Department's spokesman, had again denied any knowledge of Mr. Bundy's plans to visit the Dominican Republic. I told my passengers that I had had enough of cruising behind the general and that I wanted to stop by the embassy to see what was new there. My fellow reporters decided, however, that they wanted to continue the tour and they transferred to the other press cars. I drove alone to the embassy and parked my Land Rover in the driveway.

I walked to the door of the chancery but was barred by one of the embassy's regular Marines. He said, rather nastily, that he had strict orders to keep newsmen out of the building unless they had specific appointments. Most of the reporters had become rather unpopular with the embassy crowd and the Marines on duty were not reluctant in conveying the sentiment to us. Actually, the reasons for banning reporters from the chancery were the crowded conditions inside and the need to insure the privacy of staff members and "special guests."

It was my curiosity about the newest "special guest," of course, that had brought me to the embassy now. I told the Marine guard that I would like to see Ambassador Bennett or his deputy or anyone else he could find. The guard came back a minute later and told me, "Sorry, Mac, everybody's too busy to see you."

I went into the garden, hoping that someone I knew would poke his head out of the building and clear me to enter. As I strolled about in front of the embassy I happened, not quite accidentally, to peek into one of the offices. And there, sitting at the desk, was McGeorge Bundy. So the tip the night before from our Washington Bureau had been correct. The Administration had dispatched one of its most influential officials to Santo Domingo on what obviously was a secret mission.

I must point out, however, that as I saw Mr. Bundy's familiar profile inside the office I had absolutely no idea of all the maneuvers in Washington and San Juan involving the White House, Dr. Bosch and Mr. Guzmán. In fact, up to that moment I had heard only one mention of Mr. Guzmán's name and I'm not even sure in what context.

I sat on the steps of the embassy, smoking a cigarette and pretending to be reading a newspaper. Now that I was certain Mr. Bundy was in Santo Domingo I needed to know more about his mission. Presently a State Department official of my acquaintance came out into the garden. I beckoned to him and we walked between the trees at the far end of the parking lot. I told him point-blank that I had seen Mr. Bundy and that it might be just as well if I were told the rest of the story. I knew from experience that this kind of point-blank approach often works. I was not disappointed.

The official said: "My God, you must be the only one besides the embassy to know about this—and the President wanted the mission to be kept secret."

"I know," I said. "But so long as I know one part of the story it probably would be helpful if I found out about the rest, rather than risk printing an inaccurate story. Who else came with Bundy?"

My friend shrugged and told me that Mann and Vaughn had also come along. Just then an embassy car pulled up and I saw Mr. Martin and Deputy Secretary of Defense Vance getting out hurriedly. I turned to my friend, who now was looking most unhappy. "And what is Vance doing here?"

He told me that Mr. Bundy and the three other officials had arrived about 8 o'clock in the morning from San Juan on what he described as a fact-finding mission for the President. He said he thought the mission would remain in Santo Domingo today only or, at the most, until tomorrow morning.

I thanked him, got into my Land Rover and drove back to the Hotel Embajador as fast as I could. I assumed that no other reporter in Santo Domingo knew about the presence of the Bundy mission in the Dominican capital and, as such stories go, it was quite a nice exclusive for The Times. I found Marty Arnold and told him what I had just found out. We went to my room and I began writing the story, full of fears that the embassy would announce the Bundy mission and thus deprive me of my exclusive. I had discovered during my four years as a Washington correspondent that as soon as the White House found out that a newsman had obtained an exclusive story, it would immediately rush to make it available to everybody else. This is the kind of perversity that colors the relations between newsmen and government.

I wrote in my story that the four officials were in Santo Domingo on "a secret fact-finding mission for President Johnson on the rapidly deteriorating Dominican situation." Since I did not know about the Guzmán arrangement, this, of course, was an incomplete account. But my story remained exclusive until after the first edition of The New York Times was published that evening. About that time an embassy spokesman put out a two-line announcement that the four Presidential envoys "were in Santo Domingo today for brief consultations" with Ambassador Bennett and Mr. Martin.

I found out during the course of the evening that Secretary General Mora of the O.A.S. and the members of the peace-making commission had lunched with Mr. Bundy and his associates at the embassy. But Mr. Bundy did nothing but ask questions and therefore the Latin American diplomats, too, had no inkling of the real purpose of the mission. Likewise most people were unaware of the fact that Mr. Guzmán, Colonel Rafael Fernandez Dominguez and Colonel Enrique Herrera, the Spaniard, had also been flown to Santo Domingo aboard U.S. military aircraft during the morning.

For that matter, the embassy did not even go into the detail that Under Secretary Mann and Assistant Secretary Vaughn had arrived separately the night before and that Mr. Bundy and Mr. Vance had arrived only this morning.

While Mr. Bundy and his associates were conferring at the embassy with other American officials, the fighting in the north resumed with considerable fury. The brief informal truce for General Rikhye's benefit had ended and again there was firing everywhere.

If the Administration had not known what was happening in Santo Domingo, Mr. Bundy could hear it himself as the sounds of explosions reverberated all around the embassy.

Fanning out of the transportation headquarters, the Imbert forces were attacking the rebels in the area of the cemetery and the peanut oil factory. Led by tanks, the junta infantry advanced street by street, dislodging the "constitutionalists" from their improvised defensive positions.

Bill, my American friend at the Caamaño headquarters, telephoned me several times from downtown with reports on the fighting. Several rebels did likewise. As they portrayed it, the situation was one of "slaughter." The rebels charged that junta tanks and infantrymen were firing almost point-blank into houses in which they thought rebels might be hiding. They said that civilians—including women and children—were being indiscriminately machine-gunned.

Telephone reports from the hospitals in the rebel area and subsequent accounts by newsmen who had visited them told of hundreds of new casualties being brought in from the north. Most of them had bullet and shrapnel wounds, apparently bearing out the rebel charges that the junta soldiers were shooting civilians.

Calls for help again came from the downtown hospitals, as they had come prior to the truce. Again there were requests for plasma, antibiotics and pain killers. From the Aybar Hospital Dr. Felix A. Goico, a famous Dominican surgeon, telephoned to request the return of the Peace Corps nurses. Dr. Goico, who was briefly to be an important political figure in the Dominican crisis, had commuted throughout the long weeks of the civil war between his home in the International Safety Zone and the hospitals downtown. During the first phase of the fighting he had often been assisted by the Peace Corps nurses and now he wanted them again at his side.

Many of the reporters were shocked by what was happening. Not only was the junta shattering the cease-fire at a time when the United States Government—its sponsor—was working hard for a settlement but its soldiers were apparently engaging in atrocities. And all this was taking place virtually under the nose of one of the closest advisers of President Johnson. It was becoming increasingly difficult to make any sense out of what was occurring in Santo Domingo. The secrecy in which the U.S. was wrapping much of its activities compounded our problem.

Early in the afternoon one of the correspondents talked to Commodore Rivera Caminero, the junta's Secretary of the Armed Forces. In the light of the offensive already under way in the north the correspondent asked him whether the junta planned to respect the O.A.S. note requesting that the cease-fire be observed. The commodore winked and answered sarcastically, "You know, my boy, it may be a long time before that O.A.S. note reaches us. . . ."

And again newsmen observed convoys of Imbert troops freely crossing American checkpoints on their way to the battle zone. Marine helicopters were again shuttling high above the city between San Isidro and the uptown battlefield. United States policies were incomprehensible, to say the least, to most of us.

And to compound the chaotic situation, several of us found out that Mr. Bundy and his colleagues drove over late at night to General Imbert's house, a stone's throw from the Hotel Embajador. There, as I was subsequently to discover, Mr. Bundy broke to General Imbert the news of the incipient negotiations with Mr. Guzmán. He told "Tony" Imbert that the U.S. believed that the time had come for the creation of a provisional government, possibly under Mr. Guzmán, and that it would be helpful if the general and his junta prepared to resign.

A colleague of mine went to see Imbert later in the night. The general did not tell him about Mr. Guzmán but he did pass on the fact that he had been asked to resign. And he was absolutely furious.

"First the Americans talk me into putting together a government and now they tell me to quit," he shouted. "What the hell is the matter with you people?"

In New York, The Times was out, carrying an editorial condemning both the Imbert junta and the United States policies. It took note of the press reports that the U.S. was allowing the Imbert forces to cross its checkpoints and remarked that "trespasses should be stopped for both sides if the cease-fire is to be achieved and a new blood bath averted."

"The partisanship Washington already has shown toward the

Imbert junta has imperiled chances for establishment of a coalition government of the type President Johnson recommended this weekend," The Times editorial said. "In a country still struggling under the wounds inflicted in three decades of the Trujillo dictatorship, few figures of authority could inspire less confidence than General Imbert."

"The situation in its present form," the editorial declared, "appears incapable of solution so long as the United States favors one side against the other. The leadership and the power factors could change, and the mediatory teams of the O.A.S. and the United Nations could make progress—once it becomes clear that the cease-fire must be observed by both sides. That is the first and overriding necessity; it is also the best way to demonstrate United States neutrality in a situation in which Washington has thus far tipped all the balances."

But, as seen from Santo Domingo this Sunday evening, the United States seemed to be engaged in trying to tip the balance in both directions. In tolerating "Tony" Imbert's little blitzkrieg while attempting to convince him to resign in favor of a Bosch candidate, it was trying to eat its cake and have it, too.

Monday, May 17th.

The military briefing in the morning was held outdoors, in the white concert shell by the swimming pool, because the lights were out again at the hotel. It was a fairly symbolic beginning for another day of considerable confusion in Santo Domingo.

The military spokesmen reported on the incidents between the United States forces and the rebels in the previous 24 hours: this time there had been only 40, of which nine were said to be significant. But three more of our servicemen had been wounded.

The spokesmen had very little to say about the offensive that was now moving toward its climax in the northern part of the city. But the State Department's spokesman, relieving a military briefer at the microphones, told us innocently that he had no idea who had started the shooting in the north. We gave up asking any more questions. As usual it seemed more profitable to go out and do our own reporting.

As we did every morning after the briefing, Marty Arnold and I sat down to divide the day's reporting between us. We decided that I would look after the activities of McGeorge Bundy and his mission and the politics of it all. I asked Marty if he would keep an eye on the war, check the hospitals and so on. I disliked asking Marty to drive out to where there was shooting, but it was one of those things that had to be done.

Then suddenly I found out about Guzmán. I was crossing the hotel lobby on my way to pick up my Land Rover when I spotted a Dominican friend leaning against the front desk. He was a man whom I prefer not to identify at this time, except to say that he was a person actively engaged in the negotiations that were going on. That was why he was at the hotel.

Casually I asked him what was new. And he certainly told me. He said that Silvestre Antonio Guzmán, the former Agriculture Minister in the Bosch Government, had been flown back yesterday aboard a U.S. military plane from San Juan, where he had conferred with Dr. Bosch and Mr. Bundy. Dr. Bosch, he continued, had sent a message through Lieutenant Colonel Rafael Fernandez Dominguez advising Colonel Caamaño that Mr. Guzmán was his recommended compromise candidate for the presidency. The message further said that the Guzmán formula was also apparently acceptable to the United States—or at least to Mr. Bundy. As far as the rebel command was concerned, my friend said, there was at last the promise of a settlement.

He remarked that the apparent acceptance by the United States of the Guzmán idea signified, in effect, that the U.S. was accepting the revolutionaries' concept that there must be a restoration of constitutional government in the Dominican Republic. If so, this of course loomed as a major victory for the rebels.

Now I finally understood what had brought Mr. Bundy to Santo Domingo on his secret mission. It was not the fact-finding that we had been told about but, rather, president-finding.

As far as I knew, the other newsmen in Santo Domingo had no inkling of what was happening. I went upstairs to my room, which also served as The Times office, and asked our secretary, Ana

Teresa, to find out as much as she could about Silvestre Antonio Guzmán. Ana Teresa's great value to us was that she knew almost everybody in Santo Domingo. And if she did not know somebody, she knew those who knew him. In this case she did not know Mr. Guzmán personally but she knew his sister. She made half a dozen phone calls and within 45 minutes I had a fairly detailed picture of the man the United States now appeared ready to back.

Mr. Guzmán was 54 years old. He was a wealthy and successful planter in the Cibao Valley. He lived in a luxuriously appointed house in Santiago. He drove a yellow Mercedes Benz. He was born in La Vega, where Juan Bosch was born, and the two first met when they were attending grade school together in the little Cibao Valley town. Mr. Guzmán never attended a university but, like Bosch, was a self-taught man. He was not very well known to the Dominican masses but he was highly respected by those people who knew him. He had never been in politics, but when Bosch returned to the Dominican Republic after Trujillo's assassination Mr. Guzmán supported the Dominican Revolutionary Party, believing that the country needed the kind of reforms that his onetime schoolmate was advocating. It was only after Bosch's return in 1961 that he and Guzmán came face to face for the first time since their school days. After the elections Dr. Bosch asked Mr. Guzmán to serve as Minister of Agriculture, not because of his political views but because of his deep knowledge of the Dominican Republic's agricultural problems. Since land reform and the proper utilization of the farm areas were key issues for the new administration, Dr. Bosch wanted a highly qualified technician to run agriculture in the country. Mr. Guzmán accepted the appointment on this understanding.

Ana Teresa, who had located Mr. Guzmán's sister and other relatives of his, also reported that Mr. Guzmán was short and thin and had gray hair. She came up with the information that two of Mr. Guzmán's children had graduated from high school in Massachusetts and that his eldest son was now studying at the University of Brussels. All this was very useful inasmuch as I knew that it would be only a matter of hours before the Foreign Desk of The Times would ask for a Man in the News feature on Mr. Guzmán. This time I would be prepared.

Ana Teresa also found out through her telephone calls that Mr. Guzmán was currently staying at the house of his brother on a small street inside the International Safety Zone. She even obtained the telephone number for me but, despite hours of trying, I could not get Mr. Guzmán on the phone.

As it developed, Mr. Guzmán was extremely busy at that very moment: he was negotiating with Mr. Bundy for the creation of the proposed provisional government. Mr. Bundy was at the house where Mr. Guzmán was staying in the first of what was to be a long series of discussions between them. Although rumors circulated that Mr. Bundy or some of his mission associates had gone downtown to see Colonel Caamaño, the method that was employed in the negotiations called for Mr. Guzmán to talk with Mr. Bundy and then to go downtown and converse with Colonel Caamaño and his associates. It was a complicated and time-consuming procedure but it could not be carried out any other way if the contacts were to remain confidential. In time many Dominican figures were brought to the modest pink house on Benito Monción Street. Sometimes U.S. helicopters would fly confidential missions to the interior of the Dominican Republic, or to remote parts of the city, to bring Dominican personalities—including potential future ministers—to the site of the secret negotiations.

But if Mr. Bundy faced the difficult task of putting together a democratic government under Mr. Guzmán, the U.S. had the even more difficult task of trying to persuade "Tony" Imbert that he should bow to events and resign. It was here that U.S. policy ran into its greatest obstacle.

General Imbert not only did not propose to resign but was determined to complete his offensive in the north to obtain a military victory before Mr. Bundy or anyone else could put together a political settlement that would exclude him from the dominant role he was obviously determined to play in Dominican politics. It was again the old question of whether the U.S. could exercise real political leverage in dealing with its own protégés. As a correspondent from Detroit was to write, the United States was now faced with "a puppet who was pulling his own strings."

Unable to reach Mr. Guzmán or to see Mr. Bundy at the embassy, I went with an Associated Press reporter to the junta headquarters at the International Fair Grounds. There we found a hopping-mad "Tony" Imbert.

He said flatly that he had informed Mr. Bundy and his colleagues the evening before that he had no use for their new ideas.

"I told them," he said, "that if they wanted to turn the country over to Communism, we would have no part of it."

He described Mr. Guzmán as a "Bosch puppet" and told us that he had reminded the White House team that President Johnson had said that the mission of the U.S. forces in the Dominican Republic had been to prevent a Communist takeover.

"I made it clear," he said, "that we would continue fighting for the same objective, even if it meant that American troops would have to be turned against us. It was because of such miscalculations that Cuba fell under Communism. But we are determined that it will not happen here."

Mr. Bundy's mission had been set in motion apparently because the Administration in Washington had convinced itself that the most dangerous Communist elements in the rebel leadership—if any had existed—had been eliminated and isolated. The new policy was to go along with the thesis that the "constitutionalists" indeed enjoyed wide support in the Dominican Republic and that it would be inadvisable for the United States to remain too closely identified with the Imbert junta.

But as far as "Tony" Imbert was concerned, he had been put in power to save the Dominican Republic from Communism and he was determined to stay with this task regardless of whether or not the United States, or any other party, thought there still was a Communist danger to be fought. His forces in the northern section of Santo Domingo were mowing down rebels, suspected rebels and apparently everybody in sight.

Marty Arnold came back from the battle zone in the late afternoon and the story he wrote for the next day's paper told vividly how the Imbert forces were operating uptown. In touring the area, Marty had gone to the Salvador B. Gauthier Hospital, a few blocks from where fighting raged.

He wrote: "Inside the hospital, in a huge hall where medicine is usually dispensed, women and children in torn clothes, some naked, were milling around.

"These were among the first refugees to flee the battle zone and they told their tales quietly. 'I have a two-story house,' Mrs. Aurora Ramirez said. 'This tank came up—it was a junta tank. The man in it said they were looking for rebels. I did not even know what they were talking about, but they fired at the house and destroyed it. I ran.' "

Marty also went to the transportation battalion center, where the junta forces had their field headquarters for the operation in the north. There he discovered that the garrison had just been reinforced by about 300 of the élite Wessin troops who had in some manner reached the battlefield from San Isidro. He saw large numbers of brand-new U.S. Army walkie-talkies and other communications equipment lying on the floor in the command building. This, apparently, was the equipment that the Benoit junta had requested so desperately early in the civil war and that the United States had provided. In addition, at the junta headquarters Marty spotted several U.S. Army and Marine officers with radio-equipped jeeps. They refused to identify themselves and disappeared from sight when Marty and other reporters tried to question them about what they were doing with the Imbert troops.

However, Marty found Colonel Anselmo Pilarte, the officer in charge of the operation, wearing a neatly pressed uniform and relaxing in his chair. Marty asked him about the American officers.

"Sure we consult with the Americans," Colonel Pilarte said, "so that when we attack near their zone they know what we are doing and they don't shoot at us."

At one point Marty spoke to Elirio García, a neighborhood resident, who gave his account of how the junta forces went about their business: "The junta soldiers went into every house in the area. They said they were after rebels in hiding. They also were looking for ammunition. Every man in the street had to take off his shirt—we are peaceful home people and they were looking for rifle marks on our naked shoulders."

A woman in a small grocery told Marty that junta soldiers had broken into the store and shot the 24-year-old clerk.

"They took everything in it," she said. "Four thousand pesos and a man's life. Certainly we are for the rebels."

Later in the day several of us found General Palmer at his command post, next to the embassy. He expressed concern that the fighting might spill into the International Zone and said that certain measures might have to be taken. But he was unaware, he said, that U.S. forces were in any way cooperating with the junta, notwithstanding Marty's findings at the transportation center. General Palmer estimated that each side had committed about 1,000 troops to the battle and that casualties so far included about 200 soldiers killed or wounded.

Word from the hospitals, however, was that the toll of dead and wounded was running much higher. And again the bulk of the casualties consisted of innocent civilians.

The fighting was becoming so intense that the Dominican Red Cross appealed to both sides late in the afternoon to order a 24-hour truce beginning at 7 A.M. the next day so that the dead could be buried and the wounded evacuated. Medical stocks at the hospitals had to be replenished, too.

I called rebel headquarters and was told that Colonel Caamaño would be happy to have not only a 24-hour truce but also a permanent cease-fire. After all, the rebels' spokesman remarked, "It is we who are being attacked." But the officers at the junta office saw no need for a cease-fire—humanitarian or any other.

"Just give us another day or two and we will clean up this scum," one of the junta colonels told me.

Returning to the Hotel Embajador from my afternoon rounds, I saw the members of the O.A.S. commission and most of its secretarial staff getting into a caravan of cars. Ambassador Colombo, the chairman of the commission, was sitting in the lead car. I asked him where they were going.

"We are flying back to Washington," he said curtly. I tried to get a further explanation but the cars pulled out. Only Secretary General Mora, a singularly determined and courageous man, remained to represent the Organization of American States.

Afterward I had a chat with Dr. Mora. He did not say it in so many words but it was obvious that the O.A.S. commission had been deeply disturbed about the presence in Santo Domingo of the U.N. military adviser, General Rikhye, and the impending arrival tomorrow of José Antonio Mayobre, the special representative of U.N. Secretary General Thant.

The members of the O.A.S. commission felt that the role of the

O.A.S. was being diminished by the entry of the U.N. into the Dominican picture. Therefore they had left in a huff. Thus the entire O.A.S. presence in Santo Domingo was now limited to Dr. Mora.

A short and rather formal man, Dr. Mora had often been maligned in Washington for his alleged ineffectiveness in running the O.A.S. Whether this was true or not, in the weeks that I watched him operating in Santo Domingo I acquired a very considerable respect for him. He was not a prima donna, like so many of his Latin American colleagues, and he had the stubbornness of a terrier. He also had guts, an important commodity in a civil war. He had lost 10 or 15 pounds since coming to Santo Domingo and he looked exhausted. But he remained active in every negotiation that was being attempted in the Dominican Republic. Along with the rest of the O.A.S. he became a target of abuse from the rebels. He was criticized by the junta. And he was not even particularly trusted by the embassy. Yet in my mind Dr. Mora stands out as one of the most memorable figures in the Dominican crisis.

It was probably as ironical as everything else that had been happening that at the precise moment the O.A.S. commission was angrily leaving Santo Domingo, the United States was moving in Washington to offer to place its troops in the Dominican Republic under an O.A.S. command.

The offer was transmitted by Ellsworth Bunker, the U.S. Ambassador to the O.A.S. Council, in a letter to Assistant Secretary General William Sanders. Of course, the gesture was still symbolic inasmuch as no inter-American command had yet been created for the inter-American force the O.A.S. had voted to establish. By now we had in the Dominican Republic Honduran and Nicaraguan military contingents and a group of Costa Rican military policemen.

In the morning the military briefers had announced that the men from these three countries would be incorporated into joint military police patrols with our Marines and paratroopers. They were to act as O.A.S. troops. But later in the day we were told that this plan was being postponed. For one thing, offers of troops from other Latin American countries had not been forthcoming despite the claims in Washington that the hemisphere was solidly behind the concept of the inter-American force. Only Brazil had indicated that it would send a sizable contingent, but the Brazilians—who had international experience participating in the U.N. peace-keeping force in Suez—were not yet quite ready to come to the Dominican Republic.

In the evening Mr. Vaughn, the Assistant Secretary of State for Inter-American Affairs, quietly left Santo Domingo for Washington. But we were told at the embassy that Mr. Bundy and the two remaining members of his mission might stay on indefinitely. The negotiations with Mr. Guzmán on the one hand and General Imbert on the other were under way. In Washington, however, Administration spokesmen insisted that the sudden support for Dr. Bosch's former minister did not change basic U.S. policy.

The Administration confirmed my story that Mr. Guzmán was being considered as the most likely candidate for the Dominican presidency. As Tom Wicker, The Times Washington Bureau chief wrote, Administration spokesmen were saying that the "Johnson Administration has, from the start, sought to help construct a government of national unity from various moderate non-Communist elements and thus put an end to the fighting in the Dominican Republic."

This, of course, was not exactly the impression we had acquired in Santo Domingo during three weeks of watching the meanderings of U.S. policy. But evidently the Administration wanted to appear consistent in its efforts in the Dominican Republic.

Yet at least one more inconsistency remained visible in Santo Domingo. This was that the U.S. military command on the scene was still showing partiality to the Imbert junta's forces as they pushed on in the north, pulverizing the rebels in their advance.

Tuesday, May 18th.

There was no truce in sight in Santo Domingo. Instead, the warfare resumed with the first light of day. At 5:45 A.M. rebel snipers poured 34 rounds of small-arms fire into the camp of the First Marine Battalion in the International Safety Zone. At 6 A.M. the junta troops in the north of the city renewed their bombardment of the rebel positions and their advance across the industrial area. And at 6:15 A.M. there were four loud explosions right outside my window which nearly made me fly out of bed.

Four shells, apparently from a junta tank, had landed 250 yards west of the Hotel Embajador at the edge of the polo grounds. A Marine helicopter parked on the field suffered several dents. At the regular military briefing later in the morning none of the spokesmen had any idea why or from where the shells had been fired. But if they had landed 250 yards to the left, they would have smashed into the hotel lobby and probably killed or mangled many of the refugees and their families inside.

We asked a military spokesman if the U.S. command intended to do anything about preventing a repetition of such an incident. Obviously we felt uncomfortable about suddenly being in the fire field of the junta forces, which did not seem to know what they were doing. But the Army spokesman said that as far as he knew there were no plans to do anything about what had happened unless it happened again.

"Oh, brother," a reporter sighed.

A tropical downpour, typical of the Caribbean, was falling on Santo Domingo but it did little to dampen the intensity of the fighting in the north. The junta forces had succeeded in establishing control over most of the northwestern section of town, including the cemetery, the peanut oil factory and, to the west, the baseball stadium. Reports from the battlefield indicated that the junta commanders were now moving their troops south and east to secure the empty areas on either side of Avenida Máximo Gómez. This would bring them to the northern line of the International Safety Zone and set the stage for the second phase of the offensive—the move eastward to clean up the rebels in the city's northeastern section, above the Security Corridor.

Fleeing from the battle and the indiscriminate firing tactics of the junta troops, thousands of refugees were now pouring out of the northern district. Some fled on foot or in cars over the highway leading to Baní and set up improvised camps on either side of the highway at a safe distance from Santo Domingo. Others fled to the International Safety Zone. U.S. troops guarding the zone and the Security Corridor allowed them to enter, but only after a careful search for weapons and ammunition. The policy was that only unarmed persons, whether civilians or rebel soldiers, were allowed to cross American lines. But this policy of disarming those going through American lines was considerably less clear when it came to the junta troops moving in either direction.

Late in the morning Under Secretary of State Mann and Ambassador Bennett drove to the transportation battalion center to talk to Brigadier General Jacinto Martinez Araña, the junta's chief of staff, who had taken over the command of the operations in the north. As General Martinez Araña told Marty Arnold later, Mr. Mann and "Tap" Bennett had taken up with him the possibility that the Imbert junta might have to resign to make room for the Guzmán government that Mr. Bundy was trying to set up. But the general said his forces would go on fighting the "Communists." He said he had inquired of his two American visitors, "Why are you dropping us when we are winning? You set up our government."

Though Mr. Bundy had been negotiating for less than 48 hours, the course of the negotiations was already bringing complaints from the rebel leadership. Worried about the fighting in the north, where they were being defeated, the rebels were suspicious of U.S. motives in general. Now their spokesmen were charging that after having accepted in principle the Guzmán formula, American negotiators were trying to impose a Cabinet list of their own. "The Americans are up to their old tricks," a rebel spokesman said to me angrily over the telephone.

The rebels were upset, it turned out, because Mr. Bundy had suggested that a few prospective ministers be drawn from the National Civic Union, the right-of-center party which had been defeated by the Bosch forces in 1962. But on the whole Mr. Bundy was looking for apolitical figures for both the civilian and military Cabinet posts. Among those under discussion were an outstanding Dominican economist employed by the Inter-American Development Bank in Washington and two Dominican armed forces attachés in Washington who had not taken sides in the civil war. The problem of the military command in the future government was the most difficult. The Dominican armed forces, both those segments on the junta side and those with the rebels, formed the key element in the picture and no settlement would be possible unless new commanders generally acceptable to both factions could be found.

Meanwhile U.N. Secretary General Thant's representative, José Antonio Mayobre, arrived from New York. An immensely energetic and articulate man, Mr. Mayobre had served as Finance Minister in the revolutionary government in Venezuela that in 1958 succeeded the dictatorial regime of General Marcos Pérez Jiménez. Later Mr. Mayobre had been Ambassador to the United States. He was essentially an economist but his political instincts were highly developed and it probably is not unfair to say that his personal sympathies did not lie with the military junta in Santo Domingo.

Within an hour of his arrival at the Hotel Embajador Mr. Mayobre rushed to rebel headquarters to deliver to Colonel Caamaño the text of a cease-fire appeal from Mr. Thant. The rebel leader, Mr. Mayobre told us later, immediately expressed his readiness to accept and respect the truce. This would, naturally, have been in his interest.

Then Mr. Mayobre drove to junta headquarters for a meeting with General Imbert. He delivered Mr. Thant's cease-fire appeal but, in Mr. Mayobre's words, the junta chief spoke of "his military operation and indicated he thought he was winning and therefore could not talk of a cease-fire."

Late in the evening Mr. Mayobre called a news conference at the hotel. He announced that he had just sent a cable to Mr. Thant recommending that the U.N. Security Council act at once to bring about a truce in the Dominican Republic. He said he had made his recommendation because of General Imbert's refusal to consider a cease-fire.

"There is no prospect in sight of a cease-fire and I have so advised the Secretary General," Mr. Mayobre told us.

Then Mr. Mayobre said that he had just returned from a meeting with Mr. Bundy at the U.S. Embassy. He said he had relayed to Mr. Bundy the Caamaño complaint that U.S. forces were cooperating with the junta troops.

Mr. Mayobre said that Mr. Bundy had denied that this was the case—even though nine U.S. officers had been seen today with the junta commanders at the transportation center in the north—and that Mr. Bundy could not promise Mr. Mayobre that U.S. forces would be used to enforce a cease-fire.

Mr. Mayobre had asked Mr. Bundy why the United States, which had voted for the cease-fire resolution in the U.N. Security Council, was so reluctant to interpose its overwhelming force in Santo Domingo between the fighting factions and thus impose a truce.

Mr. Mayobre said he was not free to tell us what reasons were cited by Mr. Bundy for the refusal to intervene in the battle in the north. But I was given to understand later that Mr. Bundy had cited "political reasons," suggesting that the United States would retain greater political flexibility in the Dominican situation if it abstained from intervening in the hostilities.

Many foreign diplomats in Santo Domingo argued that the United States would have to bear the responsibility for the hundreds of deaths resulting from the Imbert offensive because of its refusal to force an end to the fighting. It was only much later that I found out what appears to have really happened. Thus I have excellent reasons to believe that Mr. Bundy personally favored some action to stop the junta advance. While the U.S. military commanders were talking of a "no-fire zone" along the northern edge of the International Safety Zone and Security Corridor to prevent the fighting from spilling into the American-held areas, Mr. Bundy reportedly developed another idea.

This idea, as I understand it, called for the U.S. troops to open a second corridor—this one running north from the Security Corridor—along Avenida Duarte. Such a corridor, if established, would have stopped the junta advance along that line and prevented further fighting. It would also have had the effect of leaving Colonel Caamaño with additional territory beyond his downtown stronghold.

Why the second corridor which Mr. Bundy seemed to have in mind was never established is one of the many unsolved mysteries of the Dominican war. It relates to the savage political in-fighting that was already developing within the Administration over the course of U.S. actions in the Dominican Republic.

There are highly informed individuals in the U.S. Government who are convinced that the main split was between Mr. Bundy on one side and Under Secretary of State Mann on the other. The intensity of the reported division between them was to become apparent to an even greater degree later.

But at this point Mr. Mann and Mr. Martin were preparing to leave Santo Domingo to return to Washington. Mr. Mann, who had not participated in the negotiations with Mr. Guzmán, was believed to be taking a dim view of the whole concept.

In any event, as he was preparing to board a helicopter to fly to the San Isidro Air Force Base en route back to the U.S., Mr. Mann turned to an embassy official and said, "I'll have to do a lot of arguing about all this when I get home."

Ony Mr. Bundy and Mr. Vance now remained in Santo Domingo to continue the attempts to form a government around Mr. Guzmán. But, with Under Secretary Mann back in Washington that same night, other influences entered the picture and, imperceptibly at first, United States policies again began to change.

Wednesday, May 19th.

Ignoring all cease-fire appeals, "Tony" Imbert's forces resumed their offensive at dawn. At 7:45 A.M., breaking through rebel defenses northwest of the Security Corridor, the junta troops captured the Radio Santo Domingo building. This was a major prize for Imbert, who six days earlier had justified the breaking of the cease-fire by charging the rebel radio with "incendiary propaganda."

As they arrived at Radio Santo Domingo the Imbert troops were met by a group of United States soldiers who had brought food and equipment for them. American reporters who accompanied the Imbert column watched U.S. Army rations being handed over to the junta forces. Then several jeeploads of American officers arrived to set up liaison with the junta commanders at the radio station.

Later in the day paratroopers of the 82nd Airborne Division, manning the Security Corridor to the east of the battle area, were seen firing at the rebels as they gradually retreated under pressure from the junta troops.

Evidence seemed to be mounting that, contrary to official pronouncements, the United States was providing considerable assistance to the Imbert advance at a time when both the U.N. and the O.A.S. were pleading for a cease-fire. In our story Marty Arnold and I wrote that in taking the radio station the junta forces had achieved a "smashing victory against the rebel regime in an offensive visibly aided by United States troops."

Our Washington Bureau, after being apprised of our story, contacted the State Department for comment. The department's spokesman said he was not aware of any help to the junta by U.S. troops and remarked: "They have no orders to do that."

Again the reporters in Santo Domingo raised the question of the U.S. cooperation with the junta forces. The military briefing officers acknowledged in effect that some rations had been given to the junta troops as they occupied Radio Santo Domingo. They also said that because of the proximity of the fighting to American lines, it had been necessary to establish a fire-control system so that the junta forces' fire would not endanger U.S. troops.

The American spokesman said there were U.S. liaison teams with the junta forces. This was the first time that the existence of these teams, which newsmen had seen earlier at the transportation center and elsewhere, had been officially confirmed. The spokesmen said that each liaison team was made up of four radio-equipped jeeps, which were used to maintain communications between the junta commanders and the U.S. military headquarters.

"This is to keep the fire out of our lines," one of the spokesmen said. But he had no comment on a report by several newsmen that once more they had seen truckloads of Imbert troops being passed through U.S. checkpoints on their way to battle.

As an afterthought the briefing officers said: "We have not joined forces with General Imbert."

Meanwhile Mr. Mayobre, on behalf of the U.N., and Dr. Mora, on behalf of the O.A.S., were striving to bring about a humanitarian truce.

Both the Dominican Red Cross and the local representatives of the International Red Cross insisted that at least a 12-hour cease-fire was necessary so that the dead could be removed from the battlefield and the wounded could be taken to hospitals. And the hospitals, after five days of heavy fighting in the northern part of Santo Domingo, were almost completely out of medical supplies.

But while the immediate objective was to achieve a humanitarian cease-fire, even if only for 12 hours, both Mr. Mayobre and Dr. Mora quietly felt that such a cease-fire, once put into effect, could be extended pending a political settlement.

Mr. Bundy was actively negotiating with Mr. Guzmán. The latter kept shuttling back and forth between the house in the International Zone where he had daily meetings with Mr. Bundy and the Caamaño headquarters downtown to keep the exchange of views going. The difficulties in the negotiations were quite considerable but I had indications from friends close to Mr. Guzmán that progress was being made. No information of any kind was forthcoming from Mr. Bundy or the embassy—U.S. policy was to keep the negotiations completely secret—but our contacts with Dominican politicians helped us to keep reasonably abreast of the story each day.

As for "Tony" Imbert, while his troops were occupying more and more rebel territory in the north, he was also busy building political support for himself. His objective was to confront the United States, and everybody else, with the accomplished fact that he had smashed the rebels and that he enjoyed the political support of Dominicans. "How can the Americans ask me to resign after all that?" General Imbert remarked to a newsman.

Shortly before noon "Tony" Imbert presided over a mass rally of enthusiastic followers who had gathered around the National Congress building at the International Fair Grounds. Addressing them from the balcony, he shouted: "We have absolute control of the Dominican Republic."

To his supporters, who were mainly well-dressed upper-class Dominicans, General Imbert said: "I guarantee to all Dominicans that I will give you peace and work."

In the afternoon "Tony" Imbert received Mr. Mayobre, Dr. Mora and the Dominican and International Red Cross representatives. They were pressing him to accept the 12-hour humanitarian truce for Friday, two days hence, after he had refused to consider it for the following day. Apparently Imbert calculated that by Friday his forces would have fully extended their control in the northern and northeastern zones of Santo Domingo. He gave an inconclusive answer to the request that he agree at once to sign the temporary truce. But in the evening he met again with the mediating officials and told them that, in principle, he would agree to the cease-fire. However, he said, he would give them his final answer at 10 o'clock the next morning after he had consulted with his military associates.

Highly pleased, Mr. Mayobre, who was thinking more of a subsequent political truce than just of the humanitarian cease-fire, announced the results of this latest meeting at a hurriedly convoked news conference at the Hotel Embajador.

But Mr. Mayobre's activities in Santo Domingo were causing consternation at the O.A.S. in Washington. The five-nation O.A.S. commission that had left in such a huff on Monday now issued a report complaining that by intervening in the Dominican situation the U.N. had "greatly obstructed" the attempts to bring peace.

Indirectly the commission suggested that Mr. Bundy's mission was also getting in the way of the O.A.S. peace efforts. Brimming with resentment, the commission proposed that it be disbanded and replaced by a special representative of the O.A.S. who could go back to Santo Domingo and take over the negotiations for a peaceful settlement.

The situation in Santo Domingo had become so improbably confused that we had not only two rival factions fighting each other—plus the U.S. forces siding increasingly with one of them—but also three separate sets of mediators ignoring each other in their individual efforts to arrive at a settlement.

The chaos was being thoroughly compounded by the tortuous

U.S. actions in Santo Domingo: Mr. Bundy was negotiating with Mr. Guzmán, who in turn was speaking for the rebels, but at the same time the United States was tolerating the anti-rebel offensive by the Imbert forces and assisting them more than anyone cared to admit.

And in the midst of all this a new tragedy exploded. We had been hearing since early in the evening heavy firing from the area around the Presidential Palace, above the embassy. Then word came of what had happened. A rebel force headed by Lieutenant Colonel Rafael Fernandez Dominguez had staged a surprise attack on the Presidential Palace, which was held by a junta detachment. Since the palace was an Imbert enclave in rebel territory, it was a constant danger to the security of the Caamaño zone.

Therefore Colonel Fernandez decided to do something about it. He was the officer who had been flown the preceding Sunday from San Juan aboard a U.S. military aircraft to carry the message from Dr. Bosch to Colonel Caamaño about the negotiations that were to open between Mr. Bundy and Mr. Guzmán. Colonel Caamaño immediately named Colonel Fernandez minister of justice and police in the "constitutionalist" regime. Colonel Fernandez was highly popular within the rebel leadership and among the rebels at large. He was considered an important force for moderation among the "constitutionalists." But now he decided to do something spectacular for the rebel cause, as if to make up for having had to sit out the initial weeks of the revolution in Puerto Rico. Leading a small force, Colonel Fernandez penetrated the gardens of the Presidential Palace. Among his men was Elio Capizzi, the gaunt Italian former Foreign Legionnaire who had been acting as Colonel Caamaño's personal bodyguard from the beginning of the rebellion. Late in the afternoon Elio had gone up to Colonel Caamaño and to Hector Aristy.

"I am getting rusty," he had told them. "I am a fighter and not a bodyguard. Now I am going to go out. Either we take the palace or Elio does not come back."

It was about 6 P.M. when Colonel Fernandez and his small force took over the palace grounds, sending the junta police detachment fleeing. There was an exchange of fire and Colonel Fernandez ran up the steps of the palace. What happened next is a matter of controversy.

The only certain thing is that Colonel Fernandez died at that moment, shot in the back by U.S. Marines. The rebels' version is that the Marines had fired at his group from across the street without provocation. The machine-gun fire also felled Elio Capizzi and several other rebels, including a top leader of the leftist 14th of June Movement. The U.S. version is that beginning at 5:45 P.M. several rounds of automatic fire were directed at paratroopers manning the end of the Security Corridor near Checkpoint Charlie. According to U.S. officers, a few minutes later 37-mm. shells were fired at the palace, two blocks away, from a nearby house. Marines occupying positions in that area radioed that they were under sniper fire and requested permission to shoot back. From then on general firing spread all over the area. The rebels as well as the paratroopers and the Marines were using heavy weapons. The rebels were said to have fired on a paratroop litter detail that was removing two wounded men to a first aid station. By then rocket launchers had been brought into action by both the paratroopers and the Marines. The rebels were firing heavy automatic weapons from surrounding buildings. It was at this point that Colonel Fernandez was killed in the general confusion.

When word of his death reached rebel headquarters it stunned Colonel Caamaño and his friends into virtual speechlessness. But then the news spread like wildfire throughout the rebel zone. Rebel youths and other hotheads started racing through the downtown streets demanding a general attack against the Americans. There were shouts of "Let's set the city on fire and get it over with."

Though Colonel Caamaño and his immediate aides were livid with fury, they marshaled all their personal prestige and influence to quiet down those demanding a general war. There are indications that the Communists and the 14th of June activists in the rebel zone were in the forefront of the demands that a holocaust be staged. At long last the rebel leaders calmed their followers and the downtown area returned to relative peace.

But these nighttime hours after Colonel Fernandez's death had been among the most dangerous of the whole civil war. And even though Colonel Caamaño was able to control his supporters, Fernandez's death had some adverse consequences for the political negotiations. The talks between Mr. Bundy and Mr. Guzmán had reached the point where all sides felt that the time had arrived for the first personal meeting between the White House envoy and Colonel Caamaño. Accordingly, plans had been made for them to meet the following day.

But now Colonel Caamaño would not hear of meeting with Americans. Mr. Guzmán, who arrived at rebel headquarters with Colonel Fernandez's wife shortly after the shooting, was also near despondency. It looked like everything was again breaking down.

I heard of Colonel Fernandez's death from Mr. Mayobre, who had been notified by rebel headquarters. I asked him if he thought this incident would interfere with the planned cease-fire and end the hopes for a political settlement.

"I just don't know. I just don't know," he said. "This is a terrible situation."

I sat at a Telex machine and sent a report on Colonel Fernandez's death to New York for the late editions of The Times. I added a message to our Foreign Desk: "Please be sure to insert it high in the story. This could be a very grave development in the kind of situation we have here."

Thursday, May 20th.

The principal result of the subtly changing U.S. policy was a decision taken in Washington, where Under Secretary Mann had returned the night before, that the United States should not interfere with the Imbert junta's drive across rebel territory in the north of Santo Domingo. McGeorge Bundy's reported suggestion for the establishment of a north-south U.S.-manned corridor to stop the junta advance was apparently not accepted.

Out of this changing policy there also emerged in Washington a deft maneuver designed to undercut the negotiations for the formation of a Guzmán government that Mr. Bundy was still actively carrying on in Santo Domingo.

That the Administration line was changing once more came as a considerable surprise to many of us—and quite possibly to Mr. Bundy. He was still committed to the idea that Mr. Guzmán could provide the best possible solution for the nearly four-week-old civil war. But it was becoming clear that other forces in the Administration—and in the U.S. Embassy in Santo Domingo—were encouraging "Tony" Imbert to proceed with his military offensive and hinting to him that if he played his cards right he might in the end emerge politically victorious as well.

The efforts initiated earlier in the week to persuade General Imbert to resign had now been completely abandoned. Mr. Bundy, who in the beginning had referred to General Imbert as "Napoleon" in telephone conversations with his White House associates in Washington, now took to calling him "Frankenstein."

And in Washington high Administration officials deliberately began to disclose their latest policy line. The twin concepts of letting Imbert win the war in the north and of killing the Guzmán formula were conveyed in a lengthy article written during the day for The Times by my Washington colleague, Max Frankel.

"Although insisting that the United States remains 'impartial' between the warring Dominican factions, Administration officials made plain their distrust of the rebel side and their bitterness over the casualties that had been inflicted upon the United States troops," Frankel wrote.

Although in a sense the United States was bound both by the O.A.S. and U.N. Security Council cease-fire appeals—for which it had voted—Max Frankel reported in his story this strange piece of Administration logic: ". . . Any move to halt the troops loyal to General Imbert was being rejected here as a violation of United States 'neutrality.' "

Max also wrote that "hopes of forming a coalition with representatives of all factions except the extreme left and the extreme right were fading"—which was an indirect way of saying that the Guzmán formula was to be regarded as moribund.

In addition, Frankel wrote that "it is conceded here that only raw demonstrations of power now have political value in Santo Domingo and that the Imbert forces are gaining because of the widespread impression that they would emerge victorious."

But, Max reported, "there is no single Administration attitude to warrant these developments." He wrote that "in fact, there is considerable dismay and frustration about the lack of purpose and decision in Washington and the absence of responsible and moderate Dominican leaders through whom a viable provisional government could be established."

Frankel then noted that "much of the confusion here has developed from the divergent views of leading officials and agencies about the nature of political life in Latin America in general, and from conflicting estimates of the rebels arising from these views."

More specifically, Frankel pointed out that in many of the policy discussions in Washington Mr. Mann and Under Secretary of State George W. Ball "are believed to have been on opposing sides, with Mr. Mann taking a graver view of the Communist threat."

Although Mr. Ball technically outranks Mr. Mann in the State Department hierarchy, the new policy shifts developing in the last 24 hours seemed to indicate that the Mann line—regarded by many Washington officials as the "hard line"—was winning. The explanation for what already loomed as a possible defeat for Mr. Bundy's efforts in the Guzmán negotiations might therefore be properly sought in Mr. Mann's attitude upon his return from Santo Domingo.

The tacit decision by the United States to let "Tony" Imbert win his northern battle before a truce was established was also becoming evident in Santo Domingo. Matching to a large extent what Max Frankel had been told in Washington during the afternoon, embassy spokesmen undertook to explain privately to a few of us in the Dominican capital the U.S. attitude in relation to "Tony" Imbert's offensive. Based on this explanation, I included the following remarks in the story I wrote later in the day:

"The United States policy was reported on high authority to be one of allowing the Imbert forces to complete without interference the clean-up of the northern area, but to hold them at the Security Corridor. This, United States sources said, would prevent the junta's troops from invading the downtown rebel stronghold and, at the same time, would seal off the Caamaño forces."

And, despite the torrential rains that continued for a second day, the junta advance continued. Marty Arnold again drove out to the combat zone and the story he wrote later in the afternoon described what life there was like. After visiting Villa Consuelo, a workers' district just west of Avenida Duarte, Marty wrote:

"There is a great deal of firing in the neighborhood, rifle and automatic, but the women are leaning out of the windows wearing the pink plastic hair curlers so popular in the Dominican Republic.

"The gunfire forms a background as continuous as traffic noise in New York. Often one cannot tell where the shots are coming from or where they are going."

On his tour of Villa Consuelo Marty found himself in the company of a Peruvian woman reporter. At an intersection, Marty wrote, he and the Peruvian woman "heard two rifle shots—a quick one-two—and then the shout, 'Agárrala, agárrala.'" This Spanish expression can mean either "get her" or "hold it" but, as Marty wrote, "whatever it meant, the bullets had been aimed from just across the narrow street, about 30 feet away, at the Peruvian woman."

Marty and the woman dropped behind a blue wooden box. Then, he wrote, "the leader of the junta squad that fired at her shouted 'Get up, get up' and 'Cross the street.'"

When he and his companion hesitated, Marty wrote, "thinking they would be shot as they walked, the squad leader pointed his rifle at them and ordered them on."

In the end the junta soldiers left them in peace. Continuing his tour, Marty found that many of the houses in the area had white sheets attached to their sides or white rags on sticks jutting from the windows, "but even these homes had been peppered with bullets and some were reduced to rubble."

A woman, pointing across the street, told Marty: "The family moved out yesterday morning; they were lucky. A cannon shell went through their window."

Other newsmen returning from the battle zone reported that they had seen a number of junta soldiers who obviously had been drinking while fighting. But the terror was not restricted to the junta forces. Bands of "Tigres," young armed hoodlums who identified themselves with the rebels, did their share of rampaging and looting on the fringes of the battle area.

And in the downtown rebel zone, on the other side of the Security Corridor, there were indications that Colonel Caamaño might be losing some control over the younger members of his movement. Although he had succeeded the night before in avoiding an explosion in the wake of Colonel Fernandez's death, tensions were still running very high.

At the funeral of Colonel Fernandez the rebels' "Minister of the Presidency," Hector Aristy, delivered a fiery speech in which he, too, warned that the rebels might burn down the city.

Whether or not it was a direct consequence of the Fernandez incident, the number of attacks on U.S. troops by rebel forces and irregular snipers had reached the record number of 95 in the 24-hour period that had ended the previous midnight. There was firing everywhere as nerves were taut and fingers were quick on triggers.

Nevertheless the mediators were making progress in their efforts to achieve a humanitarian truce. In the morning Mr. Mayobre, Dr. Mora and the Red Cross people obtained Colonel Caamaño's signature on a document calling for a 24-hour cease-fire to begin at noon of the following day. The mediators had thus succeeded in doubling the 12-hour duration of the prospective truce for the collection of the dead and the removal of the wounded to hospitals.

In the evening the mediators made the last of several visits that day to General Imbert's headquarters. He had failed to give them a positive answer at 10 o'clock in the morning, as he had promised the night before, and throughout the day he had appeared reluctant to commit himself to a cease-fire. Obviously he wanted to see his forces advance further in the north of Santo Domingo before agreeing to a truce deadline.

But finally he signed the truce agreement in the evening, though insisting that his signature not be on the same piece of paper that Colonel Caamaño had signed in the morning.

It was Mr. Mayobre who jubilantly announced at a news conference late in the day that the truce—the third one in nearly four weeks—would begin the next noon. But he was extremely cautious in his comments as to whether the "humanitarian" truce could be subsequently expanded into a more permanent arrangement that would open the doors for renewed negotiations for a political settlement.

In Washington O.A.S. diplomats showed some hope that a settlement might come after the truce. The organization's Council voted to name Dr. Mora the chief O.A.S. negotiator, replacing the five-nation peace commission that had disbanded itself the day before in anger over the U.N. activities in Santo Domingo. Since Dr. Mora had been doing nothing but negotiating anyway, the Council's action was no more than a formality.

Meanwhile the question of whether or not U.S. forces were aiding the Imbert junta continued to plague everybody in Santo Domingo. The press reports indicating that American troops were directly or indirectly helping "Tony" Imbert apparently led President Johnson to issue strict instructions to his commanders in the Dominican Republic to see to it that there should be no further acts negating the Administration's proclaimed "neutrality" policy.

In Washington Max Frankel was told that the incidents reported by us were considered "individual indiscretions, acts of bad judgment and excessive but isolated acts of camaraderie between United States and junta-led soldiers." Max reported that "messages demanding strict observance of strict neutrality are said to have been sent repeatedly to Lieutenant General Bruce Palmer Jr., commander of United States forces in the Dominican Republic." Max wrote that General Palmer said that "all they have given the junta forces was by way of two electric generators for a hospital and a mess hall, and permission for a C-47 to fly rice to the interior."

In Santo Domingo General Palmer and Deputy Secretary of Defense Vance held a late-afternoon press conference in an effort to do away with the charges that American forces were helping the Imbert soldiers.

Mr. Vance insisted that "we are impartial to both sides" and said that U.S. forces would not allow the junta troops to cross the U.S.-held Security Corridor to invade the downtown area.

Under questioning both Mr. Vance and General Palmer said that U.S. forces would not allow General Imbert to try to invade the rebels' downtown stronghold by land, air or sea. General Palmer remarked that the downtown section was regarded as an "open city" and that the U.S. forces had orders to see to it that it remained an open city.

In what turned out to be a rather tense news conference, Mr. Vance and General Palmer kept replying that the reports of U.S. soldiers letting junta troops through checkpoints were "isolated incidents." Both said that all U.S. commanders in Santo Domingo had "crystal clear orders against it."

While military fighting and political in-fighting went on everywhere, the United States also busied itself with trying to prevent a collapse of the Dominican economy.

Anthony M. Solomon, Assistant Secretary of State for Economic Affairs, had returned to Santo Domingo to coordinate the work of a special staff of more than 60 U.S. officials, some drafted from the embassy and the Agency for International Development mission in Santo Domingo and some flown in from Washington. This special staff was acting for all practical purposes as the civilian government in the Dominican Republic.

Ever since the landing of U.S. troops in Santo Domingo, hundreds of tons of food had been distributed to the population on both sides of the civil war. Huge shipments of medicine had been made available to hospitals. But now additional steps were necessary. Mr. Solomon sent out teams of his aides to different points in the interior of the Dominican Republic to look at the economic situation there. Arrangements were made to get the peanut oil factory back in operation in uptown Santo Domingo. Peanut oil is an essential ingredient in Dominican cooking. A petroleum tanker was being brought in to supply the downtown power plant so that the city would not lose its electrical services. Money was being lent to the junta to pay salaries. Thus, in every way, the United States was running the Dominican Republic.

At the little pink house on Benito Monción Street McGeorge Bundy was pursuing his difficult negotiations with Mr. Guzmán, perhaps unaware of the extent to which his efforts were already being undercut in Washington. Assisting him was Jaime Benítez, the Chancellor of the University of Puerto Rico, who had come from San Juan as "honest broker" and special adviser.

The truce was set for tomorrow, but as we ended another Santo Domingo day there was more uncertainty and confusion than ever before.

Friday, May 21st.

The 24-hour "humanitarian" truce—the third truce in the four weeks of the Dominican civil war—went into effect at noon. Immediately afterward Mr. Mayobre and Dr. Mora proposed to General Imbert that the cease-fire be extended for another 24 hours.

No secret was being made any more of the fact that the United States, as well as the U.N. and O.A.S. mediators, now hoped that the "humanitarian" truce could be parleyed into a lasting cease-fire.

In Washington the Administration reached the conclusion that with the end of the junta forces' drive across the northern part of Santo Domingo, a military stalemate had been created and that it would ultimately force both sides to accept a coalition government.

Continuing to fight until the last moment before the noontime cease-fire became effective, the Imbert army had completed its sweep across the entire northern and northeastern section of the capital, reaching the banks of the Ozama River. General Imbert thus controlled the whole northern district of Santo Domingo while Colonel Caamaño was in command of only his downtown stronghold. The United States-manned Security Corridor was a buffer between the two forces, and in the west of the city the Americans also held the International Safety Zone.

Both the Administration in Washington and U.S. officials in Santo Domingo had made it amply clear to the Imbert and Caamaño commands that neither would now be allowed to attack the other. In practice, of course, this meant that "Tony" Imbert would not be permitted to invade the rebel zone.

The Administration was certain that in having allowed General Imbert to conquer northern Santo Domingo, it had brought about a military deadlock that would convince the rebels that in the circumstances they had no choice but to agree to a compromise coalition government.

This may have seemed a sound policy back on the Potomac, but in Santo Domingo it struck a great many observers as naive. General Imbert, on the one hand, felt that his military victories had placed him in a position where he did not have to make any concessions to the rebels. He had successfully resisted the initial U.S. pressures on him to resign and now he felt stronger and more self-confident than ever before.

Colonel Caamaño, on the other hand, believed that any concession on his part beyond the acceptance of the Guzmán formula would inevitably mean the collapse of his revolution. Having fought for four weeks, Colonel Caamaño and his supporters were not prepared to consider what in their eyes would amount to a surrender. In addition, although the rebels' position had obviously deteriorated as a result of the Imbert sweep in the north, Colonel Caamaño realized that the Johnson Administration had maneuvered itself into a situation in which it could not allow a physical liquidation of the rebel zone. He knew that the United States had to contend with world opinion and therefore could no longer permit a frontal attack by the Imbert forces—or order one by its own troops—without turning Santo Domingo into a new Budapest.

Thus both sides held political advantages and, as far as we could see, it was plain wishful thinking to expect a political settlement just because a military stalemate had been created.

In mid-morning the reporters at the Hotel Embajador were advised that Colonel Caamaño would hold a news conference at his headquarters immediately after the truce went into effect. I loaded several of my colleagues into my Land Rover and we departed for downtown. As we went through the Marine checkpoint on Avenida Bolívar I suddenly became aware that the long stretch of the avenue between the American positions and the entrance to Parque Independencia was oddly deserted. In contrast to other days, there was not a single car or pedestrian along the four or five blocks of the no man's land that extended from the checkpoint to the edge of the rebel zone. It was about 11:30 A.M. and the truce was not yet formally in effect, but I saw no reason why we should not go into the rebel sector. We had been doing this almost every day without a truce.

We reached the wooden barricade at the entrance to the park but I could see no rebel soldiers behind it. I stopped the car, got out and walked to the barricade. I spotted several armed rebels around the corner of the plaza behind a wall.

"Please let us through," I shouted. "We are newsmen on our way to Colonel Caamaño's headquarters for his press conference."

One of the rebels moved up cautiously from behind the wall and started waving me away.

"You better get out of here real fast," he said. "There is a junta tank at the door of the Presidential Palace, up that street to your left, that has been firing at us for the last hour. Don't you see what it has done?"

I moved back a step or two and looked to my left. At the far end of 30 de Marzo Street, which runs from the palace to Parque Independencia, was the silhouette of a tank. I looked to my right and saw that the corner house had received several direct hits from the tank's cannon. I ran back to the Land Rover, got behind the wheel and, rather than waste precious seconds turning around, I simply drove the four blocks back to the checkpoint in reverse. Then we went south to Avenida Independencia and entered the rebel zone from the other side.

Colonel Caamaño's office on the fourth floor of the Copello Building was so full of newsmen, photographers and rebel officials that it was almost impossible to move. Juan de Onis, The New York Times correspondent in Brazil, came along with me to the news conference. He had arrived in Santo Domingo the day before to relieve me after I had been informed of a new assignment: to be The Times correspondent in Spain. The Times wanted me to get back to the United States soon and start preparing to leave for Europe. We decided that I would stay with Juan de Onis as long as McGeorge Bundy continued negotiating in Santo Domingo and then I would return to Washington. This morning Marty Arnold was out with the Red Cross people getting material for a feature story on the "humanitarian" truce.

Presently Colonel Caamaño and Hector Aristy strode into the room and sat down at a table before a bank of microphones.

Television camera lights were turned on and within seconds the place became so hot that all of us were drenched in sweat.

Colonel Caamaño was all smiles, all conciliation. He spoke highly of the United States, praised its democratic traditions and expressed hopes that the Johnson Administration would help bring about a fair settlement of the Dominican crisis.

He did not want to discuss specifically the negotiatious for a Guzmán government, but he did say that if this plan proved to be "the real solution," he would be ready to step down from his post of "constitutional president." When a newsman asked him whether he agreed with the rebels' newspaper that "Yankees" had murdered Colonel Fernandez two days earlier, Colonel Caamaño deftly made the point that the United States as a whole—or all of the Americans—could not be held responsible for an act of war involving several Marines.

In stronger terms than he had ever used before Colonel Caamaño also stressed the traditional opposition of Dominicans to Communism. And he said that today's cease-fire "may be the first step toward a possible permanent truce so that we can have talks."

Shortly before the news conference Colonel Caamaño had conferred with Dr. Benítez, whose visit marked the resumption of U.S. contacts with the rebels for the first time since John Bartlow Martin's inconclusive and frustrating final meeting with Colonel Caamaño after the formation of the Imbert junta.

Following the news conference Juan de Onis and I had a chat with Hector Aristy. He was optimistic that a Guzmán government could be formed before too long and that the rebel cause would in this manner be rewarded. We talked about the need for the rebels to control their irregulars and snipers if they did not want new problems to arise with the United States. Aristy agreed that this was indeed necessary. He said he thought that with the truce now in effect and an extension hoped for, the rebel command could take steps to discourage the snipers. Aristy mentioned that a mass rally was to be held during the afternoon at Parque Independencia and we discussed whether he and Colonel Caamaño could forestall verbal attacks on the U.S. at the gathering.

"Hell," said Aristy, "I'll do better than that. I'll see if we can call off the meeting altogether."

Apparently, however, it was too late to cancel the rally—or Aristy's associates were unwilling to do so—but the rebels did see to it that there were no anti-American pronouncements. When a young rebel grabbed the microphone to denounce the United States and praise the "socialist countries," several rebel officials bore down on him. They tore the microphone away from him and threw him bodily off the stand. Confusion ensued and several shots were fired in the air. Then the rebel "Defense Minister," Lieutenant Colonel Montes Arache, took the microphone to tell the applauding crowd that "Dominicans want Dominican solutions" and do not want to import them from other countries.

Meanwhile, the interval between the Caamaño press conference and the mass rally gave us the opportunity to have a decent meal—a rare commodity in Santo Domingo. Driving past the Marine checkpoint on Avenida Bolívar, we saw a sign that said "Restaurante Italia" on a building to the right of the avenue. Someone had told us the day before that the restaurant had reopened and we decided to try it. It was not only open but it served everything from antipasto to fine steaks. The tables were covered with clean white tablecloths, and Don Romulo, the Italian owner, had cold Dutch beer and lots of Chianti on hand. For me, after weeks of combat rations and Hotel Embajador food, it was like stumbling into a miracle.

If I forgot the war during lunch at Don Romulo's, it was quickly brought back to mind a few hours later at the hotel. Again we had power failures, the Telex lines were not working properly and in the end I had to type my story by candlelight in the manager's office while the Telex operator next door punched the tape, also by candlelight. The Telex functioned because the Marines had rigged an emergency power line from their generator outside. Then, about 7 P.M., we heard heavy firing from somewhere in the city. The truce was on, but after four weeks of civil war one couldn't make everybody stop shooting all that quickly.

However, U.S. Embassy spokesmen were not disturbed by the firing and were in fact quite optimistic about the whole situation. The State Department spokesman said the U.S. was "quite gratified" to see the truce and hoped it would be extended indefinitely. He said that Mr. Bundy and Mr. Vance were still in Santo

Domingo and that "political activity is continuing with increased intensity."

I ran into Mr. Mayobre in the hotel lobby and he told me that General Imbert had promised to let him know the next morning whether the junta would agree to a 24-hour extension of the cease-fire. He felt confident that the answer would be yes because we now knew that the United States was pressing "Tony" Imbert hard to agree to an indefinite truce.

And from Washington the news was that President Johnson had announced that about 1,700 U.S. troops would soon be withdrawn from the Dominican Republic. They were to be replaced by 1,250 Brazilian troops due in Santo Domingo in the next few days and by the 450 Honduran, Nicaraguan and Costa Rican soldiers already here. It had also been agreed in Washington that the inter-American command would be established early next week under a Brazilian general and that Lieutenant General Palmer would become his U.S. deputy.

Things, then, were looking up and, despite reports from Washington that the Guzmán formula was on its way to being derailed, there was more optimism in Santo Domingo this Friday night than at almost any time since the beginning of the civil war.

To celebrate this upturn in the situation—and also because we were anxious to eat well again—several of us decided to go to the Italia for dinner. In theory one was not supposed to drive after nightfall, even in the International Safety Zone, but with the truce in effect we saw no reason why we should be condemned to another evening of Hotel Embajador food.

The streets were empty but they were lighted for about a mile past the hotel. The rest of Avenida Bolívar was in complete darkness. We heard the crackle of snipers' rifles here and there. Farther ahead, around the Presidential Palace, there was again the sound of fairly heavy firing. It was a bit eerie. I turned off the headlights of the Land Rover on the theory, correct or not, that lights might attract sniper fire. At one of the intersections a Marine patrol in a jeep eyed us suspiciously but did not stop us. We reached the street where the restaurant was situated and parked the car on the sidewalk. There was a barbed-wire barricade across Avenida Bolívar, and a block away we could make out in the darkness the bulk of a Marine Amtrack guarding the checkpoint. Because we did not want to be shot by a suspicious Marine, I called out several times: "Anybody there? Anyone home?"

There was no answer. Only dead silence. After stepping over barbed wire that extended to the side street, we entered the restaurant. There were candles on the tables and Don Romulo greeted us enthusiastically. He already had us pegged as good customers and he could not do enough to please us.

As we worked our way through the antipasto, heavy firing erupted less than a mile off. The dishes and glasses on the table rattled. We looked at each other but nobody commented on the shooting. As if by prearrangement, all of us knew that it simply would not be the "in" thing to talk about gunfire at dinner. There were two young ladies with us—one a reporter and one a Peace Corps volunteer—and it was a matter of savoir faire to act as if we were eating at the Pavillon in New York.

Saturday, May 22nd.

Hopes had been high Friday night that the Imbert junta would agree to an extension of the 24-hour truce, which was to expire at noon Saturday. The reality of the situation was that with United States troops surrounding the rebel stronghold, General Imbert would have to smash through American lines to invade the rebel zone. The United States had made it amply clear to "Tony" Imbert that he would not be allowed to get at the Caamaño forces.

It is conceivable that, despite this, General Imbert believed that he would be allowed to complete the job of destroying the rebels if he went ahead and attacked them in their small rectangular area. There are also reasons to believe that some of his military commanders pressed "Tony" Imbert to reject the extension of the truce and mount an assault on Colonel Caamaño's positions. In a sense, United States policies had been so contradictory that it was not altogether irrational for the junta to think that it might get away with a *coup de grâce* against the revolutionaries.

In any event, when Mr. Mayobre and Dr. Mora arrived at the

junta headquarters in the National Congress Palace at 10 o'clock in the morning, General Imbert and his colleagues told them flatly that no extension of the truce would be granted. Mr. Mayobre looked angry and upset as he got into his car after the visit to the junta.

Inside the building the junta's public relations man, a Puerto Rican named Francisco Cardona, was announcing to newsmen that there would be no prolonging of the truce.

"It is a firm decision not to accede to a cease-fire extension," Mr. Cardona said.

He declared that it was for "political reasons and not for military reasons" that the junta had refused to let the truce continue. This was unquestionably true inasmuch as the real danger to "Tony" Imbert did not lie in the rebels' military potential but in the strong possibility that the U.S. would bring forth a political settlement under the Guzmán formula.

I drove up the hill to the Hotel Embajador to start planning the story for the Sunday paper. We have early deadlines on Saturdays and it is generally a good idea to have a story in shape by noon. As matters now stood, the story was going to be the junta's refusal to extend the cease-fire and speculation over what a continuation of hostilities might mean.

Despite the truce, four American soldiers had died in the preceding 24 hours in firefights with the rebels. This brought the total American casualties since the Marines and paratroopers landed in the Dominican Republic almost a month ago to 19 killed and 111 wounded.

Before I could start writing my story I was advised that Dr. Mora had gone back to see General Imbert. I jumped into my Land Rover and rushed to the Congress building. There armed junta officers and soldiers, a few U.S. officials and many newsmen were waiting in the spacious first-floor hall for the outcome of this latest conference.

Shortly before 1 P.M. General Imbert made his entrance into the Legislative Chamber, which now served as a news-conference room. Looking glum and tense, he read his surprising statement from a piece of paper he held in his hands.

General Imbert said the junta forces were not planning to

initiate "any warlike action" unless they were attacked. He said his government had to have "its hands free to repel any bellicose ing the positions we have at the present."
action" and he announced that "our troops will remain occupy-

"We seek peace, wishing to avoid the spilling of blood," he said. "We do not plan to initiate any warlike action. But, yes, I repeat, we want to be free to repel duly any warlike action that may be undertaken against us."

This, of course, meant that the junta had caved in under powerful U.S. pressure and that a *de facto* cease-fire had finally been forced upon the warring factions in Santo Domingo. It was Dr. Mora, acting with the determined support of the United States Government, who in the end had persuaded "Tony" Imbert that a situation could no longer be tolerated in which the junta remained poised for a new attack. The feeling on the part of the United States and Dr. Mora was that the time had come to start working seriously for a settlement.

We asked General Imbert to explain what had happened between 10 A.M. and 1 P.M. to change his position so radically. But he would answer no questions and marched off almost immediately.

Sentiment was growing in Santo Domingo for the establishment of some form of provisional government that would bring to an end the civil war and the division of the capital into two hostile camps headed by two rival regimes. Thus the five bishops of the Dominican Republic, led by Archbishop Octavio A. Beras, the Primate of the West Indies, issued a statement urging "a provisional government presided over by a patriotic citizen, and supported by men of goodwill from both sides."

In this manner the church, too, was taking the view that the Imbert junta should make room for another government.

This did not necessarily mean that the bishops were supporting the Guzmán formula, but it appeared likely that it would be acceptable to them.

Reports had been circulating all day that McGeorge Bundy had reached a final agreement with Mr. Guzmán—as well as with the rebel command—for the creation of a new government. My immediate problem was to obtain confirmation that this was indeed so.

It was at that point that a State Department official sought me out to inform me in the greatest secrecy that Mr. Bundy was planning to hold a background briefing for a small group of correspondents at 3:30 P.M. Nine correspondents, all of whom regularly covered Washington, were invited to this private session. It was to be held at the home of Bill Connett, the Counselor of the Embassy, and we arrived there shortly before the appointed time. We were treated to iced tea by Mrs. Connett and presently Mr. Bundy entered the room with his secretary.

What followed for the next hour and a half was without any question the most comprehensive and thoughtful analysis of the Dominican situation that we had ever been given by an American official in Santo Domingo. After a few minutes I was convinced that Mr. Bundy was probably the only high-ranking American official who had fully understood the complexities of the Dominican situation and the psychological problems inherent in it. Being fluent in Spanish, he had been able to converse and negotiate in that language with Mr. Guzmán and all the other Dominicans with whom he had dealt. Whatever other tools he had used in his painstaking negotiations, there was no question that Mr. Bundy had gained a superb insight into the whole Dominican state of affairs.

To be sure, he was extremely cautious in discussing with us the prospects for a settlement based on the Guzmán formula. He was not prepared to predict that this approach would necessarily succeed—he pointed out that the situation had many "cuts and turns"—and refused to go beyond stating that he still maintained close contact with Mr. Guzmán.

His chief assessment of the situation was that we were still dealing with "an interrupted civil war" and that the interruption was not yet quite complete.

I got the impression that matters were on the right track but not yet as far advanced as was being claimed by many of our "informed sources" in Santo Domingo.

It was probably a fitting backdrop for Mr. Bundy's remarks about the "interrupted civil war" that heavy firing broke out not more than a mile or so from where we sat just as he was explaining to us the need for solidifying the truce.

The shooting, which from the sound of it obviously involved heavy automatic weapons, made Mr. Bundy a bit jumpy. He even commented on it, interrupting his own explanation of U.S. policy. Subsequently it turned out that the firing had been the result of an accidental clash between rebels and U.S. paratroopers in the Security Corridor. The firefight had no political consequences but three more American soldiers were wounded and we were again reminded that the war was still on despite the truce.

From all I heard during the day I felt reasonably assured that a political settlement on the basis of the Guzmán formula would be reached within the next 24 or 48 hours. I was given by my Dominican sources the names of most of the tentatively accepted Cabinet members.

But I still felt a gnawing concern about the situation. Our Washington Bureau had been passing on to me reports that officials back home were increasingly doubtful of a Guzmán-type settlement. This seemed to clash with the information we were receiving from both American and Dominican sources in Santo Domingo. Yet, rather than take chances, I decided to go easy in my story for the late Sunday editions about predicting an immediate settlement. Some of my colleagues had flatly reported that a settlement had already been achieved, but I still wanted to play it safe.

The evening ended again at Don Romulo's Italian restaurant. If we couldn't have a settlement right away, at least we could have a good dinner.

THE FIFTH WEEK

Sunday, May 23rd.

This was the fifth Sunday of the civil war and probably the quietest day in Santo Domingo since the revolution erupted on April 24.

American troops and Dominican civilians went to church services throughout the city. The peace was only occasionally interrupted by the isolated crackle of a sniper's rifle.

Now that the truce seemed to be in effect permanently—or at least indefinitely—Dominicans all over divided Santo Domingo took advantage of the calm to pour out of doors. In the International Safety Zone people on foot and in cars filled the sun-drenched streets. Employes of the Dominican telephone company, aided by specialists of the 82nd Airborne Division, climbed poles to restore interrupted telephone service.

In the rebel zone people in their Sunday best strolled along Conde Street, in front of Colonel Caamaño's headquarters, and spilled into tree-shaded Parque Independencia.

Juan de Onis drove to the rebel zone in the morning and spent some time on Conde Street listening to conversations. One man, Juan later wrote in his story for the Monday paper, remarked that there could be no political settlement until the United States troops, who, he said, had been "assassinating our people," left Dominican soil. But a young rebel officer turned on him and said he was "crazy."

"Those Americans are the best guarantee that our cause has got," he said.

Actually this view was strongly held by the rebel leadership inasmuch as Colonel Caamaño and his associates had come to understand in recent days that only the shield of American forces protected them from a new assault by the apparently insatiable Imbert junta.

In fact, "Tony" Imbert went on the air in the afternoon to deliver a speech in which he warned the rebels to lay down their arms "while there is time." But the tone and content of Imbert's speech suggested that he was rather concerned about the possibility that a political settlement might indeed be built around Mr. Guzmán.

Thus he was making a new effort to persuade the United States—as well as the Dominicans—that his junta, and not Mr. Guzmán and his pro-Bosch associates, was the proper solution for the Dominican crisis.

Defending himself from charges hurled not only by the rebels but also by many other Dominicans that he could become a dictator in his own right, "Tony" Imbert said in his speech that he was neither a "reactionary" nor "the stuff of which dictators are made."

He spoke at length of the economic and social problems of the Dominican Republic and emphasized his interest in social reform. He recalled the anti-Trujillo invasion of 1959 and he even had kind words for the 14th of June Movement, which is named for the date on which that frustrated assault occurred.

Afterward "Tony" Imbert issued an indirect warning to Mr. Bundy by telling newsmen that he would "not accept impositions from anyone."

While the general was thus fighting for his political life, the balance in Washington was simultaneously tipping against Mr. Guzmán. The hints put out by some Administration officials in Washington in recent days that the Guzmán formula was moribund were turning out not to have been in vain, after all. During this quiet Sunday afternoon Mr. Bundy received from the State Department a set of new instructions which in effect meant a death warrant for the Guzmán negotiations.

I did not know at the time about the arrival of these new instructions. Nor did Mr. Bundy immediately rush to face Mr. Guzmán with the Administration's new position. But the Guzmán group, perhaps through instinct, became aware in the course of the day that something was amiss. About 5 P.M. I received a phone call from a Dominican friend, a man very close to Mr. Guzmán, asking me to come over at once. He said that what he wanted to talk to me about could not be discussed over the telephone.

My friend, who only yesterday had been the leading optimist on the subject of an imminent settlement under a Guzmán formula, now was very nervous and worried. He told me that Mr. Guzmán had earlier been given to understand by Mr. Bundy that some time Sunday the final arrangements would be completed for the creation of a government with him as constitutional president. But, my friend said, up to now no call had been received by Mr. Guzmán.

I told him that as far as I knew from American sources the Guzmán formula was still very much alive and he need not worry. In the morning I had raised the question of where we stood on the Guzmán deal when I was conversing at the embassy with a high State Department official. He had assured me that the Guzmán formula was still "very much alive."

In the evening I met an associate of Mr. Bundy in the lobby of the Hotel Embajador. Presently he came up to my room for a drink and a chat. With surprise, I realized that he was almost as disturbed as my Dominican friend.

My visitor was unwilling to go into details but he said that "certain things" were happening and that grave difficulties had arisen over Mr. Bundy's efforts to arrive at a prompt conclusion of his negotiations.

"All I can say to you," my visitor remarked, "is that today was the Black Sunday for us."

It was not until more than a week later, after I had returned to Washington, that I found out exactly what had happened.

In the meantime the supreme command of the Inter-American Armed Force was finally and formally established at a ceremony at the O.A.S. suite in the penthouse of the Hotel Embajador. Dr. Mora presided over the affair, which was attended by high U.S., Brazilian, Nicaraguan, Honduran and Costa Rican officers. In Washington during the afternoon the O.A.S. Council named General Hugo Panasco Alvim of Brazil to serve as commander-in-chief of the inter-American force. General Alvim, a grandfatherly looking but strict and outspoken officer, had been chosen because Brazil was now committed to send the largest single Latin American contingent to Santo Domingo.

General Palmer, who until now had been the military boss in Santo Domingo, was named to be the American deputy to General Alvim. As the ceremony was being held at the O.A.S. suite the consensus was that regardless of General Alvim's appointment as supreme commander in Santo Domingo, General Palmer would continue to exercise the real military leadership. After all, the United States still had more than 20,000 troops in the Dominican

Republic and most of us took it for granted that this new arrangement was only a showcase situation to convince world opinion that the intervention was truly a hemispheric affair. But, as it developed as soon as the Brazilian general arrived, he meant to be the real commander-in-chief.

While the future of the Dominican Republic continued to be decided at the highest political level, the improbable touches of daily life in Santo Domingo went on. Driving to the Hotel Embajador for the ceremony establishing the inter-American command, I heard a tremendous roar over Abraham Lincoln Avenue. I looked up and saw a U.S. Air Force C-47 flying over the avenue at no more than 150 feet. Its door was open and thousands of copies of the daily information sheet published by the United States Information Agency were being thrown out. This was the latest wrinkle in how to deliver newspapers: Air Force pilots were serving as newsboys and dropping the papers not at people's doors but onto their roofs and into their gardens.

Later in the day, as darkness began to fall over the city, I was returning in my Land Rover from a visit I had to make a few miles out of town. As I approached General Imbert's headquarters the Land Rover suddenly ran out of gas. Together with a colleague who was along, I began pushing it. Suddenly an armed junta policeman materialized out of the darkness and offered to help. We pushed the Land Rover for nearly half a mile and then, at an intersection near the Hotel Hispaniola, we were stopped by junta soldiers. They seemed to be on the verge of arresting us on suspicion of being agents of some sort. In the end we were rescued by two U.S. Marines who led us to their headquarters and made arrangements to donate five gallons of the Marine Corps' gasoline to The New York Times.

Monday, May 24th.

Today the Dominican civil war was one month old. But instead of the expected settlement, a new and hard deadlock had developed.

About 10 o'clock in the morning Mr. Bundy called again on Mr. Guzmán at the little pink house on Benito Monción Street.

However, Mr. Bundy had not gone there to finalize his negotiations, as Mr. Guzmán had expected, but to let Mr. Guzmán know that in effect the United States now took a less hopeful view of the formula that had been under discussion for eight days.

Acting on instructions that had been cabled to him the day before from Washington, Mr. Bundy told Mr. Guzmán that the United States could not support him as president unless he agreed to commit himself to expel from the Dominican Republic a number of known or suspected Communists along with certain other persons in the rebel movement who were objectionable to the Administration.

This request very effectively threw a monkey wrench into the whole negotiation, as Mr. Bundy well knew it would. Mr. Guzmán had already pledged that as soon as he became president he would deliver an inaugural speech in which comdemnation of Communism would be one of the outstanding themes. But now the problem was that under the 1963 Constitution, which Mr. Guzmán and the rebels proposed to restore, banishment of Dominicans for political reasons was not permitted.

Furthermore, Mr. Bundy conveyed the request from Washington that Hector Aristy, the rebels' "Minister of the Presidency" and Colonel Caamaño's right hand, be expelled from the Dominican Republic along with the Communists and the alleged Communists. Several U.S. officials, notably including Ambassador Bennett, had developed a deep antipathy toward Mr. Aristy and considerable suspicion of him and now the State Department felt that his departure from the country had to be an essential feature of the political settlement.

Shortly after the Bundy-Guzmán meeting, I went to see a friend who was in hourly touch with the negotiations. He told me that Mr. Guzmán had just telephoned him to narrate in general terms what had happened at the morning conference. My friend reported that Mr. Guzmán was discouraged and depressed but that he had said that the new requests presented by Mr. Bundy did not necessarily create "unsurmountable" problems.

After my return to Washington I learned that the Sunday instructions to Mr. Bundy had made it plain that the Administration was no longer interested in the Guzmán formula. And well-informed officials insisted to me that it was Under Secretary of

State Mann who was the principal force behind this latest switch in U.S. policy. According to this version, the Administration used two sets of justifications for calling off the Guzmán negotiations. One allegedly was the interception by the Federal Bureau of Investigation in San Juan, Puerto Rico, of a telephone conversation between Dr. Bosch and Diego Bordas, a successful businessman who had served as the highly controversial Minister of Industry in the Bosch regime. Dr. Bosch was reported to have told Mr. Bordas that no matter what regime would now be established, "we can have any kind of government we want within five days."

The tapped conversation did not indicate what kind of government Dr. Bosch might have had in mind when he made this remark. Nevertheless, the Administration chose to interpret his comment to mean that even if a Guzmán government were established, Dr. Bosch would waste no time in trying to force an entirely different one. All the old fears of Communist infiltration or control in the "constitutionalist" movement were thus revived.

In this connection, I also heard a report that Under Secretary Mann had expressed in a conversation with an associate the hope that "this fellow Castro would hurry up and recognize the Caamaño regime" so that it would become clear beyond any doubt that the character of the rebel movement was pro-Communist.

This, of course, was wishful thinking because the Cubans were not about to extend recognition to the rebels. As far as Colonel Caamaño and his moderate leadership were concerned, recognition by Cuba would have been the least desirable possible event.

The other justification for abandoning the Guzmán formula was a lengthy memorandum drawn up by the State Department for President Johnson pointing out that the United States had been charged with attempts to "impose a government" on Cuba when in 1933 Under Secretary of State Sumner Welles put together a new Cuban regime to replace the fallen dictatorship of Gerardo Machado. But this argument seemed utterly unrealistic. The reality was that the United States controlled all phases of Dominican life and that there could be no question but that it was actively engaged in urging, if not imposing, a government on the Dominicans as a means of settling the crisis. Nonetheless, such justifications were needed by the anti-Guzmán forces in Washington and the memorandum establishing the strange parallel between the Cuba of 1933 and the Dominican Republic of 1965 became one of the chief tools in sinking Mr. Bundy's efforts in Santo Domingo.

The word of the new complications in the Bundy-Guzmán talks spread quickly in the Dominican capital, even though the full extent of what had happened was not yet known. A close associate of Mr. Guzmán told me that he feared "everything had collapsed." At rebel headquarters Colonel Caamaño's top officials were nervously asking visiting newsmen what was going on.

As usual, the United States Embassy was not providing any guidance for correspondents. Several reporters had asked for a new background briefing with Mr. Bundy so that he could clarify the situation for us, but we were informed that he was not available. A State Department spokesman who came out of the embassy building to talk to a few newsmen in a tent set up in the garden was highly evasive. He did not want to acknowledge that the Guzmán formula was indeed "moribund" but neither would he say that it was still alive.

While Mr. Bundy held his morning meeting with Mr. Guzmán separate contacts were being pursued throughout the city. First Ambassador Bennett and then Dr. Mora met with General Imbert. Mr. Mayobre, the U.N. representative, called on Colonel Caamaño. He was told of a "new threat" that the United States was about to enlarge the Security Corridor at the expense of the rebels' territory.

It was a day of intense diplomatic activity that, if anything, only served to harden the deadlock. Then we heard that in Washington a new blow had been administered to the Guzmán plan. In a lengthy story The Washington Daily News reported that the Dominican Republic's Agricultural Bank, of which Mr. Guzmán was a director, had been involved in serious irregularities.

The article said that an audit of the bank's books by a New York accounting firm had disclosed a $75 million overstatement of assets and a shortage of thousands of notes and $1 million worth of mortgage collaterals.

When reporters in Washington inquired at the State Department about the veracity of The Daily News article, they were told by responsible officials that this disclosure could easily "throw a cloud over the candidacy of Mr. Guzmán." A State Department spokesman said that "it is up to Mr. Guzmán to explain his role in the bank."

Both the disclosure of the alleged scandal and the manner in which the State Department handled the situation were excellent examples of the way Dominican policy operated in Washington. And, chiefly, the whole episode was an extraordinary instance of how innuendo was allowed to stand unchallenged by people who really knew better.

Although The Daily News gave no source for its article on the audit, it immediately became known in Washington that the story had been supplied by a retired attorney and businessman who was an agent, registered at the Department of Justice, for the Reid Cabral Government. It also became known that a separate memorandum containing the same allegations had been supplied by this agent to the Caribbean Affairs Office of the State Department.

Inasmuch as the State Department's spokesman chose to remark that it was now up to Mr. Guzmán to clear himself, the impression was at once created in Santo Domingo that the Administration gave considerable credence to The Daily News report. But as it was to turn out the following day, all the allegations concerning the audit were completely false. And it further developed that a copy of the examination of the bank's finances had been made available to the U.S. Embassy and the U.S. Agency for International Development mission in Santo Domigo three months earlier and that a copy had been sent on to the State Department's Caribbean Affairs Office.

Therefore, to take one alternative, State Department officials had failed to read the audit either at the time they received it or when the allegations in The Daily News were published and had allowed themselves to issue formal comment without any awareness of the document's actual contents. The other alternative was that they had read the document but chose to let the charges against Mr. Guzmán stand unchallenged despite a knowledge to the contrary. I subsequently raised the question why things had happened in that manner. The reply, as given to me later by a high State Department official in Washington, was that "I guess we did not handle this one the way we should."

Coming on top of the latest difficulties in the negotiations for the formation of the Guzmán government, the Washington report on the bank audit had the effect of an electric shock on politicians in Santo Domingo—and quite possibly on Mr. Bundy himself.

During the evening I spent some time talking to Dr. Benítez, the Chancellor of the University of Puerto Rico, who had come to assist Mr. Bundy. Dr. Benítez was both discouraged and furious over what was happening. He told me he felt that in effect the Bundy mission was being torpedoed from Washington. He added that he personally had reached the point where he was ready to quit participating in the negotiations and to return to Puerto Rico with a public explanation of what he was doing. In the end Dr. Benítez decided to remain publicly silent for at least another day and to withhold his decision as to whether he should return to San Juan.

As had invariably been the case with everything concerning the Dominican crisis, once more we were faced with the fact that there was very little resemblance between the realities of Santo Domingo and the picture that the Administration, or some members of it, were painting in Washington for the benefit of public opinion.

As an Administration friend was to tell me later, there was no real unified policy in Washington: each official told newsmen what he personally believed and what best seemed to serve the interests of the faction within the Government that he represented. And, of course, it was the fate of the long-awaited political settlement in the Dominican Republic that was thus victimized by the growing tug of war within the Administration.

Tuesday, May 25th.

Now the situation was back to where it had been on the preceding Sunday when Mr. Bundy arrived in Santo Domingo. This situation was simply that there was no political solution in sight. With Mr. Guzmán discarded as prospective president for all practical purposes, the labor of negotiating a meaningful settlement had to be started again from scratch. Mr. Bundy's mission had failed because, notwithstanding his own considerable political power, other powerful officials in Washington had been able to paralyze his maneuvers.

In the morning Mr. Bundy drove for the last time to the Guzmán house. He gave Mr. Guzmán the full text of The Washington Daily News article and, as an associate of his told me later, he offered his personal apologies for the incident concerning Mr. Guzmán's involvement in the report on the alleged irregularities in the Agricultural Bank. At the same time Mr. Bundy indicated to Mr. Guzmán that he was no longer in a position to continue negotiating with him and that he would therefore be leaving for Washington the following morning.

The two men had developed a fondness and respect for each other during their daily negotiations and those who were present at this final meeting reported that there was heavy-hearted sadness at their parting. The sadness arose because, despite their best efforts, they had not been allowed to reach the settlement so painstakingly pursued.

Shortly thereafter an embassy spokesman announced that Mr. Bundy had ended his mission and would return home the next day. Embassy officials were not willing to discuss the precise status of the Guzmán formula but they left few doubts that it had died—as some Washington officials the week before had so accurately predicted it would. It was another case, then, of self-fulfilling prophecies in the Dominican crisis.

That the United States was bowing out, at least temporarily and at least overtly, from the negotiations for a Dominican settlement was indicated by the embassy officials when they said that henceforth it would be up to the O.A.S. to carry on the peace-making efforts. It was pointed out that Secretary General Mora of the O.A.S. was staying on in Santo Domingo and that the continuing efforts for a settlement would remain in his hands.

Although we knew that the whole Guzmán episode now belonged to history, several of us felt that it was nonetheless important to arrive at the truth concerning Mr. Guzmán and the alleged bank irregularities. Therefore a colleague from The Christian Science Monitor, another from The New York Herald Tribune and I spent the entire morning tracking down the story. We talked at length with the acting director of the United States A.I.D. (Agency for International Development) mission in Santo Domingo, the administrator of the Agricultural Bank and finally the auditor who had drafted the controversial report.

The documented story that emerged from these interviews added up to a complete negation of the charges that were made in Washington the day before, charges that the Administration, at least indirectly, seemed to accept as accurate.

The first point, as carefully explained to us by the auditor representing the New York firm of Ernst & Ernst, was that his report had not charged the Agricultural Bank with any irregularities. The auditor, who lives in Santo Domingo, told us that the bank had indeed increased its assets figure by $75 million but that this had been done openly and deliberately on the advice of the auditing firm and with the full concurrence of the Dominican Government and the United States A.I.D. mission. The assets figure was raised so that the bank would be more attractive to potential investors in the New York money market, and the auditor emphasized that this had been accomplished through a standard and completely acceptable bookkeeping operation.

No mortgage notes were actually missing, the auditor told us. What had happened, he said, was that a large number of the deeds had vanished from the bank's files, mainly during the Trujillo dictatorship. But, he added, since the originals were available in the National Registry Office, copies could be obtained at three pesos each. As to the shortage of funds covering some of the mortgage transactions of the bank, the auditor explained to us that there was, in fact, a shortage of about $8 million. But, he said, this shortage occurred as a result of loans made toward the end of the Trujillo regime to persons whom the old dictator chose to favor and who were not expected to repay the loans anyway.

During the Trujillo dictatorship the Agricultural Bank had been used by the Dominican Government as the principal vehicle for its transactions—many of them quite questionable—and as a sort of personal slush fund for the old dictator. After his assassination the succeeding Dominican Governments attempted to reorganize the bank's finances, and both the United States and the Inter-American Development Bank were instrumental in bringing about a reorganization.

The audit in question was ordered by the Reid Cabral Government, after the overthrow of the Bosch regime, to cover the period between Feb. 12, 1962, and March 1, 1964. It developed that it was Reid Cabral himself who had appointed Mr. Guzmán to be a member of the bank's board of directors roughly one month after the end of the period covered by the audit.

Moreover, the new administrator of the bank, freshly named by the Imbert junta, joined with the other experts in declaring that there was nothing to incriminate Mr. Guzmán in connection with the bank's operations. Not a single one of the allegations against Mr. Guzmán—and the bank—thus stood up in the light of inquiry. But these allegations had been used by Mr. Guzmán's political enemies to deal him the final blow and thereby prevent him from becoming the new constitutional president. And some key officials of the Johnson Administration had allowed themselves to be identified by implication with these allegations. This, then, was another of the many strange facets of the Dominican crisis.

About noon I drove over to the Guzmán house after I had been advised through friends that Mr. Guzmán wanted to see me and another newsman or two. This was the first time I had met him since the beginning of the negotiations with Mr. Bundy. Until now Mr. Guzmán had steadfastly refused to be interviewed by American reporters on the theory that any undue publicity could interfere with the talks.

Mr. Guzmán was meeting with one of Mr. Bundy's assistants when we arrived. As we waited for him we sat in the tiny back yard of the house under the broiling sun and chatted with several members of Dr. Bosch's and Mr. Guzmán's Dominican Revolutionary Party. I think they must have been aware that Mr. Guzmán's chances of becoming constitutional president were now dead. But they maintained their composure and showed no bitterness in discussing the situation with us.

Later, in the small sitting room inside, Mr. Guzmán himself was just as composed. He refused to enter into any discussion about the political negotiations and confined himself to reading to us a long statement denying the charges that had linked him with the bank's audit. His statement was businesslike and dispassionate. In it he discussed the situation of the bank since the end of the Trujillo dictatorship and remarked that if the text of the audit were made public, the falsity of the allegations against the bank and himself could be fully appreciated. He concluded by saying that he was not in the slightest concerned by the "gratuitous" accusations against him "because I have had more than 30 years of life dedicated to business life and everybody knows me in the Dominican Republic."

In the course of our morning investigation we had driven up and down Santo Domingo. Though there no longer existed current prospects for any political settlement, the four-day-old truce was still holding firmly and the capital was gradually returning to as much normalcy as possible for a city that remained divided.

There was a considerable amount of traffic in the International Safety Zone, and even in the rebel zone people were trying to reconstruct the customary pattern of their lives. Near the Hotel Embajador the vast outdoor market—the Matahambre—was doing a land-office business. Food was again reaching Santo Domingo in sizable quantities from the countryside, and the stalls at the market were stocked with vegetables and meat. The merchants were hawking their goods as in the old days and customers were again milling among the stands. In the industrial area in the northern district of the city—now under General Imbert's control—the peanut oil plant and the big cement factory were back in operation, even though all of the workers had not yet returned.

Only occasionally, as if to remind one that the truce did not necessarily mean peace, a sniper's shot was heard here or there. But the people, conditioned to the firing of weapons after more than a month of the civil war, were no longer paying attention. The city was reawakening.

And with this reawakening the control exercised over the capital and the countryside by the Imbert junta was growing. The obvious failure of the Guzmán formula was a major victory for "Tony" Imbert and he was taking full advantage of it in every conceivable way. His policemen were rounding up rebels, suspected rebels and political enemies at large without interference from the United States or the O.A.S. A junta official estimated that perhaps 3,000 political prisoners had been taken in recent days, not counting the armed rebels captured in combat. The baseball stadium, where fighting had raged the week before, was now being used as a processing center for the junta's political prisoners prior to their removal to regular prisons.

And one of the persons who had been arrested by the junta police was Homero Hernandez, the liaison officer between the O.A.S. and the Caamaño headquarters. While returning from a routine visit to the O.A.S. office he was arrested by Dominican policemen at a U.S. Marine checkpoint leading to the rebel zone, but neither the United States nor the O.A.S. protested this act. Only Mr. Mayobre, the U.N. representative, raised the issue of the liaison officer's fate with the Imbert junta but without success in obtaining his release.

Early in the afternoon we were summoned to the briefing room of the Hotel Embajador for a farewell background briefing by Mr. Bundy. Speaking as an "official American source," Mr. Bundy said that the President had asked him to return to Washington to report on the Dominican situation. He recounted at length the events since the outbreak of the revolution on April 24 and made the remark that the danger of a Communist take-over in the Dominican Republic had been greatly reduced. He did not elaborate on this point, although it was the fear of a Communist seizure of the revolt that had motivated the United States intervention in the first place.

Then Mr. Bundy left the hotel for what was to be his first—and last—face-to-face meeting with Colonel Caamaño. It was to develop into an extraordinary episode. The meeting had been arranged by intermediaries representing Mr. Bundy on the one hand and Colonel Caamaño on the other. Both sides agreed that the conference, to be kept completely secret, would best be held in neutral territory. Mr. Bundy and Colonel Caamaño selected the National Music Conservatory building on George Washington Avenue in the no man's land. It was, incidentally, within sight of the Marine checkpoint where the two Miami newsmen had been cut down by American fire and where I had nearly met my end several weeks earlier.

The meeting was set for 4 P.M. but Mr. Bundy and his

companions arrived at the site of the conference about 15 minutes early. With Mr. Bundy were Deputy Secretary of Defense Vance, Dr. Benítez, Secretary General Mora of the O.A.S. and Harry Shlaudeman. They had all arrived in limousines with O.A.S. markings. They had no military escort and no weapons. Mr. Bundy had assumed, for no particular reason, that Colonel Caamaño and his people had taken the necessary steps to check out the building and prepare it for the meeting. For this reason nothing had been done by the American security people. The upshot was that as Mr. Bundy and his companions reached the Music Conservatory, a modernistic white structure that had originally been built by Generalissimo Trujillo to house the offices of his official political party, they discovered that the building was locked. Since they could not get in they stood outside, waiting for Colonel Caamaño and hoping that nobody else would spot their little group.

Colonel Caamaño and his colleagues were a bit late, arriving at the Music Conservatory a few minutes after 4 P.M. It turned out that Colonel Caamaño had assumed that the Americans would check out the building—just as Mr. Bundy had assumed that the rebels would—and the colonel did not have the keys to the building, either. He and Mr. Bundy thus met in front of the door, shaking hands and exchanging pleasantries. But then the question arose how everybody would get into the building to get the conference under way. The rebels and the Bundy group tried every door and ground-floor window but found them all solidly locked. Finally one of the rebel soldiers accompanying Colonel Caamaño—he *did* bring an armed escort—produced a Swiss Army knife and used it to pry a window loose. The window was removed and one of the soldiers climbed inside to bring out a chair. The chair was placed on the outside and another chair was put against the window on the inside. Led by Mr. Bundy and Colonel Caamaño, the two delegations climbed through the window into the Conservatory building for their conference. A large room was selected for the talks, probably among the most informal in modern diplomatic history. There were not enough chairs for everybody, so the participants walked up and down the room, gathering in small groups, breaking up and regrouping. Since Dr. Mora was remaining in Santo Domingo with the mission of continuing political negotiations, it was left up to him to direct the course of the conversation—to the extent that the talks required any direction.

Mr. Bundy, as in his negotiations with Mr. Guzmán, spoke in Spanish this time, too. Those who attended the meeting reported that the conversation was extremely cordial and that Mr. Bundy and Colonel Caamaño seemed to "hit it off right away."

At one point in the discussions, which went on for four hours, Mr. Bundy undertook to explain to Colonel Caamaño why it was no longer possible for the United States to continue the negotiations for the creation of a government under Mr. Guzmán. The rebels had accepted the Guzmán formula in principle some time ago and now Colonel Caamaño showed disappointment that the negotiations had not been fruitful.

According to at least one participant in the meeting, Mr. Bundy told Colonel Caamaño that in effect the Government of the United States was not united on the question of the Dominican crisis. That, he was reported to have said, was the reason why Mr. Guzmán could not be made the new constitutional president. Subsequently, in Washington, Mr. Bundy privately denied that he so expressed himself. But whatever words were spoken at that meeting, Mr. Bundy seemed to have left no doubt in Colonel Caamaño's mind that for all practical purposes there existed a split in the Johnson Administration over the management of the Dominican crisis.

Mr. Guzmán, who had arrived at the meeting with the Caamaño group, listened mainly in silence to what in reality was a farewell to his chances for the presidency. But since he had never actively sought this post, he seemed almost relieved that he would not be saddled with the tremendous responsibility of trying to put his bitterly divided country back together again.

About 7 P.M., after nearly three hours of conversation, heavy firing suddenly broke out in the general area of the Presidential Palace, not quite two miles to the north of the Conservatory. Flushed with anger, Colonel Caamaño swore loudly and rushed out of the room in search of a telephone so he could order his men to stop firing regardless of what had set off the incident. Mr. Bundy, equally anxious that no Americans should be exchanging fire with the rebels while he was meeting with Colonel Caamaño, also rushed for a telephone.

But in the greatest piece of symbolic irony of the whole Dominican war, it turned out there was no telephone in the Conservatory building. And in a sense this sums up better than anything else a good deal of the Dominican story: the breakdown of human and political communications between Americans and Dominicans ever since the eruption of the revolution, despite so much goodwill on the part of so many.

The firing presently died down and Colonel Caamaño and Mr. Bundy went on talking a while longer. It was after 8 P.M. when everything that possibly could be said had been said. The White House emissary and the rebel colonel shook hands warmly and expressed their hopes that real peace—and real cooperation between the Dominican Republic and the United States—would soon return.

A major phase had ended in the Dominican crisis. A military truce was now in effect but a political settlement remained as elusive as ever. A patient negotiating effort had failed. The Dominican future remained uncertain.

Mr. Bundy, Colonel Caamaño and their respective associates climbed into their cars and went back to their respective zones. Night had fallen over Santo Domingo.

Wednesday, May 26th.

McGeorge Bundy left Santo Domingo early in the morning and returned to Washington after 10 days in the Dominican capital, where he had made fruitless attempts to set up a coalition government under Mr. Guzmán.

Deputy Secretary of Defense Vance, representing the United States, and Secretary General Mora, for the Organization of American States, stayed behind as the principal officials charged with whatever new steps might be taken to resume the effort to arrive at a political settlement.

Mr. Mayobre also stayed behind as the personal representative of U.N. Secretary General Thant.

But for the first time in nearly two weeks the diplomatic activity in the Dominican capital had come to a virtual standstill in light of the failure of the Bundy mission to organize a compromise government. Now all the parties were left to rethink their positions.

Meanwhile the United States was making additional moves to enhance the role of the O.A.S. in the Dominican crisis—a continuation of Washington's effort to bring the inter-American organization into the picture after the Administration had ignored it when the landing of American troops was first ordered.

New powers were vested in Dr. Mora to oversee in effect most of the political and economic activities of the war-torn country. And the first contingents of Brazilian troops had begun arriving to permit the phasing out of some of the U.S. forces.

With the arrival Tuesday of the first 200 Brazilian soldiers, 600 Marines left Santo Domingo in the morning. They were the units that had come ashore on that grim Wednesday, April 28, when Dominicans were slaughtering Dominicans at the height of the civil war.

In view of Mr. Bundy's departure, my own orders were to return to my base in Washington and prepare for my new overseas assignment. Now I was on the terrace of my hotel room watching the helicopters ferrying the Marines back to the U.S.S. Boxer, standing three or four miles offshore.

Those Marines had been in Santo Domingo for a full four weeks on one of the most exacting and difficult assignments that had confronted American troops in recent times. They had come ashore prepared for combat and some of them had engaged in combat. They had lost some of their buddies. Still others had been evacuated to hospitals back home with wounds inflicted by snipers in the night. Yet the task of these Marines had been as much to keep peace as to wage war. In many situations they had to exercise tact and understanding, living among a population not essentally unfriendly to the United States and often as confused about what was going on as the Marines themselves.

For me, the assignment in Santo Domingo had lasted one day

short of four weeks. It seemed somehow fitting that I should be departing at the same time as the Marines with whom we had come to the Dominican Republic aboard the ships of the Caribbean Amphibious Task Force.

So much had happened that I felt as if I had been in Santo Domingo for years, not weeks. The U.S. had intervened, perhaps overhastily as many of us thought at the time, but after the weeks of bloodshed and peace efforts a truce—even if a shaky one—had been achieved. The next step, sooner or later, would have to be a political settlement, even if this morning the outlook for one seemed extremely dim.

As on all the other mornings since my arrival in Santo Domingo, the sun was shining brightly over the Caribbean and the grounds of the Hotel Embajador. But, in contrast to all the other mornings, there no longer were any Marines bivouacked by the swimming pool or dug in along the perimeter of the hotel's gardens. The portable water-purification tanks set up at the edge of the pool had now been removed by the Marines. The tents had been taken down and shipped away. There were no more calisthenics, volley ball and baseball games with Marine participants and no more of the rhythmic shouts that had served as my personal reveille every morning at 6 o'clock.

Now Juan de Onis and Marty Arnold were taking over Room 321, The Times' field headquarters for this extraordinary story. Marty was to depart at the end of the week, leaving Juan, as The Times had decided that the story no longer required the presence of two or more correspondents.

I had a farewell lunch with Ambassador Varon of Israel and his wife, who had been accurate and perspicacious advisers to us at the height of the crisis, and with Juan, Marty and Ana Teresa.

Then I loaded my gear into the Land Rover and we drove a few hundred yards to the helicopter landing pad at the polo grounds—where I had arrived 27 days earlier from the Boxer—to catch a chopper ride to the San Isidro Air Force Base. We persuaded the Marine helicopter-control officer to clear us for a flight to San Isidro—now newsmen were no longer being given helicopter rides but were left to their own devices or to the services of the green Army bus—and we were off. The Marine copter headed straight toward the Caribbean, then banked north and flew over the Hotel Embajador, my home for the last four weeks. We flew over the coastline, over George Washington Avenue and over the Hotel Jaragua, where the inter-American command was already functioning under Brazil's General Alvim. I could see the black shapes of the Marine Amtracks guarding the entrance to the International Safety Zone. Farther to the left was the sprawling yellow compound of the Presidential Palace. The pilot banked the helicopter to starboard on the direct course to San Isidro. Now I could see the rebel zone and, craning my neck, the Copello Building, where Colonel Caamaño had his headquarters and where I had spent so many hours.

Again Santo Domingo looked from the air like a picture postcard: white buildings, blue Caribbean, green patches of parks and gardens. The black smoke of burning houses and the white puffs of explosions that we had seen so often on previous flights were gone. And no longer did the helicopters have to fly at top security altitude to avoid sniper fire. For the time being at least, peace had returned to the bloodied Dominican capital.

We landed at San Isidro and in front of Hangar No. 1—another familiar place of my earlier Dominican days—I found some of my Peace Corps friends awaiting the Navy courier plane to San Juan. Bob Satin was there and so was his young woman assistant, "B.J." Warren. Steve Honoré, another Peace Corps staff assistant, was also preparing for the trip to San Juan and several Peace Corps girls had come out to say good-by to their colleagues.

As usual the press plane from San Juan was late. So I invited "B.J." to walk over to the 82nd Airborne Division's temporary PX at San Isidro. We joined a long line of soldiers awaiting their turn to buy a can of cold beer from huge ice-filled buckets and there, in the sun, I drank my farewell toast to Santo Domingo.

Presently the Navy's C-54 landed and a half-hour later we were aloft. Immediately we flew into a bank of dark clouds and I did not set eyes again on the Dominican Republic. For me it was the end of the story.

In San Juan I was back in the other world. It was now evening and the streets were lighted, the sidewalks were full and there was music in the hotels.

I telephoned The Times and once more I was faced with the other dimension of the Santo Domingo story—the Washington dimension. The story written in Washington for the next day's issue of The Times conveyed the Washington version of the reason for the failure of the Bundy mission. Whereas it had been made amply clear in Santo Domingo that Mr. Bundy had discontinued his negotiations with Mr. Guzmán because the Administration no longer approved, the Washington version blamed "the recalcitrance of the junta in the Dominican Republic" for posing the fatal obstacle to a provisional government.

Our Washington story reported that Administration officials were saying that "the ambitions and defiance of the civilian-military junta led by Brig. Gen. Antonio Imbert Barreras, which the United States helped to create, were the main reasons for the failure of mediation efforts by President Johnson's special envoy, McGeorge Bundy."

As the story was being read to me over the telephone I had the strange sensation of living a fairy tale. Only three or four days ago these same officials were telling correspondents in Washington that it was the unreliable character of Colonel Caamaño and the Communist proclivities of certain members of his command that were making it inadvisable for the United States to push ahead with the Guzmán formula. But now that the anti-Guzmán forces had succeeded in sinking this formula, the responsibility was being placed upon General Imbert.

"Tony" Imbert, to be sure, had opposed the Guzmán concept with all his might. Yet we had been told repeatedly in recent days by U.S. officials that his opposition was not really such a formidable obstacle. It was pointed out to us that all the United States had to do to bring General Imbert to accept a U.S. decision would be to cut off the flow of money being made available every week to meet his payrolls.

Our Washington story also carried denials by officials that important groups in the Administration had tried to sabotage Mr. Bundy's plan to form a government around Mr. Guzmán. This was the report contained in the story I had written the day before from Santo Domingo when the details of the final round of conversations with Mr. Guzmán were made available to me.

Now Secretary of State Rusk at a Washington news conference made a point of speaking well of Mr. Guzmán and of saying that the earlier threat of a Communist take-over in the Dominican Republic had been "very substantially reduced, although not completely eliminated."

The talk in Washington now was of a coalition government—presumably between General Imbert and Colonel Caamaño—although Mr. Bundy's efforts had never really been aimed at producing such a coalition regime but rather at putting together a government which would be acceptable to a majority of responsible Dominicans, if not necessarily to "Tony" Imbert. Meanwhile, in the kaleidoscopic Dominican situation, General Imbert was again becoming the villain after the Johnson Administration had in a sense sided with him in shooting down the Guzmán formula.

It was Alice in Wonderland all over again. But now I was out of it as a reporter and all that was left for me to do before flying home was to pay a farewell visit to Juan Bosch. I left that visit for the next day.

Thursday, May 27th.

It took this final interview with Juan Bosch in Puerto Rico and the words being simultaneously spoken in Washington by a key Administration figure to emphasize once again for me how terribly different a Latin American's appreciation of events in his own country can be from the view of a United States official.

This Thursday afternoon, shortly before boarding my flight for New York, I drove out with Jaime Benítez to see Juan Bosch at his residence in a San Juan suburb.

I found Bosch dejected, depressed and discouraged. The collapse of the Guzmán negotiation had been the final bitterness for him. He was a man from under whom the rug had been pulled. He was a man who had lost his last hope that things would ultimately work out in his homeland. He said bitterly: "The United States did not have the courage to take a chance with democracy in my country."

He spoke of the setback to the cause of democracy in Latin America as a result of the U.S. actions in Santo Domingo.

But in Washington Under Secretary of State Mann was at that precise moment presenting an entirely different version of what had happened in the Dominican Republic.

In an interview with Marvin Kalb of the Columbia Boadcasting System Mr. Mann was saying that the U.S. actions in the Dominican Republic had in effect prevented the loss of another country to the "Sino-Soviet bloc."

"In this kind of situation what would have been the reaction if we had done nothing? And if the result had been a take-over of another island by the Sino-Soviet military bloc and if we had been faced with the kind of conditions that led to the October, 1962, missiles crisis," Mr. Mann was saying.

This kind of alternative, he declared, "would have had repercussions which in my opinion would have been much worse. I doubt that U.S. prestige in Latin America was lower than it was right after the Bay of Pigs when we were indecisive. . . ."

Up to now no high U.S. official had openly charged that the Dominican revolution had been a product of an actual Sino-Soviet conspiracy. But in his C.B.S. interview Mr. Mann told Marvin Kalb that this was the third time the Communists had set out to capture the Dominican Republic. The first time, he said, they attempted it in 1959, when a Castro-sponsored expedition from Cuba sought to oust the dictator Trujillo. The second time, he said, the attempt was made in 1963, during Dr. Bosch's presidency. Mr. Mann did not explain this allusion, though he did tell C.B.S. that the former President was "benevolent" and "tolerant" toward Communism. These were, incidentally, the reasons given by the right-wing military for overthrowing Dr. Bosch in September, 1963, and thus ending the brief Dominican experiment in democracy. And the third Communist attempt, Mr. Mann said, was "now."

So what to Dr. Bosch had been a U.S. failure to take a chance with democracy, to Mr. Mann became a rescue operation from a "Sino-Soviet" conspiracy.

In a sense, then, these two interviews—Dr. Bosch's in San Juan and Mr. Mann's in Washington—did perhaps more than anything else to underscore the depth of the gulf of misunderstandings dividing so many Americans and Dominicans in this crisis.

Both positions were, to be sure, extreme. Listening to Dr. Bosch, it occurred to me that when the full history of the Dominican Spring of 1965 is written one day, the truth that had eluded us in Santo Domingo in the midst of the civil war will be found somewhere between the extremes, as usually is the case.

I said good-by to Juan Bosch. Dr. Benítez drove me to the San Juan International Airport. I flew back to the United States.

An American G.I. on patrol in Santo Domingo
the day after the frequently violated Cease-Fire was signed.

UPI

Captured Marines being questioned by Rebels.
From left to right Pvt. Darrell J. Southwell, Mason, Michigan; Cpl. Reuben Garcia, New York City; unidentified Rebel officer; Rebel provisional President Col. Francisco Caamano.

UPI

U.S. Soldiers guard Dominican Rebels captured near International Zone in Santo Domingo.

UPI

Unidentified Marines wounded during Santo Domingo fighting receiving aid.

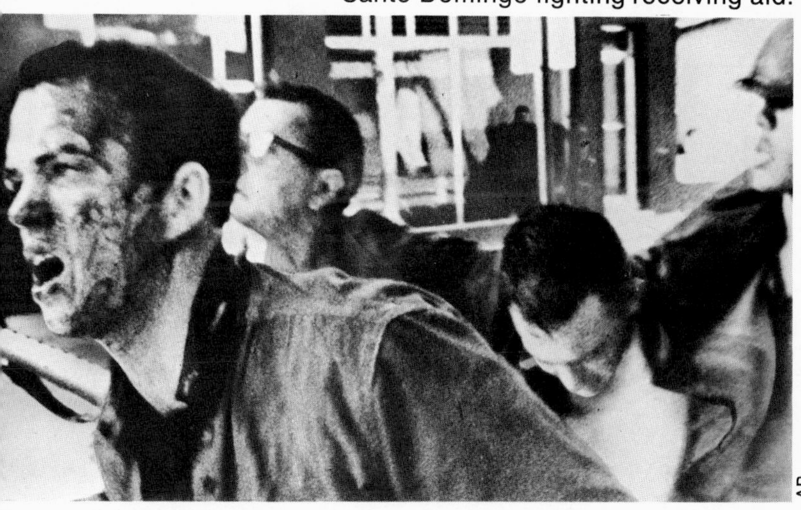

AP

A dead Dominican civilian, killed during fighting between Dominican Rebels and troops of the Inter-American Peacekeeping Force.

UPI

UPI

A U.S. Marine frisks a civilian painter
at one of the checkpoints.

U.S. Marines man sandbagged position
along George Washington Avenue.
In background is U.S. aircraft carrier Boxer.

UPI

Two American GI's control traffic in Santo Domingo.
Soldier in manhole is there to inspect underbelly of vehicles for concealed guns and ammunition as they pass checkpoint.

UPI

82nd Airborne Division band marches through Santo Domingo with civilian supporters carrying posters of President Johnson.

UPI

UPI

Lt. Gen. Bruce Palmer (left) being helped with OAS armband by Col. Carlos de Meira Mattos, Commander of Brazilian troops in Dominican Republic, just prior to signing of act which established Inter-American Peacekeeping Force.

Wide World

Deposed Junta President Donald Reid Cabral arrives at New York's Kennedy Airport accompanied by wife and daughter.

Wide World

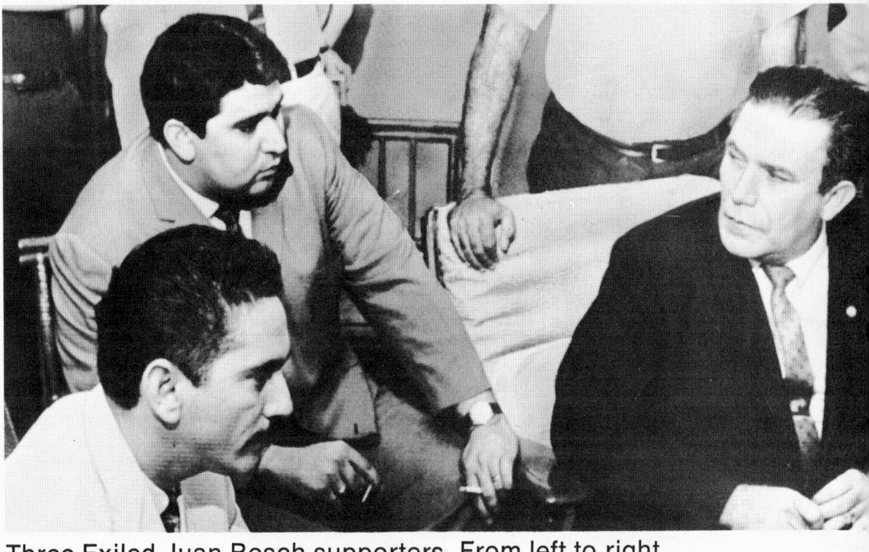

Three Exiled Juan Bosch supporters. From left to right Armando Gonzalez Tamayo, former Vice-President; Jacobo Mazluta, former Finance Minister; Angel Miolan, Revolutionary Party President.

The Principal Adversaries...

Wide World

Juan D. Bosch, Exiled President.

Wide World

Gen. Antonio Imbert Berras, Junta Leader.